Who's Who
in Fashion

Who's Who in Fashion

FOURTH EDITION

Anne Stegemeyer

Fairchild Publications, Inc.
New York

Executive Editor: Olga T. Kontzias
Assistant Acquisitions Editor: Carolyn Purcell
Editor: Sylvia Weber
Associate Production Editor: Elizabeth Marotta
Art Director: Adam B. Bohannon
Director of Production: Priscilla Taguer
Editorial Assistant: Suzette Lam
Copy Editor: Jennifer Plum, Words & Numbers
Interior Design: Ron Reeves
Cover Design: Adam B. Bohannon
Photographer: Peter Ashworth

Library of Congress Catalog Card Number: 2003102033
ISBN: 1-56367-247-2
GST R 133004424
Printed in the United States of America

Contents

Preface

who's who in fashion is a collection of brief biographies. While it deals primarily with the present fashion scene, it is also designed to help students explore the history of their chosen field—to fill in the background as it were.

The biographies trace the careers of many of the women and men who've contributed to fashion. Besides today's major figures and legendary designers of the past, there are lesser-known people and newcomers worth watching, as well as a sampling of interesting nonconformists, free spirits who prefer to work off the main fashion paths.

The picture would not be complete without the stylemakers, those with an eye and an instinct for fashion who interpret it for the public. Editors, photographers, artists—they sketch and photograph, write about fashion, and promote it. Often the first to recognize talent, they seek it out and encourage it. They may get carried away by their appetite for the new, but without their support many a designer would go unrecognized and unappreciated.

I hope this book will prove useful—to students, to professionals, to those everywhere who share my passion for this extraordinary, maddening, ever-changing business.

Acknowledgments

My warmest thanks to the many people who have helped me with this project. Thanks to the designers and their public relations representatives who returned questionnaires and supplied supplementary material—to my friends and acquaintances in the fashion field who generously shared reminiscences and personal experiences—to all those at Fairchild, Beth Applebome to Liz Marotta, who've moved the project from start to finish. And to Olga Kontzias, long my editor and source of moral support, my special appreciation.

Women's Wear Daily offices in European fashion capitals gave invaluable assistance. The librarians, Merle Thomason of *Women's Wear Daily* and Joshua P. Waller at the Fashion Institute of Technology, both earned my gratitude with their knowledge and helpfulness. Some designers, alas, sent inadequate information or ignored requests altogether. If a favorite is not found here, that could be the reason.

To all who've lent a hand, thank you again and again, I couldn't have done it without you.

Fashion–
All About Change

"Fashion isn't just clothes," designer
Ossie Clark once said, "it's what's happening in everything."
So if fashion is tied to what's going on in the world, changing
times will and must produce changes in the fashion world.
The changes on the fashion scene are obviously not in a class
with those in the real world, but attitudes change, new talents
arrive, established designers retire, and meanwhile the lowly
rag trade has been transformed into a very big business.

a new and different breed...

The most glamorous of the new giants are the luxury
conglomerates, a different breed from the familiar corporate
collections of apparel companies that have been with us for so
long. First, as the name implies, a conglomerate is not a simple group of like businesses such as dressmakers, but a con-
glomeration of disparate enterprises. Luxury is the second
unifying characteristic—each business is a producer of an extravagance, the top of the line.

Of the conglomerates, the largest and most famous is the
French Louis Vuitton Moët Hennesy (LVMH), with, at last
count, over 50 gilt-edged names in its portfolio, including couture and ready-to-wear, jewelers and watchmakers, skin care
products and much more. Second only to LVMH in size although less known is Swiss-based Richemont, strongest in
fine watches and jewelry.

Italy has Gucci with its own label for luggage, accessories,
and ready-to-wear, plus prestigious French firms. Prada is another Italian entity with its own two name brands, plus all or
part ownership of other design houses, with everything from
ready-to-wear to luggage to pricey athletic shoes.

In Europe, England, and the Far East, old fashion houses
with distinguished pedigrees have been bought up, dusted off,
and revitalized by new creative teams and hefty cash infu-
sions. Unfortunately, things are tougher for a designer starting out. With some few exceptions, newcomers have a hard
time attracting conglomerate attention, although a strong

personality and good press can sometimes bring about the desirable financial backing. This concentration of companies and capital makes establishing a business, always a chancy proposition, even more difficult.

designers as such are relative newcomers...

It's a cliché that designers are dictators who hate women and force them into bizarre styles, but designers as such are relative newcomers—and even before they existed women, and men, followed the dress conventions of their time. From ancient Crete with its improbable wasp waists through the centuries, there's been a procession of tightly laced corsets, enormous puffed sleeves, wandering waistlines, and conspicuous adornment. A cursory trip through an illustrated art history will turn up fashions that distort the bodies of both sexes in ways that can make today's most bizarre styles look pretty tame.

Back when royalty really reigned, fashion was established at the court and trickled down in diluted form to the population at large. It was at the French court that the first designer we know by name made her mark—Rose Bertin, dressmaker and confidante to Queen Marie Antoinette. Undoubtedly talented, she finally owes her place in fashion history to her domineering personality and her relationship to her royal sponsor.

With the Revolution and the Terror, French fashion went underground. It still existed—even anti-fashion is a form of it—but we don't know the dressmakers' names. Perhaps wary of too high a profile (Mlle. Bertin, after all, had to flee to England to escape the guillotine), dressmakers kept their place, more tradesman than star. It took over half a century for the next name to emerge and the dressmaker was not only a man, he was not French. He was English. The year was 1858 and the Second Empire provided a hospitable environment and a suitable patron, the Empress Eugénie.

the prototype for the designer as star

In his way a revolutionary, Charles Frederick Worth radically reshaped the manner in which dressmakers did business. Instead of making a few dresses at a time for individual clients, he designed entire collections; and instead of displaying them on dress forms or miniature dolls, he showed them on live mannequins. More significantly, except for the court, he no longer traipsed to clients' homes but required them to come to his salon. He was the prototype for the designer as star, truly the first *grand couturier.* He was also the first of the talented foreigners who have enriched French fashion, from Spanish Balenciaga to American Mainbocher to English Molyneux to German Lagerfeld to Italian Ferré to today's younger influx of English and American talent in both couture and ready-to-wear. John Galliano, Stella McCartney, Alexander McQueen, Tom Ford, Marc Jacobs, Michael Kors—the list goes on.

The end of the 19th century and the opening years of the 20th ushered in a period of prosperity and conspicuous consumption that lasted until World War I. Couture houses proliferated and so did name designers such as Paul Poiret, who worked for several fashionable couturiers before setting up on his own in 1904. With a genius for publicity equaled only by his talent, he became the best-known designer of his era but he was by no means the only one—Lanvin, Callot Soeurs, and Chanel in her first incarnation were among the many. A number of the English—Lucile, for example, and the tailors Redfern and Charles Creed—also established themselves in Paris.

As World War I ended, there was a burst of creativity in the arts matched in fashion by an explosion of fresh design talent—Vionnet, Chanel, Schiaparelli, Balmain, Nina Ricci, Rochas, and Grès were only the most prominent. Most had begun working before the war but came fully into their own in the heady days of peace.

...it took another war

The United States, like the rest of the western world, had relied on Paris for fashion direction and might have done so indefinitely if not cut off from Europe by two cataclysmic wars. During World War I, *Vogue* promoted the creations of American designers and luxury stores depended on them for high-end glamour, but with peace Paris regained its primacy as fashion arbiter. And so things remained between the two great conflicts.

There were, however, signs of change. A burgeoning American ready-to-wear industry was beginning to recognize the value of original native talent and rely less on copyists. While most designers were still anonymous, a handful became known to the public and their names appeared on labels, notably Claire McCardell, Vera Maxwell, and Clare Potter for sportswear, Norman Norell in luxury ready-to-wear, and Sylvia Pedlar for lingerie. There were others, but it took another war and another forced separation from Europe to bring wider recognition to home-grown designers and turn the United States into a major fashion force.

World War II brought another disruption in the flow of fashion ideas but with its end Paris resumed its leadership role—familiar names resurfaced and new ones appeared, memorably Christian Dior. Once again, serious attention was paid to each French fashion edict as fine stores across the country and the fashion press resumed their twice-yearly pilgrimages to the couture showings.

There were premonitions of change. The increasing importance of ready-to-wear became so obvious that even the French couturiers had to recognize it, and as they tired of seeing their ideas knocked off by others, they began to produce their own boutique or diffusion collections. Dior and Balmain, Fath and Saint Laurent, one by one they joined the ready-to-wear parade and the *prêt-a-porter* showings became another reason to make the Paris journey.

...the Youthquake felt round the world

BY THE LATE 1950s AND early 1960s revolutionary rumblings were forecasting the shift of fashion focus from the mature, elegant client of the couture to the young and irreverent consumer who wanted to wear nothing that would be suitable for her mother. Centered in London, the Youthquake's seismic shock was felt around the world. Young, uninhibited designers—Mary Quant, Ossie Clark, Vivienne Westwood, Zandra Rhodes, among others—gained attention and customers with their anti-establishment ideas, and London became a major stop on the fashion professional's itinerary. In Paris, Emmanuelle Khanh and Kenzo (the first of his Japanese countrymen to make an international reputation) took up the cause of youth; Betsey Johnson joined in gleefully in New York and has never stopped.

Meanwhile, on the couture level and in luxury ready-to-wear and knits, Italy became a force and the Spanish couture was briefly heard from. But for nearly two decades after World War II, the French couture maintained its primacy and American retailers and manufacturers continued to look there for ideas.

Today, ready-to-wear designers in New York, London, and Milan propose trends, and ideas circulate in all directions; but, like it or not, Paris remains the lodestar of the fashion firmament. However, whether or not the French care to admit it, much of the ferment of new ideas in Paris these days comes from abroad. Designers from the United States, Austria, Belgium, England, Germany, Italy, and The Netherlands show in the city, and many of the most illustrious French houses are under the creative guidance of foreigners. Karl Lagerfeld has the longest tenure with over 20 years at Chanel, John Galliano keeps making waves at Christian Dior, Tom Ford is given credit for reviving Saint Laurent Rive Gauche. The list goes on.

Here in the United States we've produced a number of world-class designers at the couture level—Mainbocher worked in Paris between the two World Wars, Charles James was recognized there, and more recently Oscar de la Renta made Balmain one of the few profitable couture operations. It is through ready-to-wear, though, that we've been most influential and more specifically, through sportswear and the ideal of style wedded to comfort. You could say that our major contribution to world fashion is jeans. There are very few places in the world where jeans have not become a staple of dress, if not always a mark of fashion.

...a commitment to change...

TODAY, PERHAPS 1,500 WOMEN IN the entire world buy from the couture, and only a tiny number of them buy more than a piece or two and make regular purchases. It's even doubtful that the couture is the incubator of new ideas it once was. Its customers, the wealthy women who once set the standards, have been supplanted for the young and hip by newer role models—film stars, pop music divas, and celebrities of all kinds. Increasingly the person interested in cutting-edge fashion is very young, eager for novelty, and either ignorant of or not interested in the finer points of dressmaking. There is, however, a reassuring emphasis on quality among our younger designers, which bodes well for the future of fashion.

In her book *Seeing Through Clothes,* art historian Anne Hollander says "...the commitment to change that is the essence of fashion must often rely heavily on the effect of shock." Obviously, not everyone is ready for shock. The tiny fraction of the population that cares passionately about clothes and about the newest thing is and always has been outnumbered by the more timid and conventional. For every person who yearns for the newest look and the attention it brings there are many, many more who feel uncomfortable with either one.

If these were the only customers, fashion would be nothing more than a trade and a business, and certainly not a lot of fun. Fortunately for the designer, a core of dedicated fashion lovers hangs in there, enthusiasts who recognize and appreciate creativity wherever they find it. These are the people, stylemakers and customers alike, who give talented people the encouragement they need to survive and to generate the ideas that keep fashion alive and move it ahead. They are the supporters who, amused by its whims and thrilled by its successes, treasure fashion for the variety and enrichment it brings to their lives. As long as there are enough of them who care, it will be well worth every bit of effort, every ounce of skill and daring, every iota of artistry it takes to survive in this difficult calling.

A

Joseph Abboud

Adolfo

Adri

Adrian

Miguel Adrover

Agnès B

Alaïa

Victor Alfaro

Linda Allard

Hardy Amies

John Anthony

Maria Antonelli

Arkadius

Giorgio Armani

Laura Ashley

Joseph Abboud

Born Boston, Massachusetts, May 5, 1950
Awards Cutty Sark Men's Fashion Award *Most Promising Menswear Designer* 1988 ·
Woolmark Award for Distinguished Fashion, 1989 · Council of Fashion Designers
of America (CFDA) *Menswear Designer of the Year:* 1989, 1990

Abboud brings a fresh viewpoint to the conservative realm of men's clothing, fusing a European aesthetic with American practicality. His clothes are exceptionally well made of beautiful fabrics, classic but with a contemporary attitude, combining colors and textures to give classicism a modern edge.

Of Lebanese descent, Abboud came to designing with a strong retail background—12 years in buying, merchandising, and sales promotion at Louis of Boston. He went to work there part time in 1968 during his freshman year at the University of Massachusetts, and worked full time after graduation. He also studied at the Sorbonne in Paris, where he fell in love with the European sense of style. He left Louis in 1981 for a job as sales representative at Polo/Ralph Lauren, joined the design team, and became associate director of men's wear. Following a year at Barry Bricken, Abboud was ready to form his own company in 1986.

In addition to the signature Abboud collection, there are shirts and ties, casual sportswear and golf clothes, loungewear, sleepwear, robes, rainwear, and men's scarves, as well as home products ranging from bedding to bath accessories to flatware. The label is sold at fine specialty stores and in Abboud boutiques around the United States. Internationally it is distributed in Canada, Great Britain, Japan, and Taiwan.

Joseph Abboud (above) and a sweater from his Fall 2001 sportswear collection (left).

Adolfo

Born Adolfo Sardina; Havana, Cuba, February 13, 1933
Awards Coty American Fashion Critics' Award *Special Award* (millinery): 1955, 1969

when Adolfo announced his retirement in March 1993, he had been established in fashion for 25 years. First as a milliner, then with custom-made and ready-to-wear, he turned current trends into wearable, elegant clothes for countless socially prominent women and notables such as Nancy Reagan. His knitted dresses and especially his Chanel-inspired knit suits became daytime uniforms, while for evening he created extravagant gowns in luxurious fabrics and characteristically subtle color combinations.

Adolfo demonstrated an early interest in fashion, encouraged by an aunt, Maria Lopez. She took him to Paris to see the designer showings and introduced him to both CHANEL and BALENCIAGA, where he began his career as an apprentice. After a year's apprenticeship, he came to New York in 1948 as designer for Danish-born milliner Bragaard. In 1953 he moved to the milliner Emme where he quickly gained recognition; in 1956 his name appeared on the label as Adolfo of Emme.

In 1962 he opened his own millinery firm with the help of a $10,000 loan from Bill Blass. Among his many

Adolfo designs from 1984 (left) and the designer in his studio, 1992 (above).

successes were the Panama planter's hat in 1966 and the shaggy Cossack hat in 1967, plus huge fur berets and such non-hats as fur hoods, kidskin bandannas, and long braids entwined with flowers worn attached to the wearer's hair. His declining interest in hats coincided with their disappearance from the heads of fashionable women and Adolfo gradually added clothing, finally switching entirely into apparel.

In addition to knits and the suit homages to Chanel, each collection included classic silk print dresses, often paired with the suit jackets, and one or two beautifully tailored coats and suits. His twice-a-year showings invariably brought out a large audience of faithful clients, usually with three or four of them in the same suit or dress. He also faithfully promoted his clothes with trips to stores around the country.

Since closing his apparel business, he has concentrated on his licenses, including perfume, men's wear, luggage, handbags, sportswear, furs, and hats.

Adri

Born Adrienne Steckling; St. Joseph, Missouri, c. 1935
Awards Coty American Fashion Critics' Award "*Winnie*," 1982

ADRI SPECIALIZES IN SOFT, REALITY-BASED clothes in the best American sportswear tradition, giving simple, wearable shapes an unexpected edge, using unusual fabrics in interesting mixes. Her supple, weightless fabrics—such an integral part of her designs—come largely from Italy's finest mills, with some selections from specialized French, American, and Irish houses. These are truly investment clothes to be worn and appreciated indefinitely.

Adri studied design at Washington University in St. Louis and was a guest editor at *Mademoiselle* magazine during her sophomore year. She continued her studies at Parsons School of Design in New York where CLAIRE MCCARDELL was her critic. McCardell, with her belief in functional, comfortable clothes, proved an important and lasting influence. In October 1971 Adri's clothes were included in a two-designer showing at the Smithsonian Institution in Washington, D.C. The theme was Innovative Contemporary Fashion; the other designer honored was Claire McCardell.

Adri worked at B.H. Wragge for eight years then went on her own. She had a succession of businesses, designing leisure wear as well as ready-to-wear. Deciding that the time had come for a smaller operation, she formed Adri Studio Ltd. in 1993 as a new way of marketing better-priced clothing. With this approach, and working with her partner, Nadia, she designs a collection of thoughtfully integrated outfits, which is then cut to order for private customers and a select group of retail stores.

She has been a critic at Parsons since the early 1980s.

Adri design sketch, Spring/Summer 2003.

Adrian

Born Adrian Adolph Greenburg; Naugatuck, Connecticut, March 3, 1903
Died Los Angeles, California, September 13, 1959
Awards Neiman Marcus Award, 1943 · Coty American Fashion Critics' Award
"Winnie," 1945 · Parsons Medal for Distinguished Achievement, 1956

A top Hollywood studio designer of the 1920s and 1930s, Adrian was also successful at made-to-order and ready-to-wear.

In 1921 he began studies at The New York School of Fine and Applied Arts, now Parsons School of Design. In 1922, he transferred to the school's Paris branch, and in the process changed his name to Gilbert Adrian. After six months in Paris he met Irving Berlin, who saw a costume Adrian had designed for a classmate to wear to the annual Bal du Grand Prix. Berlin offered him a job designing for the *Music Box Revue.* He then returned to New York, where he continued to work on stage productions, including the Greenwich Village *Follies* and George White's *Scandals.* In 1923,

Rudolph Valentino's wife, director Natacha Rombova, lured Adrian to Hollywood to design costumes for her screen idol husband.

In 1926 he started working for Cecil B. DeMille, and in 1928 moved with DeMille to MGM where he soon began designing for that studio's pictures.

As the studio's chief designer, Adrian created costumes for such stars as Greta Garbo, Joan Crawford, Katharine Hepburn, Rosalind Russell, and Norma Shearer, nearly 200 films in all.

The association with MGM lasted until 1941, when he left the studio to open his own business, Adrian Ltd., for couture and top-ticket ready-to-wear. He closed his Beverly Hills salon in 1948 but continued in wholesale until a 1952 heart attack forced his retirement. Following his recovery, he and his wife, actress Janet Gaynor, retired to their farm in Brazil where he concentrated on landscape painting, a longtime avocation.

Adrian returned to Hollywood in 1959 to design the costumes for the Lerner and Loewe New York production of *Camelot,* on which he was working when he died suddenly of a cerebral hemorrhage.

In general, the Adrian look was sleek and modern, a silhouette marked by exaggeratedly wide shoulders tapering to a small waist. He was a master of intri-

cate cut—stripes were worked in opposing directions on shapely, fitted suits, and color patches and bold animal prints were set into sinuous black crepe evening gowns. Diagonal closings, dolman sleeves, and floating tabs were recurring details. In addition, he did draped, swathed late-day dresses and romantic organdy evening gowns such as the "Letty Lynton" gown designed for Joan Crawford, which was widely copied. It is said that more than 50,000 were sold at Macy's alone.

In addition to women's clothes and stage costumes, Adrian also produced several men's wear collections, and had two perfumes, *Saint* and *Sinner.*

Joan Crawford (left) in the "Letty Lynton Dress"; from Adrian's 1946 ready-to-wear collection (right). *Also see Color Plate 20.*

Miguel Adrover

Born Calonge, Mallorca, Spain, December 14, 1965
Awards Council of Fashion Designers of America (CFDA) · *Perry Ellis Award for Women's Wear*, 2000

Miguel Adrover appeared on the fashion scene in 1999 as an original—no prestigious design school, no apprenticeship with established designers. He left school at the age of twelve to work on his family's almond farm, completed his compulsory military service, and in his teens paid a visit to London, which introduced him to both punk rock and the new romanticism. He arrived in New York in 1991, supported himself as a janitor, and in 1995 teamed up with a tailor friend, Douglas Hobbs, to do a clothing line called Dugg. They opened a shop in the East Village called Horn, dedicated to the new and experimental.

Four years later, Adrover showed his first collection, put together with the help of his friends. These were the now famous pieces made, because he couldn't afford fabric, from a recycled Burberry coat (turned inside out and backwards), a Vuitton bag, and ticking allegedly taken from the late Quentin Crisp's mattress. They were put together with solid design and tailoring skills, and were also well made.

His Spring 2002 collection, shown on Monday, September 10, 2001, was called brilliantly inventive, creative, and sophisticated. But between the September 11 disaster and his backers' financial difficulties, the Adrover enterprise was closed down the following month. He resurfaced in mid-2002 and showed in the New York collections that September.

Miguel Adrover, 2001.

Agnès B.

Born Agnès Troublé, Versailles, France, 1942

Agnès B. is the inspiration for a generation of laid-back sportswear dressing. After graduating from the École des Beaux Arts in Versailles and an editorial stint at *Elle* magazine, she worked as an assistant to Dorothée Bis and as freelance designer for several clothing firms before going into business for herself. She initiated her style in the early 1970s as a reaction to what she felt were the too dressy, too trendy clothes available at the time in Paris. Her unforced, airy, low-key clothes, essentially sports separates and accessories for women, men, and children, are sold primarily in her own stores around the world, including New York, Amsterdam, London, and Tokyo. Her output now includes a perfume, skin care and cosmetics products, and a maternity collection.

Alaïa

Born Azzedine Alaïa; Tunis, Tunisia

Fashion connoisseurs now consider him a genius and one of the last true couturiers but until 1980 when Alaïa presented his first ready-to-wear collection, he worked in obscurity, known only to a select group of adventurous customers who also bought from the great couture houses. For the previous 18 years he had worked out of his

apartment, with a list of knowledgeable clients ranging from Paloma Picasso to Dyan Cannon and Raquel Welch.

Raised in Tunis by his grandmother, Alaïa studied sculpture at the École des Beaux-Arts of Tunis, and while in art school worked for several dressmakers. In 1957 he went to Paris where he had been promised a job with Dior. Arriving a few months before Dior's death, he did indeed get a job in the Dior cutting room but lasted only five days. For the next few years he supported himself by working as an *au pair,* at the same time making clothes for his fashionable young employers and their friends. By 1984, he had become so commercially successful that he bought his own townhouse in the Marais section of Paris.

Alaïa's first international notice was for an accessory—black leather gauntlets studded with silver rivets. His original clothes, said to be the sexiest in Paris, were seamed, molded, and draped to define and reveal every curve of a woman's body. Translating these techniques from woven cloth to knits is probably his greatest ready-to-wear achievement.

After 1992, Alaïa stopped runway shows and essentially dropped off the fashion radar. Although he continued to design for a few select customers, his deliveries to retail establishments were so sporadic that few stores were willing or able to cope. He has reappeared in the new century as if reborn, both in his influence on younger designers toying retrospectively with the 1980s, and in his own collections. These, while unmis-

takably Alaïa, are totally without nostalgia and entirely contemporary.

In 2001 he sold a minority share of his business to Prada, and in July of that year staged a small showing of just 22 pieces in his own home and headquarters to a select audience of barely 100 people. It was considered one of the most exhilarating and influential collections of the year—only his fourth showing in ten years—and confirmed his standing as probably the least derivative designer of our time. "I try to go my own path. I don't like to go out and find influences for collections. That's not my way. I just do what I do."

Alaïa's unique draping, inspired by the work of the great Madeleine Vionnet, is the heart of his style—the key to his design is his belief that fashion should be timeless.

Designer Alaïa, 2000 (above). Design from 2001 (left).

A

Victor Alfaro

Born Chihuahua, Mexico, May 26, 1963
Awards Vidal Sassoon, Excellence in New Design, 1993 · Omni-Mexican Award for Best Latin American Designer, 1994 · Dallas Fashion Award *Rising Star Award*, 1994 · Council of Fashion Designers of America (CFDA) *Perry Ellis Award for New Fashion Talent*, 1994

Alfaro takes his inspiration from the fabric, draping directly on the form. Without exaggeration or gimmicks, his work melds talent, intelligence, and technique, for sophistication with a contemporary edge. He attended the Fashion Institute of Technology from 1983 to 1986, and got his first job with Mary Ann Restivo. After two years with Restivo he went to JOSEPH ABBOUD, remaining there until 1991 when he opened his own business. For several years he worked in Milan for the cashmere company Tse and subsequently moved his own business to Milan.

Alfaro specializes in designer sportswear and in evening clothes, combining casual ease with unabashed luxury for an effect of contemporary, unforced, elegance-on-the-move.

Design by Alfaro, 2001.

Linda Allard

Born Akron, Ohio, May 27, 1940
Awards Dallas Fashion Award: 1986, 1987, 1994

Linda Allard for Ellen Tracy is a label familiar to women who need career clothes that are up to the minute but not over the top, excellent quality at prices that won't break the bank. Cut from fine fabrics, including precious fibers such as cashmere, the clothes reflect the designer's belief that what a woman wears should be an extension of her own style and personality, helping her to look her best and conferring a feeling of confidence and power.

Allard has spent her entire career at Ellen Tracy, where she got her first job after leaving Kent State University in 1962 with a degree in Fine Arts. Starting out as assistant designer, she became design director in 1964, a position she's held ever since. Her name went on the label in 1984. In addition to the signature collection, there is Company by Ellen Tracy for casual sportswear, both collections available in special sizes. Licenses extend to fragrances, leather outerwear, shoes, belts, scarves, eyewear, and hosiery. The Ellen Tracy company was sold to Liz Claiborne in 2002.

Allard actively supports her own industry and other community and cultural activities, serving on the boards of the Council of Fashion Designers of America (CFDA), American Ballet Theater, New York's Garden Conservancy, and Kent State, her alma mater.

Cindy Crawford wearing an Allard design for Ellen Tracy from Fall 2001 collection.

Sir Hardy Amies

Born Edwin Hardy Amies; Maida Vale, London, England, July 17, 1909
Died "at his country home" in the English Cotswold, March 5, 2003
Awards KCVO (Knight Commander of The Royal Victorian Order), 1989

Dressmaker to Queen Elizabeth II for over 50 years, Hardy Amies has always specialized in tailored suits and coats, and cocktail and evening dresses. The house also makes breezy, more contemporary women's clothes such as pantsuits and casual classics. Men's wear has become a major part of the business.

Hardy Amies and a typical ballgown, 1960.

Amies succeeded in fashion without formal design training; his mother, however, worked for a London dressmaker and as a child he was sometimes taken there as a treat. After leaving school, he spent several years in France and Germany, becoming fluent in both languages, returning to England when he was twenty-one to work for a manufacturer of scales.

In 1934 he became designer for Lachasse, a London couture house owned by his mother's former employer, and within a year was managing director. He left Lachasse in 1939 to serve in the British Army Intelligence Corps. During his Army career he gained the rank of lieutenant colonel and in 1944 was head of the Special Forces Commission to Belgium.

While in the service Amies was given two months' leave at the request of the Board of Trade to make a collection of clothes for South America. These, designed in his spare time at the War Office, were his first steps toward his own business. In 1945 he was mustered out to take part in a government-sponsored collection designed in accordance with the rules of the wartime Utility Scheme. In 1946 he opened his own

dressmaking business, added a boutique line in 1950 and men's wear in 1959. Starting with ties and shirts, the men's wear business progressed to made-to-measure suits and soon extended to firms in the United States, Canada, and Japan.

In 1984, at age seventy-five, Amies announced plans to leave his multimillion dollar fashion business to the members of his staff but denied any intention of an early departure. Ten years later he was still actively engaged in his businesses.

In May 2001 he sold his business to Luxury Brands Group, which also acquired Norman Hartnell, another classic British house that had dressed the queen. In November of that year Amies announced his retirement, at age 93, and Jacques Azagury, a Moroccan-born designer with his own label, was made head of couture for the house. A new ready-to-wear line was also planned. Besides the men's wear, licensing agreements have included jewelry, small leathers, luggage, and bed linens. Among Sir Hardy's publications are: *Just So far,* 1954; *ABC of Men's Fashion,* 1964; *Still Here,* 1984.

John Anthony

Born Gianantonio Iorio, New York City, 1938
Awards Coty American Fashion Critics' Award "Winnie," 1972; Return Award, 1976

Anthony's strength is in sophisticated, feminine clothes of refined elegance, marked by a feeling for asymmetry, a sensuous suppleness, and masterly tailoring. In each collection he has confined himself to a few lean, simple shapes in luxurious fabrics, a limited color palette, and a small group of key textures.

At the High School of Industrial Arts (now High School of Art and Design), Anthony won three European scholarships. He spent one year at the Accademia di Belle Arti in Rome before returning to New York and two years at the Fashion Institute of Technology.

His first job was a nine-year stint with Devonbrook, followed by three years with Adolph Zelinka. John Anthony, Inc. was established in January 1971 and closed in 1979.

After a number of years spent in made-to-order fashion and in recovering the use of his own name, Anthony reopened for fall 1986, showing a small ready-to-wear collection out of his couture salon. Since then he has been in and out of ready-to-wear, in recent years concentrating entirely on custom work with its emphasis on luxurious materials and impeccable handwork, and the perfect fit that comes only with clothes made on the person who wears them.

Maria Antonelli

Born Tuscany, Italy, 1903
Died Rome, Italy, 1969

Antonelli started as a dressmaker in 1924, and soon became known and respected for the exceptional tailoring of her coats and suits. One of the pioneers of Italian fashion as it came into prominence in the 1950s, she participated in the first showings at Florence in 1951. Antonelli Sport ready-to-wear was begun in 1961 with the assistance of her daughter Luciana.

Both André Laug and Guy Douvier, who became successful designers on their own, trained with Antonelli. Her list of clients was international in scope and included many film and stage personalities.

In 1958 she was made a Cavalier of the Republic by the Italian government in recognition of her contributions to Italian fashion.

A

Arkadius

Born: Arkadius Weremsczuk, Lublin, Poland, July 5, 1969
Awards: British Fashion Council *New Generation Award,* September 2000 · *Elle*
Awards, Warsaw, Poland *Best Designer of the Year,* October 2000

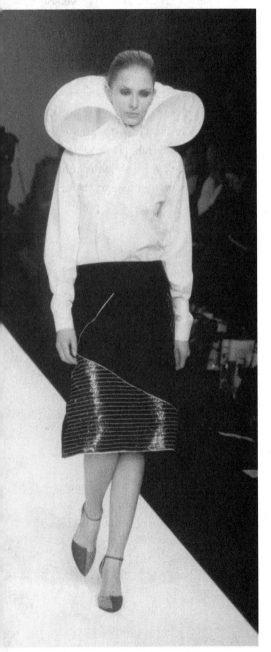

From the start Arkadius has amused, and sometimes enraged, fashion onlookers with wildly creative shows of clothes that are alternately calmly wearable and provocatively outrageous; his fine tailoring skills and imaginative cutting go hand-in-hand with a taste for ornate decoration and eccentric presentations. Half creator, half businessman, he has been described as bizarrely talented and hailed as the next John Galliano.

Born into a family of teachers, Arkadius set his sights on London and on fashion while still in college in Krakow, leaving before graduation to pursue his dream. He reached London in 1994 after side excursions to Tuscany and Munich, his goal, Central St. Martins College of Art and Design. He first had to learn enough English to walk through its doors but managed to enroll in September of that year. During his third year he was invited to work in Alexander McQueen's design studio, and his July 1999 graduation collection earned both a double first and a sponsor for his debut collection that September at London Fashion Week.

Appearing to have found a happy medium between commercialism and art, Arkadius has since added ready-to-wear, men's wear, and jeans.

Designer Arkadius (left) and design from 2001 (far left).

12

Giorgio Armani

Born Emilia-Romagna, Italy, July 1934
Awards Neiman Marcus Award, 1979 · Council of Fashion Designers of American (CFDA)
International Award, 1983

Armani designs, 1994 (above) and 2002 (left). *Also see Color Plate 8.*

After brief tries at medicine and photography, Armani began his fashion career in 1964, first as a window dresser, then as assistant buyer of men's clothing for La Rinascente, a large Italian department store. During the seven years he spent there he developed his ideas on men's dress and a dislike for what he considered a stiff, formal look that disguised individuality.

His next job, as designer for a men's wear company of the Cerutti group, gave him even greater knowledge of the practical and commercial aspects of the clothing business. From there he went on to design for a number of companies including Ermenegildo Zegna and UNGARO.

Armani produced his first men's wear collection under his own label in 1974, incorporating the ideas he had developed while working for others. An

unconstructed blazer was his first attention-getter. He moved into the area of women's wear in 1975, bringing to it the same perfectionist tailoring and fashion attitude applied to his men's clothes. From day into evening, Armani's emphasis is on easy, uncontrived shapes cut from exquisite Italian fabrics, tailored with absolute mastery. Color and fabric are primary considerations. His preference is for neutrals such as taupe, beige, black, and infinite tones of gray. He claims to have taught women to dress with the ease of men but always with a feminine turn to even the most masculine cut. His work is not intended to shock and he is not interested in trends; he aims for a soft, light silhouette, emphasizing femininity and gently disguising imperfections.

Armani business interests now include perfumes and accessories for men and women sold in fine retail stores and free-standing shops in Italy and around the world. The Emporio label and shops were developed to bring Armani styles to young men and women who could not afford the regular line, and A/X: Armani Exchange, is younger and sportier still. Armani has also done film work.

Armani devotes himself to work singlemindedly, supervising every aspect of his collections, which are shown in his own theater. He does not use stylists and insists on complete control, down to such details as the models' hairstyles and makeup.

In October 2000, a 25-year Armani retrospective opened at the Guggenheim Museum in New York, moving in March 2001 to the museum's outpost in Bilbao, Spain, and in 2003 to Berlin, Germany.

Laura Ashley

Born Merthyr Tydfil, Wales, 1926
Died Coventry, England, September 17, 1985

Romantic and innocent, the Laura Ashley look consisted of dresses with long, soft skirts in small flower prints, sweetly trimmed with lace. It would appear to have little connection with life and fashion in the 21st century yet its influence can still be seen on city streets, worn in ways the designer would probably not have imagined—with backpacks and work boots—and in the collections of cutting-edge designers from Italy to the United States.

In 1953 Ashley and her husband began printing textiles on the kitchen table of their London flat. The couple began with towels, scarves, and placemats, which Bernard carried around to the major London stores and sold so successfully that the Ashleys formed their first company in 1954. As their business and family expanded, they moved from London to Wales, setting up a factory at Carno, Montgomeryshire. In the early 1980s the family moved into an 18th century chateau in Northern France, although the business remained centered in Wales.

Laura Ashley died in 1985 as a result of a fall, but the company has endured. Reaching its apogee in the 1960s, 1970s, and early 1980s, it went public in 1985. At its height, there were Laura Ashley stores in cities as diverse as New York, Paris, Geneva, and San Francisco, dispensing the distinctive prints in decorative fabrics and clothes, bringing the cozy warmth of an English cottage into the harsh city environment.

The final three percent of the company owned by the family and the Ashley trust was sold in June 2001.

B

Badgley Mischka
Balenciaga
Pierre Balmain
Travis Banton
Jhane Barnes
Neil Barrett
John Bartlett
Geoffrey Beene
Eric Bergère
Rose Bertin
Laura Biagiotti
Dirk Bikkembergs
Manolo Blahnik
Bill Blass
Marc Bohan
Veronique Branquinho
Tom Brigance
Donald Brooks
Bruce
Stephen Burrows
Barbara Bui

Badgley Mischka

Born Mark Badgley; East St. Louis, Illinois, January 12, 1961
James Mischka; Burlington, Wisconsin, December 23, 1960
Awards Mouton Cadet *Young Designer Award*, 1989

Badgley attended UCLA and Mischka took a B.A. in Managerial Science at Rice University in Houston—they met at Parsons School of Design where both graduated with B.F.A. degrees in Fashion Design. After Parsons, their paths diverged, Mischka going to WilliWear from 1985 to 1987, Badgley successively to Jackie Rogers and DONNA KARAN. The two young designers teamed up in 1988 to form their own company. In January 1992 the firm was acquired by Escada, the large German fashion company, but the two designers retained creative control and a financial stake in the business.

Badgley Mishka evening gown, Spring 2003 (left). Designers Mark Badgley and James Mischka, 2000 (right).

The designers are best known for their beaded evening wear, favored by celebrities from New York to Hollywood. They describe their clothes as modern and sleek, appropriate for dinner and dancing. However, they have broadened their focus to include daywear, separates, and a collection of bridal gowns with the clean, elegant lines and the luxurious beading and ornamentation that distinguish their clothes for evening.

Balenciaga

Born Cristobal Balenciaga; Guetaria, Spain, January 21, 1895
Died Valencia, Spain, March 24, 1972

Master tailor, master dressmaker, Balenciaga was a great originator, possibly the greatest couturier of all time. Of them all, only he could do everything—design, cut, fit, and sew an entire garment. He worked alone, using his own ideas, putting together with his own hands every model that later appeared in his collections. His clothes, so beautiful and elegant, were also so skillfully designed that a woman did not have to have a perfect figure to wear them. They moved with the body and were comfortable as well as fashionable.

The facts of Balenciaga's origins and early life are so obscured by legend that it is difficult to know where reality begins and myth ends. His father, for example, has been said to have been both captain of the Spanish royal yacht and captain of a fishing boat. It is known that after his father's death, the boy and his mother moved to San Sebastián where she became a seamstress. The son followed in her footsteps to become a skilled tailor. As the story goes, his career in fashion began when the Marquesa de Casa Torres allowed him to copy a DRÉCOLL suit he had admired on her, later sending him to Paris to meet the suit's designer. The Marquesa encouraged him to study design and in 1916 helped him set up his own shop in San Sebastián. This was the first of three houses named Eisa; the others were in Madrid and Barcelona.

Balenciaga designs from *Women's Wear Daily,* 1947 to 1957.

Balenciaga evening gown in raw silk from 1965. *Also see Color Plate 21.*

Balenciaga moved to Paris in 1937, returning to Spain at the beginning of World War II. After the war he reopened in Paris on avenue George V, where he established himself as the preeminent designer of his time, one of the most imaginative and creative artists of the Paris couture.

A great student of art, he understood how to interpret his sources rather than merely copy them. The somber blacks and browns of the old Spanish masters were among his favorite colors and the influence of such early moderns as Monet and Manet can also be found in his work. His interest in the post cubists and abstract expressionists can be seen in his late designs.

His innovations, especially during the 1950s and 1960s, are still influential: the revolutionary semi-fitted suit jacket of 1951; the 1955 middy dress, which evolved into the chemise; the cocoon coat; the balloon skirt; and the flamenco evening gown cut short in front, long in back. To achieve his sculptural effects he worked with the Swiss fabric house, Abraham, to develop a heavily sized silk called gazar, very light but with a capacity for holding a shape and floating away from the body.

In 1968 Balenciaga abruptly closed his house and retired to Spain. There has been speculation concerning his reasons but perhaps he was simply tired—he was seventy-five years old. He came out of retirement to design the wedding dress of Generalissimo Franco's granddaughter, whose marriage took place in 1972 just two weeks before Balenciaga died.

A shy and private man who loathed publicity, Balenciaga was seldom photographed, never appeared in his own salon, and, except for his perfumes, refused to have anything to do with commercial exploitation. Since his death, he has been honored by a number of exhibitions: in New York in 1973 at the Metropolitan Museum of Art and in 1986 at the Fashion Institute of Technology; in France in 1985 at the Museum of Historic Textiles in Lyons, the center of the French silk industry. The label was revived for ready-to-wear in the 1990s as Balenciaga Le Dix, with Joseph Thimister as head designer (1992–1997), and upon his departure with NICOLAS GHESQUIÈRE. In July 2001, the house was bought by Gucci, which allotted a nine percent share to Ghesquière as creative director.

Balenciaga's sense of proportion and balance, his mastery of cut, his touches of wit, the architectural quality and essential rightness of his designs still inspire awe and admiration. He is rightly considered one of the giants of 20th-century couture.

Pierre Balmain

Born St. Jean-de-Maurienne, France, May 18, 1914
Died Paris, France, June 29, 1982
Awards Neiman Marcus Award, 1955

BALMAIN CLAIMED CREDIT for beginning the New Look—critics and writers divided it between him, DIOR, FATH, and BALENCIAGA. It is true that his first collections accentuated the femininity of the figure with a small waist, high bust, rounded hips, and long, full skirts—all New Look characteristics. He continued making clothes of quiet elegance, and at his death had just completed the sketches for his fall collection.

An only child, Balmain was only seven when his father died. He was raised by his mother, who later worked with him in his couture salon. In 1934, while studying architecture at the École des Beaux Arts in Paris, he began sketching dresses and took his designs to Captain MOLYNEUX. The British-born designer allowed the twenty-year-old to work for him in the afternoons while continuing school in the mornings, finally advised him to devote himself to dress design. Molyneux then gave him a job and Balmain remained with the house until called into the Army in 1939. After the fall of France in 1940, Balmain

"Scotch" from the Balmain 1962–63 Fall-Winter collection.

returned to Paris to work for LUCIEN LELONG, where he stayed until 1945 when he left to open his own house.

In 1951 he opened a New York ready-to-wear operation, for which he designed special collections, and he also did theater and film work. In addition to Balmain boutiques there were perfumes, *Vent Vert* and *Jolie Madame,* and over 60 licenses including men's wear, jewelry, luggage, and accessories. The fragrance business was bought by Revlon which introduced new fragrances *Ivoire* in 1981 and *Opera* in 1994.

After Balmain's death the business continued until January 1990 with Erik Mortensen in charge of couture. When the house was sold, Mortensen, who had been there for 42 years, was replaced and when ownership changed once more, OSCAR DE LA RENTA moved in as couture designer. His first collection was for Spring 1993, his last for Fall-Winter 2002-2003. He was succeeded by Frenchman Laurent Mercier who was fired in June 2003. No replacement was named.

B

Travis Banton

Born Waco, Texas, 1894
Died Los Angeles, California, February 2, 1958

Banton was with Paramount Pictures for 14 years, designing elegant, sophisticated clothes for some of the screen's most legendary actresses—Claudette Colbert, Marlene Dietrich, Carole Lombard, and Mae West among them. He favored glow and shimmer over sparkle and shine and was especially partial to the bias cut. With an extraordinarily long career, Banton is remembered particularly for what became known as "The Paramount look." He produced clothes of the highest quality, often cut on the bias, superb in fabric, workmanship, and fit. The effect was dreamy, elegant, understated.

His parents moved to New York City when Banton was two years old. He briefly attended Columbia University, transferred to the Art Student's League and then to the School of Fine and Applied Arts. His apprenticeship to Madame Frances, a successful New York custom dressmaker, was interrupted by naval service in World War I, but not before he established himself as a designer. On his return he worked for a number of custom houses, including LUCILE, training ground for Howard Greer and a number of other designers, then opened his own salon. There his designs included elaborate costumes for the Ziegfeld Follies.

At the instigation of Walter Wanger, he went to Hollywood in 1924 to design costumes for Leatrice Joy in Paramount Pictures' *The Dressmaker From Paris.* He stayed on at Paramount and in 1927,

when Howard Greer left to open his own custom business, became the studio's head designer. At the expiration of his Paramount contract in 1938, Banton joined Howard Greer as a private couturier. A year later he went to 20th Century Fox, then worked off and on for Universal Studios. Meanwhile, he conducted his own dressmaking business, turning to ready-to-wear in the

Banton designs for Marlene Dietrich in *Shanghai Express,* 1932.

1950s. He designed Rosalind Russell's wardrobe for the stage production of *Auntie Mame,* and dressed Dinah Shore for both her television appearances and her private life.

Jhane Barnes

Born 1954
Awards Coty American Fashion Critics Award *Men's Wear*, 1980; *Men's Apparel*, 1981;
Men's Wear Return Award, 1984 · Council of Fashion Designers of America (CFDA)
Outstanding Menswear Designer, 1981

Barnes established her own company in 1977 when she was twenty-three. While known mainly for men's sportswear, she has also made sportswear for women. Her designs are unconstructed, beautifully tailored in luxurious and original fabrics, many of which she designs herself. They are marked by innovative details, carefully thought out and carried through. She is original and creative, with architectural insight into clothing, now confined exclusively to men's wear, from belts and neckwear to sportswear, suits, and outerwear, sold through a few fine stores and her own Web site.

Other design commitments include textiles and carpets for the office environment and furniture—tables, chairs, and upholstered furniture—as well as a collection of throws for the home.

Neil Barrett

Born South Devon, England, 1965

Barrett grew up in southwestern England on the stormy English Channel, as he describes himself, "a very practical kid who went out dressed for all kinds of rough weather." His family, master tailors, made uniforms for British naval officers.

In 1989 after college (Central St. Martin's and the Royal College of Art), Barrett went to work, first for Gucci then for Prada Uomo, before joining the Belgian luggage company Samsonite. There he designed a collection of men's clothes intended specifically for travelers. These included the time-travel jacket with built-in watch, a travel jacket with built-in earplugs and inflatable neck pillow, and multipocket, crease-resistant pants. Intended not as fashion but as practical things for travel, they were greeted enthusiastically by the fashion press.

Neil Barrett, 2000.

Barrett's first collection to appear under his own name was strictly men's wear—described as haute utilitarian—spare, durable clothes designed not just for the runway but to be worn. His first capsule collection for women appeared in Milan in January 2000, shown with his men's collection. Before that women would raid men's stores for items such as his motorcycle jackets and sweaters. For both women and men, Barrett thinks not of the ultra-fit, ultra-thin model but of the real people with less-than-perfect bodies who will be wearing the clothes. His strength lies in fabric innovation (he has been a consultant to the Italian textile industry), in subtle colors and clever details, and an ability to make clothes that are individual fashion and also wearable.

B

John Bartlett

Born Columbus, Ohio, March 22, 1963
Awards Woolmark *Cutting Edge* Award, 1992 · Fashion Institute of Technology
Alumni Award, 1994 · Council of Fashion Designers of America (CFDA) *Perry Ellis
Award for New Fashion Talent*, 1993; Men's Wear Designer of the Year, 1997

Bartlett has, from the beginning of his career, put an unconventional spin on his approach to men's wear, giving familiar pieces a fresh, younger look with altered scale and proportions and unexpected mixes of texture and pattern. His body-conscious clothes, while firmly grounded in the American sportswear tradition, are not for the timid or unimaginative, but rather for free-thinking men with minds of their own. He has also produced collections for women with the same edgy viewpoint as his clothes for men.

Bartlett graduated from Harvard in 1985 with a B.A. in Sociology, went on to the Fashion Institute of Technology's men's wear program, graduating in 1988 with the Bill Robinson Award. He interned with WILLI SMITH, Bill Robinson, and RONALDUS SHAMASK, spent a year as men's designer for WilliWear from 1988 to 1989, and was design director for Shamask from 1989 to 1991. He established his own label in 1992. Despite critical acclaim, he has struggled over the years to find stable financial backing to build his business, and in November 2002, announced he was closing down and leaving fashion.

Geoffrey Beene

Born Haynesville, Louisiana, August 30, 1927
Awards Coty American Fashion Critics Award "*Winnie,*" 1964; *Return Award,*
1966; *Hall of Fame,* 1974; *Hall of Fame Citation,* 1975; *Special Award (jewelry),*
1977; *Special Award (contribution to international status of American fashion),* 1979; *Special Award (women's fashions),* 1981; *Hall of Fame Citation,*
1982 · Neiman Marcus Award: 1964, 1965 · Council of Fashion Designers of
America (CFDA) *Special Award,* 1985; *Special Award Designer of the Year,* 1986;
Special Award for fashion as art, 1989

Long considered the most original and creative designer in American fashion, Beene is noted for his subtle cut, imaginative use of color, and luxurious fabrics. Making clothes that fit the life of the modern woman has been a major preoccupation—he believes that clothes must not only look attractive but also must move well, be comfortable to wear, and easy to pack. Year by year he has refined his style and continued to work toward greater simplicity, with increasing emphasis on cut and line and the lightest, most unusual fabrics.

The grandson and nephew of doctors, Beene came to fashion after three years in pre-med and medicine at Tulane University in New Orleans. Deciding that medicine was not for him, he went to California and while waiting to enroll at the University of Southern California, worked in window display at I. Magnin, Los Angeles. There his talent was recognized by an executive who suggested he make a career of fashion.

He attended Traphagen School of Fashion in New York for one summer and in 1947 went to Paris to study at L'École de la Chambre Syndicale and

Académie Julian. While in Paris he apprenticed with a tailor who had worked for the couturier MOLYNEUX, a master of tailoring and the bias cut. Returning to New York in 1950, Beene designed for several small custom salons and for Samuel Winston and Harmay. In 1958 he joined Teal Traina and for the first time had his name on the label. He opened his own business in 1962.

Beene's first collection, shown in Spring 1963, had elements characteristic of his work throughout the 1960s: looser fit, eased waistlines, bloused tops, flared skirts. Each collection in-

Designs from 2000 (above).

cluded at least one tongue-in-cheek style to stir things up, such as a black coat paved with wood buttons and a tutu evening dress with sequined bodice and feather skirt. Among the memorable Beene designs are long, sequined evening gowns cut like football jerseys complete with numerals, tweed evening pants paired with jeweled or lamé jackets, a gray sweatshirt bathing suit, and soft evening coats made of striped blankets from the Hudson's Bay Company.

Coat from 1964.

B

Designer Geoffrey Beene in 1987. *Also see Color Plate 12.*

He has, at various times, designed furs, swimwear, jewelry, scarves, men's wear, and Lynda Bird Johnson's wedding dress, he has had a boutique collection, fragrances for women and men, and licensed his name for shoes, gloves, hosiery, eyeglasses, loungewear, bedding, and furniture. Beene has shown his clothes in Europe with great success—in Milan in 1975, and at the American Embassies in Rome, Paris, Brussels, and Vienna. In December 1989 he opened his first retail shop in the Sherry Netherland Hotel on Fifth Avenue.

In 1988 he was honored by a retrospective of his work at the National Academy of Design, "Geoffrey Beene: The First Twenty-Five Years," to celebrate the 25th anniversary of his business. In the fall of 1993, he commissioned a 30-minute film to mark his 30th year in this own business. In February 1994, The Fashion Institute of Technology mounted "Beene Unbound," a 30-year retrospective of his designs.

In late 2001 he gave up his wholesale operation, electing to sell only to private clients.

Eric Bergère

Born November 6, 1960, Troyes, France

ERIC BERGÈRE began his fashion career early, studying clothing techniques in his native Troyes, a center of knitting industries, before moving to Paris and further studies in fashion design. He started working at Hermès when he was just twenty years old and stayed eight years, designing everything from women's sportswear to furs and swimwear.

In 1988 he began a seven-year period of freelance work—for Erreuno in Milan, for LANVIN, Jun Ashida, and Inès de la Fressange in France—spanning the range from coats and suits to evening clothes and wedding dresses. He also designed eyeglasses, shoes, and collections of leather and fur for various firms.

His first collections under his own name were for both women and men and appeared for Summer 1996. Subsequent collections—tailored clothing and sportswear for men, dresses, sportswear, and career clothes for women—have been described as elegant clothes with "clean, wearable shapes and subtle detail . . . classics with a twist . . . what French design should be about." In addition to his own Paris boutique, the clothes are sold in fine stores in Europe and Asia, and also on the Internet.

Eric Bergère, 2001.

Rose Bertin

Born near Abbeville, France, July 2, 1747
Died Epinay, France, September 22, 1813

At sixteen, Bertin became an apprentice in the Paris millinery shop of a Mlle. Pagelle. When sent to deliver hats to the royal princesses at the Conti palace, she was noticed by the Princesse de Conti, who became her sponsor. Nine

Marie Antoinette, patroness of Rose Bertin.

years later in 1772, having become a partner in the shop, Bertin was appointed court milliner. She was introduced to Marie Antoinette and became her confidante.

With such connections her establishment, *Au Grand-Mogol,* became extremely successful, not only with the French court but with the diplomatic corps. She executed commissions for dresses and hats to be sent to foreign courts, thus becoming one of the early exporters of French fashion. She also produced fantastic headdresses reflecting current events, enormously costly and symbolic of the excesses that led to the French Revolution.

Bertin could be considered the first "name" designer. She was celebrated in contemporary memoirs and encyclopedias and has left behind a reputation for pride, arrogance, and ambition. So influential was she that she was dubbed "The Minister of Fashion." With the onset of the Revolution, she fled to England to escape the Terror but remained loyal to the Queen. She returned to France in 1800 and eked out her last impoverished years selling trinkets.

At her death, an obituary recognized her accomplishments: "Mlle. Bertin is justly famous for the supremacy to which she has raised French fashions and for her services to the industries that made the material she used in her own creations and those that she inspired others to make."

Laura Biagiotti

Born Rome, Italy, 1943

Biagiotti graduated from Rome University with a degree in archaeology, then went to work at her mother's clothing company where she began producing clothes for other designers. Her first collection under her own label appeared in Florence in 1972. Soon afterwards she bought a cashmere firm and thus discovered her true métier.

She became known as the "Queen of Cashmere," producing beautiful sweaters in that precious fiber for both men and women. Exceptional in their colorings and quality, these were sold under the Macpherson label.

For her label Laura Biagiotti Roma, Biagiotti has collaborated with her daughter, Lavinia Cigna, to produce women's clothes that are feminine and

wearable, interestingly detailed, and of excellent workmanship, with a refined mastery of knitwear. Her first fragrance *Fiori Bianchi* appeared in 1982, followed over the years by numerous others for women and men.

Biagiotti has been honored by her government for her consistent support of Italian culture and trade, both at home and abroad.

Dirk Bikkembergs

Born Germany, January 2, 1959
Awards *Golden Spindle* award for *Best Young Designer in Fashion,* 1985.
Moët & Chandon *Esprit du Siècle* award, 2000

A 1982 graduate of the Royal Academy of Fine Arts in Antwerp, Bikkembergs is one of the wave of designers to come out of Belgium since the early 1980s. He first worked at various Belgian fashion firms before the Golden Spindle award led to a collaboration with a Belgian shoe manufacturer and his first collection of men's shoes in 1986. Men's clothing followed, then knits, and in 1988 his first full collection in Paris.

His first women's collection in 1993 shared the runway with the men's—essentially the same garments but fitted for a woman's body. The collection now spans the range from outerwear to evening. He has since added, for both women and men, a second diffusion line and a collection of jeans and active sportswear. Bikkembergs sees the same person wearing pieces from each collection.

His aim is to make clothes and shoes that are beyond fashion and will not be dated after six months but will endure for years.

Manolo Blahnik

Born Santa Cruz de la Palma, Canary Islands, November 28, 1942
Awards Council of Fashion Designers of America (CFDA) *Special Award (Outstanding Excellence in Accessory Design):* 1987, 1989; *Stiletto Award,* 1997

One of the world's most creative and influential shoe designers, Blahnik is based in London, where he turns out four collections a year of his fantastical, elegant shoes. His designs are sold through a very few fine specialty stores worldwide and in his own boutiques to such celebrity customers as Bianca Jagger, Cher, Madonna, PALOMA PICASSO, and Sarah Jessica Parker. They have frequently been chosen for runway presentations by designers as different in approach as ZANDRA RHODES and BILL BLASS. He has done collections for PERRY ELLIS, CALVIN KLEIN, and ANNE KLEIN, and men's shoes for SAINT LAURENT.

Blahnik's father was Czech and his mother was Spanish, an elegant woman who shopped for clothes in Paris, Monte Carlo, and Madrid. His mother exposed Blahnik to the great designers of the day—DIOR, BALENCIAGA, and Spain's famous cobbler, Rius. He attended the University of Geneva, first studying politics and law, soon switching to literature and architecture. He then moved on to Paris where he studied art for two years at l'École du Louvre, moved to London around 1968.

Early in 1971 Blahnik traveled to New York, where his friend PALOMA PICASSO arranged for him to show his stage designs to *Vogue* editor DIANA VREELAND. She was so impressed by the shoes in his sketches that she urged him to go into shoe design and helped him connect with an Italian manufacturer. Now he employs four Italian factories, spending nearly three months a year in Milan supervising the translation of his ideas into reality. As a designer he works alone without assistants, drawing as many as 300 designs a year, often even whittling the original lasts. The shoes are fantastically expensive, each pair made by hand from the costliest fabrics and finest leathers, with a few rare designs studded with diamonds and other precious gems. While he does make a few low-heeled designs, Blahnik is mainly identified with the extravagantly high, spiky heel.

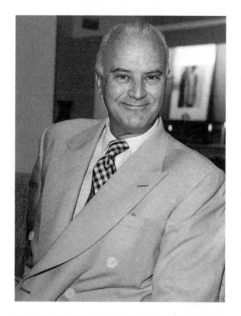

Manolo Blahnik, 2000.

A man of prodigious energy, Blahnik personally cuts 80 or more samples each season, a skill it took him 7 years to acquire. He draws and paints, but mainly he thinks about shoes. He has filled two floors and the attic of his weekend house in Bath, England, with his collection: one shoe of each pair he has ever made. He is constantly traveling between London, Milan, the United States, and Asia. An avid movie buff, he uses his New York business trips to catch up, sometimes seeing as many as four movies in a day.

Bill Blass

Born Fort Wayne, Indiana, June 22, 1922
Died New Preston, Connecticut, June 12, 2002
Awards Coty American Fashion Critics' Award "Winnie," 1961; *Return Award*, 1963; First Coty Award for *Men's Wear*, 1968; *Hall of Fame*, 1970; *Hall of Fame Citation*, 1971, 1982, 1983; *Special Award (furs for Revillon America)*, 1975 · Neiman Marcus Award, 1969 · Council of Fashion Designers of America (CFDA) *Lifetime Achievement Award*, 1986; *Dom Pérignon Award*, 1995; *Special Award The Dean of American Fashion*, 2000

In Late 1999 when Bill Blass announced his retirement and the sale of his business, anguished cries went up from the members of the New York social establishment, of which he was an acknowledged member. For these women and their sisters around the country, he had produced high-priced, high-quality clothes, for more than 30 years, first for other labels and finally under his own name.

Blass was a quintessentially American designer, and his work, from the most glamorous evening clothes to simple, elegant daytime fashions, reflected that attitude. Evening clothes could resemble dressy sportswear with skirts of crisp taffeta or sheer chiffon topped by cashmere twin sets. Interesting mixtures of patterns and textures were expertly coordinated to create a polished, worldly look, investment clothes for women with active social lives.

Blass graduated from Fort Wayne High School in 1939, then studied fashion in New York for six months. He got his first fashion job in 1940 as sketch artist for David Crystal, resigning to enlist in the Army in World War II, where he was assigned to the 602nd Camouflage Battalion engaged in counter intelligence. After the War he worked briefly for Anne Klein (who informed him that he had good manners but lacked talent), and in 1946 became designer at Anna Miller & Co. When the company merged with Maurice Rentner, Blass stayed on as head designer; his name went on the label when Rentner

B

died in 1960. Ten years later Blass bought the company and renamed it Bill Blass Ltd.

In addition to his designer clothes for women, the Blass design projects have included Blassport women's sportswear, rainwear, Vogue patterns, loungewear, scarves, and men's clothing. His name has also been licensed for automobiles, uniforms for American Airlines flight attendants, even chocolates. *Bill Blass* perfume for women was introduced in 1978.

Blass gave time and support to his industry and was an early vice presi-

Designer Bill Blass, 1987 (above). Typical Blass designs for day and evening from 1994 (below, left) and from 1986 (above, left).

dent of the Council of Fashion Designers of America. He was also a perceptive and generous supporter of design talent in others. In January 1994, he donated $10 million to the New York Public Library.

The label has continued under successive designers.

Marc Bohan

Born Paris, France, August 22, 1926

chief designer and artistic director of CHRISTIAN DIOR from 1960 to 1989, Bohan was responsible for the couture and ready-to-wear collections, as well as accessories, men's wear, and bed linens. Refined and romantic, his clothes were also very wearable, notable for beautiful fabrics, and exquisite workmanship. He always maintained that elegance consists of adapting dress for the place, the atmosphere, and the circumstances.

The son of a milliner who encouraged his early interest in sketching and fashion, Bohan had a solid background when he took over design direction at Dior. He was assistant to ROBERT PIGUET from 1945 to 1953, worked with Captain MOLYNEUX and MADELEINE DE RAUCH, had his own couture salon, which closed after one season due to undercapitalization. He was head designer at JEAN PATOU starting in 1954, after a few years left Patou to freelance, working briefly in New York for Originala.

Marc Bohan (right) and from his 1987 Spring/Summer collection for Christian Dior (left).

In August 1958 Bohan went to work for Dior, designing the London, New York, and South American collections. When SAINT LAURENT was drafted into the army in September 1960 Bohan was chosen to design the January collection. In 1989, after 29 years as chief designer, Bohan left Christian Dior and in September of the same year became fashion director for NORMAN HARTNELL, the British fashion house. His first collections were couture, followed by ready-to-wear in Fall 1991. He left Hartnell when the house closed in 1992.

B

Veronique Branquinho

Born Vilvoorde, Belgium, June 6, 1973
Awards VH1 *Fashion Award for Best New Designer*, 1998 · Moët & Chandon *Fashion Award 2000*

one of the many fresh talents nurtured and based in Belgium, Branquinho first studied painting at the Saint Lucas School of Art in Brussels before switching to fashion studies at the Royal Academy of Fine Arts in Antwerp. She graduated in 1995, and worked briefly for several commercial labels before opening her own business in 1997. In August of that year she showed her first collection in the trendy Paris store, Colette, attracting both favorable press notice and orders. Since then she has designed two collections for the Italian leather firm Russo Research, which routinely hires young designers for limited stints, has participated in fashion events in Italy at the Venice Biannale, in Japan, South Korea, and at the Fashion Institute of Technology in New York. She also designs shoes.

Branquinho works with a light touch in the designer range, very much aware of current trends while going her own distinctive way. Even the most tailored pieces—jackets, pants, coats, or

Veronique Branquinho (above) and design from her Spring 2002 collection (right).

leathers—have a relaxed, easy assurance, while the dresses, blouses, and knit pieces are fluid and feminine with a certain mysterious elegance. Far from imposing a certain look, she is pleased to see women make her clothes personal by mixing them with things they already own.

Tom Brigance

Born Thomas Franklin Brigance; Waco, Texas, February 4, 1913
Died New York City, October 14, 1990
Awards Coty American Fashion Critics' Award *"Winnie" (for revolutionizing the look of American women at the beach)* 1953 · International Silk Citation, 1954 · National Cotton Fashion Award, 1955 · Italian Internazionale delle Arti *(for foreign sportswear)*, 1956

PROBABLY best known for his swimwear, Brigance designed everything from coats and suits to day and evening dresses and blouses, before finding his true calling in sportswear. His early beach outfits could be ultra-feminine with ruffles and frills or ultra-sophisticated in fabrics such as grey flannel and black velvet. At Brigance's death, the head of Gabar, where he worked for two years prior to his retirement, said that a Brigance-designed, skirted swimsuit was still one of his company's best-selling styles.

The son of an English mother and French father, Brigance studied at Parsons School of Design and the National Academy of Art in New York, and later at the Sorbonne in Paris. On his return to New York his talent was recognized by Dorothy Shaver, president of Lord & Taylor, and in 1939 he became the store's designer. He spent the war years in Air Corps Intelligence in the South Pacific, returning to Lord & Taylor in 1944. In 1949 he opened his own firm on Seventh Avenue. In the 1960s and 1970s he concentrated primarily on swimwear, designing for Sinclair, Water Clothes, and Gabar. He retired in the late 1970s but continued to lecture extensively on fashion throughout the United States.

Brigance trained as a couturier in Paris and sold sketches to French and English designers but whatever he de-signed bore an unmistakably American viewpoint. In an interview in 1960, he said that "the secret of a woman being well dressed lies in her being appropriately dressed for her way of life."

Separates from 1941 (left) and swimsuit from 1946 (right).

B

Donald Brooks

Born New York City, January 10, 1928
Awards National Cotton Fashion Award, 1962 · Coty American Fashion Critics'
Award *Special Award (influence on evening wear)*, 1958; *"Winnie,"* 1962; *Return Award*, 1967; *Special Award (lingerie design)*, 1974 · New York Drama Critics'
Award for costumes (for *No Strings*), 1963 · International Silk Association
Award, 1954 · Parsons Medal for Distinguished Achievement, 1974

NOTED FOR ROMANTIC EVENING DESIGNS and uncluttered day clothes, Brooks has also designed extensively for theater and film. He is known for his use of clear colors in unexpected combinations, careful detailing, and dramatic prints of his own design.

Brooks studied at the School of Fine Arts of Syracuse University and at Parsons School of Design in New York City.

Donald Brooks with models in 1974.

He had his own company from 1964 to 1973 and has freelanced extensively, specializing in better dresses. He has designed collections for Albert Nipon and exclusive designs for Lord & Taylor. He costumed Diahann Carroll in the Broadway musical, *No Strings,* and Liza Minelli in *Flora the Red Menace.* His ten movie credits between 1963 and 1987 include costumes for Julie Andrews in *Star* and *Darling Lili.* He has also designed furs, bathing suits, men's wear, shoes, costume jewelry, wigs, and bed linens.

Bruce (Daphne Gutierrez, Nicole Noselli)

Born both in New Jersey, 1972
Awards Council of Fashion Designers of America (CFDA) *Perry Ellis Award for Womenswear, 2001*

The designing partners of Bruce met while studying at New York's Parsons School of Design and started their collaboration soon after graduation in 1995. Their day jobs in and out of the fashion industry convinced them that they wanted to follow a more individualistic route, designing clothes unique to the wearer and with details and shape that require a closer look. They presented their first capsule collection for Fall 1997, and their first formal show for Spring 1998, receiving a positive critical response while keeping hype to a minimum.

The pair is lauded for skillful cutting techniques, immaculate execution, and an absorption with fit, producing clothes with a subtle edge of sensuality. They do not design for an ideal Bruce Woman but expect their customers to be as individual as their designs. They would never expect a woman to wear Bruce head to toe. The clothes are in the upscale sportswear category and are sold at fashion-forward stores such as Barney's in New York, Wilkes Bashford in San Francisco, and Harrod's in London.

From Bruce's Fall 2001 collection.

B

Stephen Burrows

Born Newark, New Jersey, September 15, 1943
Awards Coty American Fashion Critics' Award *Special Award (lingerie)*, 1974;
"Winnie," 1977

BURROWS HAS ALWAYS GONE HIS own way in fashion, favoring soft, clinging fabrics such as chiffon and matte jersey, and with a partiality for the asymmetrical. He used patches of color for a mosaic effect in the early 1960s, topstitched seams in contrasting thread, and finished edges in a widely copied, fluted effect known as "lettuce hems."

He started making clothes as a young boy under the tutelage of his grandmother, studied at the Philadelphia Museum College of Art and the Fashion Institute of Technology in New York. In 1968 he and an F.I.T. classmate, Roz Rubenstein, joined forces to open a boutique. The next year both went to work for Henri Bendel—Rubenstein, as accessories buyer, Burrows as designer in residence. In 1973 they formed a partnership and a firm on Seventh Avenue and in November of the same year Burrows was one of five American designers to show in France at a benefit for the Versailles Palace, an event which proved a smash success for the Americans. A few years later KARL LAGERFELD pronounced him "the most original American talent since Claire McCardell."

Burrows and Rubenstein returned to Bendel's in 1977, remaining until 1981

when the store was sold. Since then, Burrows has been in and out of business a number of times, ascribing his lack of commercial success at least partly to a lack of business skills and an unwillingness to acquire them. He has supported himself by making theater costumes, by designing for the licensing divisions of

Stephen Burrows with models in 1979 (below) and from the Summer 2002 collection (left).

other designers, and by the occasional private client. He has also done furs. In January 2002 he was back as house designer at Bendel's, with an in-store studio and staff and a small collection sold only at the Fifth Avenue store.

Barbara Bui

Born Paris, France, circa 1960

Bui came to fashion self-taught and by a route as diverse as her French-Vietnamese origins—first studies in literature then classes in theater. It was in her theater classes that she met her future partner, William Halimi. When they tired of theater in the 1980s, the pair opened a boutique to sell her designs and called it Kabuki, later renaming it Barbara Bui.

After successful showings in Paris, Bui withdrew from runway presentations until the mid-nineties, when she showed in New York. Her several collections include suits, dresses, furs, evening wear, separates, bags, and shoes.

She sees her clothes as balancing the masculine and feminine, delicacy and assertiveness, for women with a strong point of view who feel themselves citizens of the world.

In addition to a boutique and a café in Paris there are shops in Milan and New York.

B

C

Callot Soeurs

Giuliana Camerino

Albert Capraro

Ennio Capasa

Roberto Capucci

Pierre Cardin

Hattie Carnegie

Carven

Bonnie Cashin

Jean Charles de Castelbajac

Consuelo Castiglioni

Edmundo Castillo

Sal Cesarani

Hussein Chalayan

Gabrielle Chanel

Aldo Cipullo

Liz Claiborne

Ossie Clark

Clements Ribeiro

Robert Clergerie

Anne Cole

Kenneth Cole

Sybil Connolly

Jasper Conran

André Courrèges

Jules-Francois Crahay

Charles Creed

Angela Cummings

Callot Soeurs

Founded 1895
Closed 1937

Founded by three sisters, the couture house of Callot Soeurs was noted most particularly for formal evening wear of intricate cut and rich color. It was famous for its delicate lace blouses, and use of gold and silver lamé, floating fabrics such as chiffon, georgette, and organdy, and flower embroidery and embroidery in Chinese colors. The high standard of excellence maintained in collection after collection over many years built the Callot reputation, and the world's most fashionable women went there to dress. Among them was the noted Spanish-American beauty Mrs. Rita de Acosta Lydig, who was rumored to be a financial backer of the house.

The sisters were daughters of an antiques dealer who specialized in fabrics and lace. He was also said to be a painter. All three were talented but it was Mme. Gerber, the eldest, who was the genius. Tall and gaunt, her hair dyed a brilliant red, she was usually dressed in a baglike costume covered with oriental jewelry and ropes of freshwater pearls. Mme. Gerber possessed great technical skill—she was also an artist of impeccable taste, an originator. Her two sisters eventually retired and she became the sole proprietor of the house, which at one time had branches in London and New York.

Henri Bendel was a great admirer of Mme. Gerber, referring to her as the backbone of the fashion world of Europe. She was an early influence on MADELEINE VIONNET, who worked for some time at Callot. During the 1920s the house produced every up-to-the-minute look, always with such taste, subtlety, and superb workmanship that the clothes had the timelessness and elegance of classics.

Tulle evening gown with velvet bands, from 1931. *Also see Color Plate 7.*

Giuliana Camerino (Roberta di Camerino)

Born Italy, circa 1920.
Awards Neiman Marcus Award, 1956

camerino began designing and making handbags during World War II in Switzerland, where she had taken refuge with her banker husband and infant son. When they returned to Venice in 1945 the family established a firm to produce her designs, which she named "Roberta," after her favorite movie.

The Roberta name was established with beautiful and original handbags, especially the striped velvet satchels and pouches with carved motifs and the exceptional leathers. At its peak, the business, which began with one employee, employed over 200, plus more than 3,000 freelance artisans. Velvets were woven and cut by hand in the ancient, time-consuming manner; frames, handles, and locks were produced in Camerino's own factories. She operated a tannery for her leathers, a fabric-printing plant, and factories producing clothes and umbrellas. The business expanded to include ready-to-wear, knitted fashions, furs, fragrances, and luxurious accessories for women and men. Camerino was praised by Stanley Marcus for her creativity and constant flow of new ideas.

After dropping from sight in the mid 1980s, the handbags enjoyed a revival in the early 21st century in a new age of opulence. Once again, the elegance of the designs, the beauty of the materials, and the perfection of workmanship were recognized for the precious rarities that they are.

Giuliana Camerino, 2000.

Albert Capraro

Born New York City, May 20, 1943

A graduate of Parsons School of Design, Capraro worked for LILLY DACHÉ as an associate and from 1966 to 1974 as associate to OSCAR DE LA RENTA. He established his own business for designer ready-to-wear in 1975.

Capraro's first public notice came when Mrs. Gerald Ford, then First Lady, invited him to bring his collection to the White House. He closed the business in 1985, but continued to design for individual clients such as Mrs. Ford under the label Albert Capraro Couture. On the wholesale side, he designed exclusively for the specialty shop Martha, since closed.

In June 1990 he joined ADELE SIMPSON as designer of a new collection while continuing to design his private collections, but left in December of the same year when the future of the firm was uncertain. In recent years he has shown in Milan.

Ennio Capasa (Costume National)

Born Lecce, Italy, 1960

Ennio Capasa, 2001 (above) and from Spring/Summer 2001 (left).

capasa's parents owned up-scale boutiques in Lecce, a city on the heel of the Italian boot. Growing up there he hated fashion, which he considered to be for "tired rich people." But after graduating from the Milan Academy of Fine Arts in 1982 and wanting to avoid Italy's mandatory military service, Capasa looked for work in industrial design in Japan, and instead found a job in fashion design with

YOHJI YAMAMOTO. It was there that he learned to drape, cut, and sew.

After three years it was time to move on, and in 1987 he left Yamamoto with the older designer's suggestion that he start his own label. Rather than use his own name, Capasa chose Costume National, from the title of an antique book on French uniforms.

He felt that it was the moment for a new silhouette—more relaxed, closer to

the body from the shoulder down—more style than fashion. His first collection for women was based on the skimpy proportions of Charlie Chaplin and was greeted with disdain by the Italian fashion press. Since then he has gone from success to success quietly, without the press hype usually considered necessary to gain recognition. The first men's collection was in 1993; there are now bags, belts, and leather goods. His cool, hip clothes for women and men have found a receptive audience worldwide, sold by forward-thinking retailers such as Barney's New York and in his own boutiques in Milan, Rome, Tokyo, and New York.

Roberto Capucci

Born Rome, Italy, 1929

scion of a wealthy roman family, Capucci first studied art at the Accademia di Belle Arti in Rome. In 1950, at the age of twenty-one, he opened a small fashion house in Rome and showed successfully in Florence the same year. He opened a house in Paris in 1962, moved back to Rome seven years later.

Considered a genius ranking with Balenciaga and Charles James, Capucci has experimented daringly with cut and fabric to achieve dramatic sculptural and architectural effects. Fittingly, because he has raised dressmaking to the level of an art, his clothes are shown in

Capucci design, 1985.

total silence without histrionics. He does not use design assistants.

In early 2003, still doing couture on a limited basis, Capucci entered into an agreement for a ready-to-wear collection under his name. This was to be designed by three young designers, including the Spanish Sybilla and the American Tara Subkoff of Imitation of Christ, working not as a team but individually, in turn, and drawing on his archives for inspiration. The first showing was scheduled for Milan in February–March 2003.

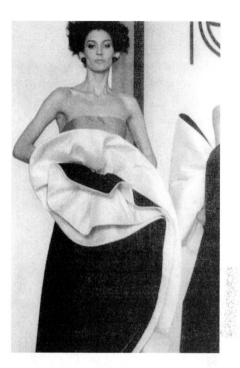

Pierre Cardin

Born Venice, Italy, 1922

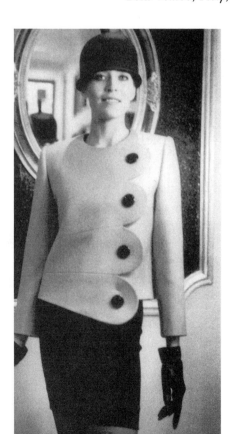

cardin is considered one of the most creative, intellectual, and avant-garde couturiers of the 1950s and 1960s. He showed the first nude look in 1966, followed by metal body jewelry, unisex astronaut suits, helmets, batwing jumpsuits, and other clothing then considered suitable for space travel.

The son of Italian immigrants, Cardin grew up in St. Etienne, France, and moved to Vichy at the age of seventeen. He worked there as a tailor, left Vichy for Paris at the end of World War II and went to work at Paquin. At Paquin he executed

Cardin design, 1991.

costume designs based on sketches by Christian Bérard for Jean Cocteau's film, *La Belle et la Bête,* and was introduced by Cocteau to Christian Dior. He worked briefly for Schiaparelli, then as assistant to Dior, where in 1947 he headed the coat and suit workroom. He left Dior to form his own business, showing his first collection in 1950.

Boutiques followed for men and women—men's ready-to-wear appeared in 1958, children's apparel ten years later. From there he went on to label the world with the Cardin name—more than 600 licenses extending from wines to bicycles, jewelry to bed sheets, food to swimwear to toiletries. In 1970 he established his own Paris theater, L'Espace Pierre Cardin. Cardin now owns the famous Paris restaurant, Maxim's. In 1979 he entered into a trade agreement with the Peoples Republic of China to produce Cardin clothes there. A Maxim's has been established in Beijing.

In July 1987 he named his long-time collaborator, André Oliver, artistic director of the couture house, while continuing to share the design duties. In the wake of Oliver's death he reassumed artistic direction of the house.

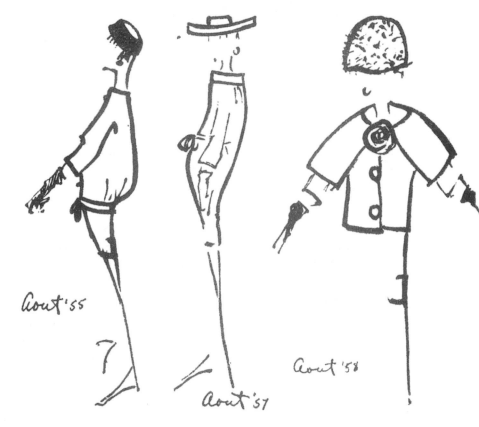

Sketches made by Cardin exclusively for *Women's Wear Daily* (above). Pierre Cardin, 1992 (left).

Hattie Carnegie

Born Vienna, Austria, 1889
Died New York City, February 22, 1956

Hattie Carnegie began as a milliner, opening her first shop when she was just twenty. By the end of her life, she had a multi-million dollar business, including two resort shops, made-to-order workrooms, ready-to-wear factories, millinery, jewelry, and perfumes. She is said to have been the first American custom designer to go into ready-to-wear. Her knack for discovering design talent was legendary—JAMES GALANOS, NORMAN NORELL, PAULINE TRIGÈRE, and CLAIRE MCCARDELL all worked for her.

Carnegie's designs were youthful and sophisticated, never faddish, never extreme, eternally Carnegie whatever the current trends might be. Less than five feet tall, she was noted for suits with nipped waists and rounded hips that were especially becoming to smaller women, as well as embroidered, beaded evening suits, theater suits, at-home pajamas, and long wool dinner dresses. Beautiful fabrics and excellent workmanship were hallmarks and anything but the best was abhorrent to her.

She arrived in America when she was eleven and started working in her early teens—first as a messenger at Macy's, then in a millinery workroom, later as a millinery model. In her spare time she designed hats for neighborhood women. She changed her name from Henrietta Kanengeiser to Carnegie in emulation of Andrew Carnegie, "the richest man in the world." In 1909 she opened her own hat shop, and in 1915, a custom dress-making salon on West 86th Street near fashionable Riverside Drive. Her partner, Rose Roth, made dresses; Carnegie made hats and waited on customers. She did not know how to cut or sketch, and never learned. What she did have was great fashion flair and an acute business intelligence. In 1917 she bought out her partner.

Her first buying trip to Europe occurred in 1919, and from then on she went four times a year, bringing back quantities of Paris models, which she would adapt. She dressed society beauties, movie and stage stars such as Constance Bennett, Tallulah Bankhead, and Joan Crawford. In the early 1930s, recognizing the hard facts of the depression, she opened a ready-to-wear department in her shop where a good Vionnet copy could be had for as little as $50.

She was married briefly in 1918, again in 1922. In 1928 she married Major John Zanft, who survived her. Her clothing business continued for some years after her death.

Theater suit from 1950.

Carven

Founded Paris, France, 1944

carven (madame carven mallet) built her success on attractive, wearable apparel for petite women like herself, specializing in imaginative sports, beach, and dress-up clothes; accessories, too, were kept in proportion to the small figure. An ardent traveler, she was inspired by her travels, as shown in such silhouettes as the Greek amphora and in a use of Egyptian pleats.

The daughter of an Italian father and a French mother, Carven had planned to study architecture and archaeology. It is said that she was diverted into dressmaking by the fact that her tiny size made it difficult to find beautiful clothes, which were always created for taller women. Following her retirement, the house remained in business for couture, and, at one time or another, with Carven lines for children and teenagers and men. Among her fragrances, *Ma Griffe* and *Monsieur Carven* have been especially successful.

Bonnie Cashin

Born Oakland, California, 1915
Died New York City, February 3, 2000
Awards Coty American Fashion Critics' Award "*Winnie,*" 1950; *Special Award (for leather and fabric design),* 1961; *Return Award,* 1968; *Hall of Fame,* 1972 · Neiman Marcus Award, 1950

Bonnie Cashin in her studio.

cashin always worked in her own innovative idiom, uninfluenced by Paris. She especially believed in functional layers of clothing and showed this way of dressing long before it became an international fashion cliché. From the beginning she specialized in comfortable clothes for country and travel, using wool jersey, knits, canvas, leather, and tweeds in subtle, misty colors.

Some dominant Cashin themes were the toga cape, the kimono coat and the shell coat, a sleeveless leather jerkin, the poncho, the bubble top, the hooded jersey dress, and a long, fringed, plaid mohair at-home skirt. Signature details included leather bindings and the use of toggles and similar hardware for closings. Clothes were coordinated with hoods, bags, boots, and belts of her own design. Her clothes are included in the costume collections of museums, colleges, and design schools around the country.

A third generation Californian, Cashin was raised in San Francisco where her father was an artist, photographer, and inventor; her mother was a custom dressmaker. She played with fabrics from an early age, was taught to sew, and her ideas were encouraged. She studied at the Art Students League of New York, then returned to California where she designed costumes for the theater, ballet, and motion pictures—*Anna and the King of Siam* and *Laura* are among her 60 picture credits. She moved back to New York in 1949.

From 1953 Cashin freelanced, designing collections for sportswear houses Adler and Adler and Philip Sills, and bags for Coach Leatherware. In 1967 she started The Knittery, limited edition collections of hand knits and cashmeres from Scotland, also concentrating on coats and raincoats.

In the early 1980s she established The Innovative Design Fund, a public foundation, with herself as president.

Its purpose was to nurture uncommon, directional ideas in design—clothing, textiles, home furnishings, or other utilitarian objects—with awards to be used solely for producing prototypes. Another fund, "The James Michelin Distinguished Lecturer Program," at the California Institute of Technology at Pasadena began operation in 1992. Its purpose is to bring the arts and sciences together. British playwright Tom Stoppard was the 1994 lecturer.

A Cashin sketch (left) and layers in tweed and suede (right), 1968.

Jean-Charles de Castelbajac

Born Casablanca, Morocco, 1950

Part of the ready-to-wear movement that burgeoned in France in the 1960s and came into full flower in the 1970s, Castelbajac is best known for the fashion flair he gives to survival looks—blanket plaids, canvas, quilting, rugged coats—and sportswear for both men and women. He has been called "the space age BONNIE CASHIN."

Castelbajac's parents moved to France when he was five. His mother started her own small clothes factory and he went to work for her when he was eighteen. He designed for Pierre d'Alby, joined a group of young designers in 1974, then opened his first retail shop. He has collaborated with COURRÈGES on ready-to-wear, designed for a number of manufacturers, including some in Italy, and has done theatrical costumes.

Consuelo Castiglioni

Born Italy, ca. 1959

castiglioni became a fashion designer more by chance than by plan when her husband's family firm was having difficulties—as Italy's foremost supplier of top-quality fur pelts to houses such as FENDI and PRADA, they were suffering from the anti-fur movement of the early 1990s. Although she had never been involved in fashion, Consuelo decided in 1993 to design a small fur collection called Marni, to present to the press during the Milan ready-to-wear showings. Her first attempts attracted little or no attention and it wasn't until 1999, when she showed a colorful "deluxe hippy" collection of patchwork coats, tie-dyed crushed velvet dresses, and multi-colored fur jackets, that the firm took off. The house has since split off to become a separate fashion entity.

Using luxurious materials such as cashmere, silk, and fur, Castiglioni creates young, pretty clothes with a modern edge. They are sold in fine retail stores and, increasingly, in the company's own boutiques.

From the Marni Spring 2002 collection.

Edmundo Castillo

Born San Juan, Puerto Rico, April 13, 1967

Awards Council of Fashion Designers of America (CFDA) *Perry Ellis Award for Accessories*, 2001

Even as a teenager Castillo was a shoe addict, obsessed with having the newest and best sneakers. He began his design studies with one year at the Altos de Chavón School of Design in the Dominican Republic before moving to New York and stints at both the Fashion Institute of Technology and Parsons. After a succession of jobs working in shoe stores where his passion for shoes blossomed, he began his real training in shoemaking in 1989 in the men's and women's footwear division at Donna Karan. "If it weren't for her I wouldn't know half of what I know now. . ." He stayed there eight years as a shoe designer, moved to Polo Ralph Lauren for one year as senior design director before returning to Karan to design the Donna Karan and DKNY men's shoes. In 1999 he began work on his own line of women's shoes.

Castillo's focus is on feminine, sexy shoes designed along classic lines with a modern edge and made of only the finest materials—shoes that women want to wear and also collect. He views them as more makeup for the feet than mere foot-coverings, "The beauty of a shoe is in how it transforms and takes life when it makes contact with the foot. . ."

Edmundo Castillo, 2001.

C

Sal Cesarani

Born Salvatore J. Cesarani, New York City, September 25, 1939
Awards Coty American Fashion Critics' Award *Special Award (men's wear),* 1975,
1976; *Men's Wear Return Award,* 1982 · Fashion Group of Boston Award, 1977

The son of Italian immigrant tailors, Cesarani graduated from the High School of Fashion Industries and the State University of New York. He developed his color sense and knowledge of merchandising as fashion coordinator at the prestigious men's store Paul Stuart (1964-1969), then worked successively at Polo by Ralph Lauren, Country Britches, and Stanley Blacker, be-

Cesarani's 1994 collection.

fore forming Cesarini Ltd. in 1976. He has produced women's fashion but has mainly concentrated on dressing men.

Essentially a traditionalist, Cesarani handles modern trends in a classic way. Cut and tailoring are impeccable: pants break at precisely the right point, jackets fit exactly with contemporary ease. As befits a classicist, he favors natural fibers—fine woolens and tweeds for fall and winter, linens and cottons for the warm months.

Cesarani has taught men's wear at the Fashion Institute of Technology and Fabric Selection and Design Styling Theory at Parsons School of Continuing Education, and has served on the Advisory Board of the Fashion Crafts Educational Commission of the High School of Fashion Industries. He is further involved with fashion education as a member of the Advisory Board of the Kent State University School of Fashion in Ohio. He has been recognized both nationally and by New York City for his distinguished design career and for his dedication to community service.

Hussein Chalayan

Born Huseyin Caglayan, Nicosia, Cyprus, 1970
Awards *British Designer of the Year*, 1999, 2000

Chalayan went to boarding school in England and to college in Cyprus. After college, he enrolled at London's Central St. Martin's College of Art and Design, and while still in school apprenticed with a Savile Row tailor. His highly eccentric 1993 graduation collection was featured in the window of one of London's most adventurous boutiques, which immediately established him as a hot new talent.

Subsequent collections have included unrippable paper clothes and sharply-tailored suits printed with illuminated flight patterns, showing his continuing interest in technology-inspired fabrics. In various financial ups and downs, Chalayan has been in and out of business but has managed to get new backing and continue producing collections.

Chalayan has shown the total dedication and complete self-belief necessary for survival in his chosen field. His work, with its clearly-defined, minimalist silhouettes, has ranged from the wildly conceptual to the highly wearable designs he produced for Tse, the New York-based cashmere house. In 2001 it was included in the exhibition "London Fashion" at New York's Fashion Institute of Technology. He is admired by such unconventional fashion thinkers as Rei Kawakubo and Alexander McQueen and has been mentioned as a possible designer for several major European houses.

Gabrielle "Coco" Chanel

Born Saumur, France, 1883
Died Paris, France, January 10, 1971
Awards Neiman Marcus Award, 1957

In evaluating Chanel, some place her alongside such giants as Vionnet and Balenciaga, while others see her as more personality than creator, with an innate knack for knowing what women would want a few seconds before they knew it themselves. Certainly her early designs exerted a liberating influence and even the evening clothes had a youthful quality that was all her own.

She purposely obscured the details of her early life but it is now said that she was one of five children born to an unmarried mother. By the time Chanel was twelve, her mother was dead, her father had deserted his family, and Gabrielle had been sent to an orphanage run by nuns. There she spent six years and there she learned to sew. She started in fashion making hats—first in a Paris apartment in 1910, later in a shop in Deauville. In 1914 she opened a shop in Paris, making her first dresses of wool jersey, a material at that time not considered suitable for fashionable clothes.

Her business was interrupted by World War I but she reopened in 1919, by which time she was famous in the fashionable world. Slender and vital, with a low, warm voice, she was a superb saleswoman and undoubtedly her personality and private life contributed to her success. Misia Sert, the wife of the Spanish painter, Jose Maria Sert, was a friend and introduced her to such leading figures of the 1920s art world as Diaghilev, Picasso, Cocteau, dancer Serge Lifar, and decorator/designer Leon Bakst. She was famous for feuds with other designers, notably Schiaparelli. Although she never married, there were many love affairs. Grand Duke Dmitri, grandson of Czar Alexander II, was a frequent escort and a three-year liaison with the Duke of Westminster may have contributed to her longstanding use and appreciation of Scottish tweeds.

Chanel closed her couture house in September 1939 at the outset of World War II. During and after the Occupation she shared her life with a German officer, for which many refused to forgive her. She managed to leave Paris for Switzerland in 1945, remaining there in exile for eight years.

At the age of seventy she decided to go back into business, presenting her first postwar collection on February 5, 1954. A continuation of her original themes of simplicity and wearability, it received a brutal reception from both the Paris and English press, still under the influence of the waist cinchers and pads of the New Look. By the end of the year, however, it was clear that once again Chanel had seized the moment when women were ready for change; the dresses from the reviled collection sold very well, especially in America but also in France. Her success continued into the 1960s when her refusal to change her basic style or raise hemlines led to a decline in her influence. Inevitably, the pendulum swung back and in 1969 her life was the basis for *Coco,* a Broadway musical starring Katharine Hepburn.

Chanel's daytime palette was neutral—black, white, beige, red—with pastels introduced at night. Trademark looks included the little boy look, wool jersey dresses with white collars and cuffs, pea jackets, bell-bottom trousers, and her personal touches of suntanned skin, bobbed hair, and magnificent jewelry worn with sportswear.

In her second, post-World War II period, she is best remembered for her suits made of jersey or the finest, softest Scottish tweeds. Jackets were usually collarless and trimmed with braid, blouses soft and tied at the neckline, skirts at or just below the knee. Suits were shown with multiple strands of pearls and gold chains set with enormous fake stones. In her own case, these were mixed with real jewels. Other widely-copied signatures were quilted handbags with shoulder chains, beige sling-back pumps with black tips, flat black hair-bows, and a single gardenia.

In addition to couture, Chanel's empire encompassed perfumes, a costume

Chanel suit (left), 1929. Chanel (right), 1972. *Also see Color Plate 5.*

jewelry workshop, and for a time, a textile house. *Chanel No. 5* was created in 1922. In 1924 Parfums Chanel was established to market the perfumes, which have continued to proliferate. A line of cosmetics was introduced after her death.

Chanel, "La Grande Mademoiselle," died on a Sunday night in January 1971, to the last working on a new collection. The House of Chanel has continued, directed by a succession of designers. Ready-to-wear was added in 1977 with Philippe Guibourgé as designer. KARL LAGERFELD has since taken over design duties for both the couture and ready-to-wear and is credited with bringing the house into the modern era.

Chanel remains a legend for her taste, wit, personal style, and for her unfaltering dedication to perfection. Hers was a luxury based on the most refined simplicity of cut, superb materials, and workmanship of the highest order.

Chanel suits from 1957, 1958, and 1960.

Aldo Cipullo

Born Rome, Italy, November 18, 1936
Died New York City, January 31, 1984
Awards Coty American Fashion Critics' Award *Special Award (men's wear/jewelry)*, 1974 ·
Diamonds Today Competition, 1977

cipuLLo is probably best known for the gold "love bracelet" he designed while at Cartier in 1969. Coveted by both men and women, it fastens on the wrist with a screw, comes with its own small vermeil screwdriver, and is still carried by Cartier. He enlarged the scope of men's jewelry with the wrap-around gold nail bracelet, lapel pins to replace the boutonniere for evening, and pendants. His work also included more conventional adornments: rings, cuff links, studs, and buttons.

Born into a family that owned a large costume jewelry firm, Cipullo studied at

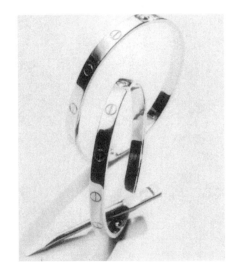

the University of Rome, came to New York in 1959 and attended the School of Visual Arts. He worked as a designer at David Webb, Tiffany, and Cartier, and in 1974 opened his own design studio. Cipullo's design projects extended from jewelry to silverware to textiles, included placemats, china, stationery, leather goods, and desk accessories. His design objectives were simplicity, elegance, function, and style.

The Cartier love bracelet by Cipullo, 1969.

Liz Claiborne

Born Brussels, Belgium, 1929
Awards Council of Fashion Designers of America (CFDA) *Special Award,* 1985;
Humanitarian Award for the Liz Claiborne and Art Ortenberg Foundation, 2000 ·
Dallas Fashion Award, 1985

cLaiborne made her name in sportswear, where her strength lay in translating new trends into understandable and salable clothes. They were simple and uncomplicated with an easy, natural look and were in the moderate price range. She was known for sensitive use of color and for excellent technical knowledge of fabric. As her company expanded into other areas, such as dresses, men's wear, and children's clothes, she came to function largely as editor of the work of other designers.

The daughter of a banker, Claiborne spent her early childhood in New Orleans, went on to study painting in Belgium and France. Her career in fashion began in 1949 when she won a trip to Europe in a *Harper's Bazaar* design contest. On her return to the United States, she worked as a model sketcher, as assistant to TINA LESER, OMAR KIAM, and others. She was top designer at Youth Guild for 16 years. In February 1976 she formed Liz Claiborne, Inc., with her husband, Arthur Ortenberg, as business manager.

She has served as critic at the Fashion Institute of Technology and has received numerous awards from retailers and industry associations. In 1989, she and her husband retired from the company to devote themselves to environmental issues. The company has since expanded to giant size through acquisitions, including KENNETH COLE and Ellen Tracy.

Ossie Clark

Born Raymond Oswald Clark, Liverpool, England, June 9, 1942
Died London, England, August 6, 1996

In his heyday in the 1960s, Ossie Clark was the top designer for English film and rock stars, entirely in touch with everything going on: music, art, politics, film, photography. He dressed Julie Christie and Brigitte Bardot, was painted by David Hockney, vacationed with the Rolling Stones, and put the Beatles in the front row of his shows, setting precedents that designers still try to follow. The difference was that those were his friends, not celebrities invited for their publicity value.

Clark entered Manchester Regional Art College at sixteen, immediately becoming part of a circle that included the actor Ben Kingsley and Celia Birtwell. Birtwell was a textiles student who created brightly-colored, naïve prints that Clark used in his designs; she later became his wife. In 1962 Clark won a scholarship to the Royal College of Art in London where he met David Hockney, also a student.

In 1965, Clark and Birtwell, with fellow designer Alice Pollock, started a shop called Quorum in Chelsea, just off the King's Road at the heart of swinging London. Clark was the "King of King's Row." By the early 1970s, drugs, numerous affairs with women and men, and erratic work habits had undermined his life. Birtwell took their two sons and left him in 1973, and Quorum closed two years later. By the end of the decade, Clark was broke and living in a tiny public housing flat.

In the late 1980s Clark had become converted to Buddhism and begun to rebuild his life. He was once again beginning to be recognized. CHRISTIAN LACROIX went to London to meet him and both RIFAT OZBECK and JOHN GALLIANO greatly admired him and invited him to their shows. In 1995, several of his pieces were included in an exhibition of street fashion at the Victoria and Albert Museum. Then in 1996 he was murdered—by a drug addict with whom he had lived for nearly a year but whom he had kicked out.

Clark's success was based on two things: he loved women's bodies and made clothes for them that were sexy but not too obvious; his designs were based on his genius as a master cutter—he cut directly into the fabric, requiring neither patterns nor templates. He studied the masters—Vionnet, Chanel, Poiret—and picked up ideas such as bias-cut bodices or Peter Pan collars, which he then translated into something entirely his own.

In the endless recycling of past fashion, a number of today's designers have borrowed references from Clark for their work. His dresses have been commanding hefty prices in vintage shops, and are once again making celebrity appearances.

Designer in his studio, 1977.

Clements Ribeiro

Born Suzanne Clements, England, 1969
Inacio Ribeiro, Brazil, 1963

cLements and Ribeiro trained at Central St. Martins College of Art & Design in London, both graduating in 1991 with first class honors. They married a year later. Before moving to London to get formal training, Ribeiro had worked as a designer for several years; Clements had a fledgling knitwear line carried at Harrod's and Liberty. After graduation, they went to Brazil where they worked as design consultants, returning to London in 1993.

Their first collection under the Clements Ribeiro label was in October 1993—crisp separates in cotton pique, hand-painted silk chiffons, and textured linen. They quickly became known for uncluttered, exuberant designs featuring bold stripes of color and for luxurious cashmeres. In 1995 they gave their first solo presentation at the Brazilian Embassy during London Fashion Week. A shoe collection was added in 1996. In 2001 the couple was hired by the French firm Cacharel, meanwhile continuing to design for their own label.

Robert Clergerie

Born Paris, France, July 18, 1934

cLergerie arrived in the shoe business by the unlikely route of Army service in Algeria and a job as salesman of concrete pipe for road construction. He was general manager of women's shoes for Xavier Danaud, a subsidiary of Charles Jourdan, before setting up his own company in 1978.

He derives inspiration from architecture, painting, the street, "everything but shoes." Never exaggerated or trendy, Clergerie shoes are elegant and refined with a strong element of architectural balance.

Designer Robert Clergerie with some of his designs.

Anne Cole

Born Los Angeles, California

Awards Dallas Fashion Award, 1987 · Otis College of Art and Design *Fashion Achievement Award*, 1993, 2001

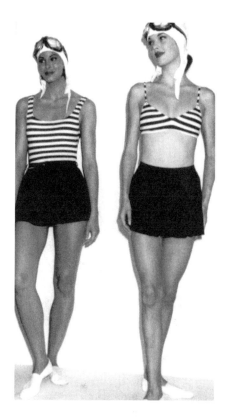

Anne Cole (left) and selections from her 1994 collection.

The daughter of Fred Cole, one of swimwear's great innovators, Anne Cole was born into the beachwear business. She studied at UCLA and Holy Names College before joining the family firm in 1951, after a brief fling in the theater. Once in the company she had to work her way up, moving from the mailroom to posting orders to taking trunk shows on the road.

Being drafted into the family business was a Cole tradition; Fred Cole was starring in silent movies when his mother decided it was time he joined their firm, West Coast Knitting Mills. The factory made drop-seat underwear until Fred started them knitting women's swimsuits. Taking what had been a drab and shapeless garment, he lowered the back and defined the bust

and waistline; these became the first fashion swimsuits. He also introduced brilliant colors. He continued to innovate, working with Margit Fellegi, a Hollywood costume designer. They introduced the cotton suit puckered with rubber threads, and during World War II when rubber was restricted, originated the two-piece "swoon suit" that laced up the sides of the trunks and had a tie bra. The name of the company was changed to Cole of California in 1941. After the war came plunging necklines, cut-outs, bare midriffs, suits in sequins, gold lamé jersey, and water-resistant velvets.

When her father sold Cole of California to Kayser-Roth in 1960, Anne Cole left the company but was lured back to establish Cole's New York office and become stylist and company spokesperson. The firm has since had several owners, most recently Los Angeles-based Authentic Fitness, which also includes Speedo and Catalina.

The Anne Cole Collection, launched in 1982, is the expression of Anne Cole's most advanced fashion ideas. She sees swimsuits as existing somewhere between fashion and beauty aids, reflecting current trends but with the prime function of enhancing the appearance

of the wearer. She is given credit for introducing the tankini, the popular two-piece suit with a tank top and bikini bottom.

The 2001 Otis award was in recognition of her design innovations and of her efforts as a mentor to fashion design students at the school. At that time she was still actively engaged in swimsuit design, as she put it, "the oldest living swimwear designer in the world."

Kenneth Cole

Born Long Island, New York, ca. 1955

Awards Council of Fashion Designers of America (CFDA) *Dom Perignon Award for Humanitarian Excellence,* 1996 · Fashion Footwear Association of New York (FFANY) *The Fashion Medal of Honor Award,* 1997

COLe couLd be considered an example of creative entrepreneurship and downright chutzpah, valuable qualities in his chosen field. He grew up on Long Island, in his spare time working as a stock boy at the local shoe store. After graduation from Emory University in 1976, he worked for the shoe business his family owned in Brooklyn before deciding he was ready to go on his own. In 1982, with limited money for an introductory splash, he launched his company Kenneth Cole Productions from a 40-foot trailer parked across the street from the hotel where the shoe show was taking place. While supposedly shooting a full-length film, he was actually showing his shoes and sold out his production quota in two and a half days. Since then, the company has expanded beyond shoes for men and women to clothing for men, women, and children as well as luggage, accessories, and, of course, fragrance. These are sold worldwide in fine stores and in his own retail shops. He has also designed uniforms for the W hotel chain.

Designer Kenneth Cole, 2001 (above). Left, from 2002 sportswear collection.

Cole is nearly as well known for his provocative, socially-conscious advertising and active participation in causes—from AIDS awareness to homelessness to abortion rights—as for his cool, hip fashions. He has been recognized for his fashion and humanitarian work by organizations ranging from New York Magazine to Amnesty International, and with honorary degrees from Manhattanville College and the University of Illinois School of Public Health.

Sybil Connolly

Born Swansea, Wales, January 24, 1921
Died May 1998

America discovered Connolly in the early 1950s, thanks to CARMEL SNOW of *Harper's Bazaar* and to the Fashion Group of Philadelphia who were visiting Dublin. In 1953 she took a collection to the United States, where her one-of-a-kind designs and beautiful Irish fabrics made a strong impression. In 1957 she set up her own firm, with a special boutique for ready-to-wear. Her clothes were simple in cut, extremely wearable, notable for fabric and workmanship, especially the iridescent Donegal tweeds and the evening dresses made of gossamer Irish linen worked in fine horizontal pleats.

When she was fifteen years old, Connolly's father died and her mother moved the family to Waterford in southern Ireland. In 1938 she went to work for Bradley's, a London dressmaker, returning to Ireland at the outset of World War II as buyer for Richard Alan, a Dublin specialty shop. By the time she was twenty-two, she was a company director. She built the store's couture department into a thriving business and when their designer left in 1950 designed a small collection, the start of her designing career. Her clothes have been carried by fine specialty stores across the United States.

Irish linen evening separates, 1957.

Jasper Conran

Born London, England, 1959
Awards British Fashion Council *Designer of the Year,* 1986

As the son of Sir Terence Conran, the founder of Conran's Habitat stores, Jasper Conran would seem to have been predestined for a design career. He was educated at Bryanston School in England until the age of sixteen, when he was accepted at New York's Parson's School of Design. He studied there for 18 months, leaving in 1977 for a brief stint with Fiorucci, then returned to London the same year. In 1978 he produced his first independent show and the next year became a member of London Designer Collections.

Conran's continued success is solidly based on his technical ability—fine tailoring and thoughtful details—executed in luxurious fabrics. His clothes are original in cut, designed for a sophisticated and elegant woman, none of the legendary English dowdiness here. Other design projects have included fine crystal and a deluxe automobile model.

André Courrèges

Born Pau, France, March 9, 1923

courrèges emerged on the fashion scene in 1962 as a brilliant tailor. Using fabrics with considerable body, he cut his coats and suits with a triangular flare that disguised many figure defects, the balanced silhouettes defined by crisp welt seaming. His aim was to make functional, modern clothes for active modern women. Among his successes—many of them widely copied—were all-white collections inspired by his Basque heritage and tunics worn over narrow pants with flared bottoms that slanted from front to back. There were squared-off dresses ending above the knee, short, white baby boots, industrial zippers, and zany accessories such as sunglasses with slit "tennis ball" lenses. He was called the couturier of the space age.

Courrèges studied civil engineering before switching to textiles and fashion design. His first job was with Jeanne Lafaurie. From 1952 to 1960 he worked as a cutter for BALENCIAGA, whose influence showed clearly in his early designs. In 1961, with the blessing of the great designer, Courrèges and his wife Coqueline, who became his close collaborator, left Balenciaga to open their own business. Together they designed, cut, sewed, and presented their first collection in a small apartment in the avenue Kleber.

Courrèges was so widely plagiarized that the couple sold the business in 1965, then spent two years working for private clients and setting up their own

Courrèges in 1984 (right). Sketches by the designer from *Women's Wear Daily* (above), 1965.

manufacturing and production. They returned in 1967 with Couture Future deluxe ready-to-wear and the distinctive ac logo displayed on the outside of the clothes, another fashion first. There were see-through dresses, cosmonaut suits, knitted "catsuits" with flowers appliquéd on the body, and knee socks. The Courrèges name also extended to accessories, luggage, perfumes, men's wear, and boutiques in the United States and other countries. These carried everything from sports separates to accessories to Couture Future. The name continued on a ready-to-wear line designed by Courrèges in collaboration with other designers.

In 1996 the couple regained the company, which has continued in business with Madame Courrèges in active control, Courrèges himself having retired in 1995 to devote himself to painting and sculpture. The clothes are still made in their own factory to the original patterns in the same fabrics and sold in their own shops and in fine specialty stores. Madame Courrèges has said that they were always designing for the year 2000 and in 2001 the Courrèges influence was noted on numerous collections by other designers.

Jules-François Crahay

Born Liege, Belgium, May 21, 1917
Died Monte Carlo, Monaco, January 5, 1988
Awards Neiman Marcus Award, 1962

Recognized for his thoughtful, interesting cuts, Crahay was deeply influenced by fabrics and liked to design his own. He was probably best known for his use of folklore themes, admiring their rich mixture of color, materials, and embroidery.

Crahay literally grew up in the fashion business, starting to work at age thirteen as a sketcher in his mother's couture house. After studying couture and painting in Paris (1934-1935), he returned to Liege to work for his mother (1936-1938). His army service during World War II ended in capture by the Germans and imprisonment in Germany from 1940 to 1944.

In 1951 he opened his own fashion house in Paris, which closed within a year. He then went as chief designer to NINA RICCI, receiving his first credit as sole designer in 1959. He stayed at Ricci until 1964 when he moved to the House of LANVIN, succeeding Antonio del Castillo as head designer. According to published reports, he was the highest paid couturier of his time. For 20 years he created and maintained a recognizable Lanvin look, civilized and wearable, with his own flair for original details. He retired from Lanvin in 1984 and the following year started a ready-to-wear collection under his own name in Japan.

Hard working and never satisfied, he is quoted as saying "I like ready-to-wear. I want to have fun making dresses. It is my love, it is my life." Shy and solitary, he had just a few close friends who served him as a surrogate family.

Charles Creed

Born Paris, France, 1909
Died London, England, July 1966

Creed's family was established in London as men's tailors in 1710. His grandfather, Henry Creed, opened a Paris establishment in 1850, earning a reputation for the finest tailored riding habits for women in Europe. The client list included the actress Réjane, Empress Eugénie of France, England's Queen Victoria, opera singer Mary Garden, and the spy Mata Hari. Under the direction of Henry's son, the house expanded into tailored suits, sports clothes, even evening dresses.

Charles Creed entered the family business in Paris in 1930 after studies in France, Berlin, Vienna, Scotland, and the United States. He opened his own London house in 1932, closed the Paris business a few years later with the advent of World War II. In the 1950s he designed wholesale lines for firms in London and the United States, closed his couture house in March 1966 to concentrate on ready-to-wear. The house was distinguished for sound traditional tailoring and excellent fabrics, elegant suits for town, country, and evening, and bright printed blouses of sheer Rodier wool.

He was married in 1948 to Patricia Cunningham, a fashion editor of British *Vogue*, who later went to work for him. The house closed with his death.

Angela Cummings

Born 1945

cummings works in the classic tradition in 18 karat gold, platinum, or sterling silver, yet her work is far from conventional, often combining materials such as wood, gold, and diamonds. As thoroughly versed in gemology and goldsmithing as she is in jewelry design, Cummings has revived old techniques including *damascene,* the ancient art of inlaying iron with precious metal. Much of her inspiration comes from nature and organic forms, including silver jewelry derived from the leaf of a ginkgo tree and pieces influenced by the exotic orchids that she raises. She finds rings the most difficult to design because they must be entirely three dimensional, yet balanced, and must look good on the finger.

The daughter of a German diplomat, Cummings graduated from art school in Hanau, Germany, and studied at the Art Academy of Perugia, Italy. She joined Tiffany & Co. in 1967, remaining there until 1984 when she left to open her own business. The first Angela Cummings jewelry boutique was at Bergdorf Goodman, followed by others coast to coast and in Canada and Japan. In April 2003, she announced she was closing shop as of June 1, except for her TV work with QVC. The TV sales are confined entirely to sterling silver.

Angela Cummings, 2002 (right) and jewelry from her earlier collection (left).

D

Lilly Daché

Wendy Dagworthy

Sandy Dalal

Oscar De La Renta

Diego Della Valle

Louis Dell'Olio

Pamela Dennis

Madeleine de Rauch

Jean Dessès

Christian Dior

Dolce & Gabbana

Drécoll

Gilles Dufour

Randolph Duke

Stephen Dweck

Lilly Daché

Born Beigles, France, ca. 1904

Died Louvecienne, France, December 31, 1989

Awards Neiman Marcus Award, 1940 · Coty American Fashion Critics' Award *Special Award (millinery),* 1943

vivacious and feminine, Daché brought an inimitable French flair to American fashion at a time when no woman was considered fully dressed without a hat. She left school at fourteen to apprentice with a milliner aunt, at fifteen was an apprentice in the workrooms of the famous Paris milliner Reboux, and later worked at Maison Talbot. She came to the United States in 1924, spent one week behind the millinery counter at Macy's, then, with a partner, opened a millinery shop in the West Eighties. When her partner left, Daché moved to Broadway and 86th Street in the same neighborhood as HATTIE CARNEGIE.

Her next move was to Madison Avenue and, finally, to her own nine-story building on East 57th Street. This contained showrooms, workrooms, and a duplex apartment on the roof where she lived with her husband Jean Despres, executive vice president of Coty. By 1949 Daché was designing dresses to go with her hats. She also undertook lingerie, loungewear, gloves, hosiery, men's shirts and ties, and even a wired strapless bra. The hairdresser Kenneth worked in her beauty salon before going into business for himself.

Her major design contributions were draped turbans, brimmed hats molded to the head, half hats, colored snoods, romantic massed flower shapes, and visored caps for war workers. She was considered America's foremost milliner and influenced many others in this country, including HALSTON. She closed her business in 1969 upon her husband's retirement.

From Daché's spring 1940 collection.

Wendy Dagworthy

Born Gravesend, Kent, England, 1950

one of the second wave of young London fashion designers, Dagworthy studied at Medway College of Art from 1966 to 1968, majored in fashion for three years at Hornsey College of Art. After graduating with honors, she designed for a wholesale firm for one year, opening her own company in 1972. In 1975 she joined the London Designer Collections, a cooperative of London designers. Her clothes are finely detailed and extremely wearable.

Since 1988 Dagworthy has been designer and consultant to other firms and devoted much of her time to fashion education, both at Central St. Martins College of Art & Design and the Royal College of Art.

Sandy Dalal

Born Sandy Agashiwala, New York, 1977
Awards Council of Fashion Designers of America (CFDA) *Perry Ellis Award for New Talent in Menswear, 1998*

sandy DaLaL first became interested in making clothes when he was ten years old and went with his mother on a trip to the Far East, where

she was checking out factories to make clothing for designers. He himself started sewing at fourteen and by his senior year in high school had made over 30 pieces, mostly shirts and pants—any jacket designs were sent to a tailor to execute. At eighteen he felt ready to begin a design career but at his family's insistence enrolled at the University of Pennsylvania, majoring in international trade and marketing. He also was on the fencing team but always continued to sew.

In 1996 he made his first tailored suit by himself. The next year, using Dalal, his mother's maiden name, he established his own business. This was financed with a few thousand dollars saved from summer jobs, plus the backing of family and friends. The clothes were cut with clean, simple lines, and made of beautiful fabrics—a cross-breeding of 1960s Swinging London and colonial India, appealing to men with a sense

Sandy Dalal (above). From his 2001 collection (left).

of adventure and a taste for luxury. They have been well received by such stores as Barney's in New York and Fred Segal of Los Angeles. He has also worked for Italian and Japanese firms while continuing to design for his own label.

D

Oscar De La Renta

Born Santo Domingo, Dominican Republic, July 22, 1932
Awards Coty American Fashion Critics Award "*Winnie,*" 1967; *Return Award, 1968;
Hall of Fame, 1973* · Neiman Marcus Award, 1968 · Numerous awards from the Do-
minican Republic · Council of Fashion Designers of America (CFDA) *Women's Wear
Designer of the Year,* 2000

De La Renta is known for sexy, ex-travagantly romantic evening clothes in opulent materials. His daytime clothes, sometimes overshadowed by the more spectacular evening designs, have a European flavor—sophisticated, feminine, and eminently wearable.

Educated in Santo Domingo and Madrid, De La Renta remained in Madrid after graduation to study art,

Above and left, day and evening looks from Oscar De La Renta, Spring/Summer 2003. Right, the designer, 2002.

– – – – – – – – – – – – – –

intending to become a painter. His fashion career began when sketches he made for his own amusement were seen by the wife of the American ambassador to Spain, who asked him to design a gown for her daughter's debut. His first professional job was with BALENCIAGA's Madrid couture house, Eisa. In 1961 he went to Paris as assistant to Antonio de Castillo at Lanvin-Castillo, in 1963 went with Castillo to New York to design at Elizabeth Arden. He joined Jane Derby in 1965, was soon operating as Oscar De La Renta, Ltd., producing luxury ready-to-wear.

A signature perfume introduced in 1977 has been enormously successful; a second fragrance, *Ruffles,* appeared in 1983. He has also done boutique lines, bathing suits, wedding dresses, furs, jewelry, bed linens, and loungewear. In 1992 he took over the design of the BALMAIN couture collection remaining until his retirement in late 2002. He continues to design his own New York collection.

Diego Della Valle (J.P. Tod's)

Born San Eupidio a Mare, Italy, December 30, 1953

Diego Della Valle grew up in Italy's Marche region, the grandson of Filippo Della Valle, a cobbler who began a modest business in 1924 making fine shoes by hand. His son, Diego's father, developed the company to large-scale industrial production but it was Diego who gave it glamour.

He attended Law School in Bologna, and spent a year in the United States before returning to Italy to enter the family business. With an excellent design sense and a flair for promotion he has expanded the business and brought the company international recognition, linking up with such prominent designers as Gianfranco Ferré, Fendi, Lacroix, and Azzedine Alaïa.

Under the Diego Della Valle label the firm continues to make exquisite, one-of-a-kind shoes on special order, as well as fine, traditional, ready-to-wear footwear. It is, however, best known for J. P. Tod's, the leather driving shoe with the American-sounding name he introduced in 1987. This is a moccasin with 133 small leather pebbles, or *gommini*, set in the sole and running up the heel. Available in countless materials and colors, it's the casual shoe of choice for celebrities worldwide. The company also produces boots, loafers, and handbags, and a less expensive collection of casual shoes called Hogan.

Louis Dell'Olio

Born New York City, July 23, 1948
Awards Coty American Fashion Critics' Award "Winnie" (with Donna Karan), 1977; Hall of Fame (with Donna Karan), 1982; Special Award (women's wear, with Donna Karan), 1984

Dell'Olio is best known for his years at Anne Klein, first as co-designer with Donna Karan and then as sole designer when she left to open her own house. After her departure he continued the direction begun with Karan—a modern, sophisticated interpretation of the classic Anne Klein sportswear—clothes in the deluxe investment category marked by clean, sharp shapes in beautiful fabrics. His other design projects included furs for Michael Forrest.

In 1967 Dell'Olio received the Norman Norell Scholarship to Parsons School of Design, from which he graduated in 1969, winning the Gold Thimble Award for coats and suits. He assisted Dominic Rompollo at Teal Traina, was designer at the Giorgini and Ginori divisions of Originala. In 1974, he joined Karan, a friend from Parsons, as co-designer at Anne Klein & Co. Spring 1985 was their last joint collection. Dell'Olio continued as sole designer for Anne Klein until 1993, when he was replaced by Richard Tyler. He has continued to design on a freelance basis.

Dell'Olio with model for Anne Klein Collection, Fall/Winter 1993.

D

Pamela Dennis

Born Newark, New Jersey, August 24, 1960

Dennis has carved a distinctive niche for herself in the designer evening category. Without formal training, she came into design by chance when, invited to a wedding and with nothing to wear, she took a few yards of silk to a tailor and had him make it into a columnar dress. Another wedding guest, a photostylist, asked to use the dress in a diamond commercial, which led to three more commercials and inspired Dennis to design her first collection.

Her clothes are distinguished by simple shapes in luxurious fabrics—silk crepe, chiffon, georgette, charmeuse, wool bouclé, stretch crepe—enhanced with crystals or hand-beaded lace. They have been sold nationally and internationally to fine boutiques and specialty stores and worn by celebrities ranging from Calista Flockhart to Joan Rivers to Whitney Houston.

In 2000, with the aim of adapting her signature styles for a more accessible price range, Dennis sold her company to a newly-formed luxury conglomerate. The move proved disastrous with an acrimonious parting of the ways in early 2001. By March 2002, though still not yet able to use her own name, Dennis was back in business on a limited basis with plans for future expansion.

Madeleine de Rauch

Starting in 1928 with a single worker, de Rauch grew and stayed in business for 45 years. The house was known for beautiful, wearable, functional clothes. Soft fabrics were handled with great fluidity, draped close at the top of the figure. Wide necklines were often framed with folds or tucks.

Plaids, checks, and stripes were treated with simplicity and precision, so perfectly done they seemed to have been assembled on a drawing board.

An accomplished sportswoman, de Rauch began in the 1920s to design her own clothes for active sports. When friends persuaded her to make clothes for them, she opened a business called the House of Friendship in 1928, employing a single worker. With the help of her two sisters, the business grew and in the 1930s evolved into the House of de Rauch overlooking the Cours de Reine. It closed in 1973.

Jean Dessès

Born Alexandria, Egypt, August 6, 1904
Died Athens, Greece, August 2, 1970

Dessès is remembered primarily for draped evening gowns of chiffon and mousseline in beautiful colors, and for the subtlety with which he handled fur. Of Greek ancestry, he was as a child interested in beautiful clothes and designed a dress for his mother when he was only nine. He attended school in Alexandria, Egypt, studied law in Paris, and in 1925 switched to fashion design. For 12 years he worked for Mme. Jane on the rue de la Paix and in 1937 opened his own establishment.

Dessès visited the United States in 1949. He admired American women and in 1950 designed a lower-priced line for them called Jean Dessès Diffusion. This is seen as the beginning of French couture expansion into ready-to-wear.

A gentle man of refined and luxurious tastes, Dessès was inspired in his work by native costumes he saw in museums on his travels, especially in Greece and Egypt. Customers included Princess Margaret, the Duchess of Kent, and the Queen of Greece. Other designers worked for him—VALENTINO in the 1950s, also GUY LAROCHE. Dessès gave up his couture business in 1960 due to ill health, continued the ready-to-wear until 1965, when he retired to Greece. With the recent renewed interest in vintage couture his beautiful classic gowns have had a second coming, no longer hidden in museum collections but showing up on the backs of celebrities such as Renée Zellweger, who wore one to the 2001 Academy Awards.

Sketch from *Women's Wear Daily* of Jean Dessès gown, 1949.

Christian Dior

Born Granville, France, January 31, 1905
Died Montecatini, Italy, October 24, 1957
Awards Neiman Marcus Award, 1947 · Parsons Medal for Distinguished Achievement, 1956

The name DIOR is most associated with the New Look. This silhouette was, in essence, a polished continuation of the rounded line seen in the first postwar collections, appearing at the same time at a number of design houses. Dior's was a dream of flowerlike women with rounded shoulders, feminine busts, tiny waists, and enormous spreading skirts. Everything was exquisitely made of the best materials available.

Dior was the son of a well-to-do manufacturer of fertilizer and chemicals from Normandy. He wished to become an architect—his family wanted him to enter the diplomatic service. He studied political science at L'École des Sciences Politiques, performed his obligatory military service, and in 1928 opened a small art gallery with a friend. This was soon wiped out by the Depression, which also ruined Dior's family. In 1931 he traveled to Russia, returned disillusioned with Soviet Communism, and for

Dior's New Look from 1947 (left) and a cowl-back jacket from 1957 (above).

the next few years lived from hand to mouth, eating little and sleeping on the floor of friends' apartments.

He became seriously ill in 1934 and had to leave Paris. During an enforced rest in Spain and the south of France he learned tapestry weaving and developed a desire to create. He returned to Paris in 1935, thirty years old and without means of support. Unable to find any kind of job he started making design sketches and also did fashion illustrations for *Le Figaro.* That year he sold his first sketches—for 20 francs each.

His early hat designs were successful, his dresses less so. In 1937, after a two-year struggle to improve his dresses, he sold several sketches to

Robert Piguet and was asked to make a number of dresses for an upcoming collection. He was hired by Piguet in 1938 but in 1939 went into the Army. The fall of Paris in June 1940 found him stationed in the south of France. Asked by Piguet to come back to work, Dior delayed his return until the end of 1941, by which time another designer had been hired. He then went to work for Lucien Lelong, a much larger establishment. At the end of 1946 he left Lelong to open his own house.

Dior was backed in his new project by Marcel Boussac, a French financier, race horse owner, and textile manufacturer, who originally was looking for someone to take over an ailing couture

house he owned. Instead, Dior persuaded Boussac to back him, and in the spring of 1947, presented his wildly successful, first New Look collection.

He continued to produce beautiful clothes in collection after collection, each evolving from the one before, continually refining and expanding his talent. In 1952, with the sensuous line, he began to loosen the waist, freed it even more with the H-line in 1954, the A- and Y-lines in 1955.

Dior described himself as a silent, slow Norman, shy and reticent by nature, strongly attached to his friends. He loved good food, and for relaxation and pleasure, he read history and archaeology and played cards. His chief passion was for architecture. Like many designers he was superstitious and believed in the importance of luck, consulting fortune tellers on the major decisions of his life. Since his death, the House of Dior has continued under the

direction of other designers: YVES SAINT LAURENT until 1960, MARC BOHAN until 1989, then GIANFRANCO FERRÉ, and since 1996 by JOHN GALLIANO. Christian Dior, Inc. has become a vast international

merchandising operation with the Dior label on jewelry, scarves, men's ties, furs, stockings, gloves, ready-to-wear and, of course, perfume. Dior-Delman shoes were designed by ROGER VIVIER.

— — — — — — — — — — — — — —
Dior in his studio, 1947.

D

Dolce & Gabbana

Born Domenico Dolce; Polizzi Generosa, Palermo, Italy, September 13, 1958
Stefano Gabbana; Venice, Italy, November 14, 1962

Members of the avant-garde of Italian fashion, Dolce and Gabbana came to their craft by disparate routes: Domenico Dolce, whose father had a small clothing factory in Sicily, attended fashion school, but Stefano Gabbana was totally lacking in fashion background, having studied graphics and worked in an advertising agency.

The two met in Milan in 1980, became assistants to a Milanese designer, and in 1982 joined forces in their own business,

Left, designers Dolce and Gabbana, 2002. Right, from the Spring/Summer 2003 collection.

----

working as consultants to other companies while creating their own line. Their first international recognition came in 1985 when they were chosen by the Milano Collezioni as one of three young Italian talents to be given formal presentations. Their first knitwear collection appeared in 1987; they have since added

men's wear and in 1994, a lower-priced collection called D & G.

Dolce & Gabbana continue to evolve along their own highly individual path. Their look, based on body clothes, seasons the modern with romantic historical references, the pieces designed to be worn in different ways in different situations. In their men's clothes, a Sicilian-influenced combination of strict, structured tailoring with avant-garde shirts and accessories appeals to the man who is not afraid of attention.

Drécoll

Founded Paris, France, 1905
Closed 1929

The House of Drécoll was established in Vienna by a Belgian, Baron Christopher Drécoll. His designer bought the name and moved the business to Paris, where it survived the first World War only to perish like the dinosaur when it could not change with the times. Drécoll was never one of the top Paris houses but in the pre-war period of conspicuous display of wealth, its elaborate clothes fitted in and the house prospered. After the war, new attitudes and women's changed expectations demanded new clothes. Unable to change direction, the house was forced to close.

Gilles Dufour

Born Lyon, France

Dufour established his own prêt-à-porter label in March 2001 after an already extensive career, including collaboration with KARL LAGERFELD at Chloé and Fendi and 15 years as Lagerfeld's number two at Chanel. He has freelanced in New York and Paris for ready-to-wear, leathers, and furs, and put in three seasons as prêt-à-porter stylist at Balmain. He graduated from l'École Supérieure des Arts Décoratifs in Paris and studied in New York at the School of Visual Arts, after which he worked at CARDIN on both ready-to-wear and couture.

Extremely versatile, Dufour has designed just about everything a woman could wear, from accessories to bridal to furs to sportswear, and in addition, sportswear for men. He has also created sets and costumes for ballet, opera, and film. His assured designs show a light touch—witty trompe-l'oeil knits, sexy sweaters and little-black-dresses, and trademark T-shirts bearing naughty legends that vary with each collection.

Gilles Dufour, 2001.

D

Randolph Duke

Born Las Vegas, Nevada, January 14, 1958

Duke studied at the university of Southern California and at the Fashion Institute of Design and Merchandising in Los Angeles, from which he graduated in 1978 with the Bob Mackie and Peacock awards. He began his career immediately as a swimwear designer, working successively for various West Coast companies—Jantzen, Cole of California, the Anne Cole Collection—and until 1987 for Gottex.

To establish his own label, Duke relocated to New York. For a time he had a shop on the Upper West Side of Manhattan and a wholesale business, closed in 1992. He then joined a private label concern producing exclusive signature collections for retail stores.

In 1996 he became creative director for the newly-resuscitated Halston label, where over several seasons he oversaw its revival with clothes of an American smartness consistent with the Halston name, glamorous and luxurious.

He has sold his clothes successfully in personal appearances on the QVC shopping channel and created collections of apparel and accessories for the Home Shopping Network, meanwhile selling his signature collection through select specialty stores such as Neiman Marcus, Saks Fifth Avenue, and Barneys. Duke's attention-getting evening dresses have been chosen for awards appearances by numerous actresses, including Jennifer Aniston, Minnie Driver, Angelina Jolie, and Hilary Swank.

Stephen Dweck

Born Brooklyn, New York, August 10, 1960

Graduating from New York's School of Visual Arts in 1980 with a gold medal in sculpture, Stephen Dweck went into business as a jewelry designer the same year in partnership with his brothers. Working with sterling silver, vermeil, and bronze, he combines the metals with natural minerals and semiprecious stones for jewelry that is modern with overtones of fantasy and hints of ancient cultures. He utilizes natural forms such as beetles and butterflies, leaves and vines, for his jewelry and for the collections for the home, which he creates for others. These have included china for Sasaki and sterling silver gifts and accessories for Lunt Silversmiths. He has also designed a belt collection.

Necklace and earrings from Dweck's collection.

E

Florence Eiseman
Mark Eisen
Alber Elbaz
Perry Ellis
Elizabeth Emanuel

Florence Eiseman

Born Minneapolis, Minnesota, September 27, 1899
Died Milwaukee, Wisconsin, January 8, 1988
Awards Neiman Marcus Award (the first children's designer recipient), 1955 ·
Swiss Fabrics Award, 1956 · Dallas Fashion Award, 1980

Eiseman's all-time best-selling jumper and T-shirt from 1976-1979 (top); sailor top and culottes for resort 1982 (bottom left); the "hello" dress from the early 1950s (bottom right).

TWO FLorence Eiseman sayings are: "Children have bellies, not waists" and "You should see the child, and not the dress first." Ruled by these precepts, and by her belief that children should not be dressed in small versions of adult clothing, Eiseman produced simple styles distinguished by fine fabrics and excellent workmanship, with prices to match. The clothes were so classic and so well made they were frequently handed down from one generation to another.

Florence Eiseman took up sewing as a hobby following the birth of her second son, Robert. As her children grew she turned out quilts and clothing for them and for her neighbors' children. In 1945, when family finances were pinched, her husband Laurence took samples of her organdy pinafores to Marshall Field & Co. in Chicago. The $3,000 order he came away with put them in business with her as designer, him as business manager/salesman.

Mrs. Eiseman first worked out of her home, enlisting other women to sew for her in theirs. Next, with two sewing ma-chines, she took over a corner of her husband's toy factory. Within a few years, Laurie Eiseman gave up his toy business to devote himself to the cloth-ing firm, which in a short time grew into a large concern, with sales across the United States and abroad. Mrs. Eiseman functioned successively as vice presi-dent, president, and chairman.

She became known as the "NORMAN NORELL of children's clothes," making dresses and separates, swimsuits, play-clothes, sleepwear, and boys' suits. In 1969 she added less expensive knits, brother-sister outfits and, for a short time, a limited group of women's clothes. In 1984 the company was asked by Neiman Marcus to do a luxury collec-tion of dress-up clothes at prices begin-ning where the regular collection left off. The result was Florence Eiseman Couture, not custom-made but using rich fabrics and many hand touches. Its introduction in September 1984 coin-cided with Mrs. Eiseman's eighty-fifth birthday, finding her still actively in-volved in the company she founded. The same year, the Denver Art Museum pre-sented a retrospective of her work. On her death, she was praised for her role in raising the standards of fashion and quality in children's clothes and for en-couraging manufacturers to trade up.

Mark Eisen

Born Cape Town, South Africa, September 27, 1958

Mark Eisen grew up in Cape Town, always interested in art and design. His father had little faith in fashion as a career and urged him to explore other options, so Eisen enrolled in a business course at the University of Southern California, where in 1982 he earned a B.S. degree. While in school, he designed a gold and red Trojan army helmet, which he sold to fans of the USC football team (the Trojans) to make extra money. The project was so successful that it was mentioned in *Newsweek* magazine, and made him even more determined to go into fashion.

He began his own company in Los Angeles in 1988 and in 1993 moved to New York, bringing with him some of the freedom and relaxed feeling of California design.

While early on he did Mick Jagger's clothes for the 1994 Rolling Stones tour, Eisen has built his success on clean, sleek clothes for women, simple but sensuous. His primary focus has been on women's designer sportswear, but his business interests include couture, ready-to-wear for women and men, shoes, and custom-tailored clothes, and extend worldwide.

He has been a critic in the Fashion Design Department of Otis College of Art and Design in Los Angeles; in 1988 he was honored by the USC Business School as Alumnus of the Year.

From Mark Eisen's Fall 1994 collection.

Alber Elbaz

Born Morocco, 1961

Designer Alber Elbaz.

ELbaz grew up in Tel Aviv, where he graduated from the Shenkar College School of Fashion and Textiles. He served three years in the Israeli Army and, when he was twenty-five, left Israel for New York, where he had a brother living in Queens. He immediately started working on Seventh Avenue, designing inexpensive evening dresses, and a few years later was introduced to GEOFFREY BEENE, who hired him on the spot. He worked for Beene for seven years as a design assistant before moving to Paris in 1996 and the top job at GUY LAROCHE.

After successfully invigorating Laroche, he was hired away in 1998 to become head women's designer at Yves Saint Laurent Rive Gauche. In 1999, when Saint Laurent was bought by Gucci, he was supplanted by Tom Ford. He then worked briefly for KRIZIA in Milan before being hired as creative director for LANVIN late in 2001.

The Elbaz style is based on classic shapes, beautiful, womanly clothes without elaborate trimming or silhouettes, in flattering colors, and with a few feminine turns such as beading or ribbons to give them pizazz. Without losing sight of wearability, he is fascinated with new ways of cutting fabric or placing a seam, visualizing a client who wants something both beautiful and comfortable. For evening he aims at glamour but never extravagance: "When a woman walks into the room, no one will faint, but she will be noticed."

Elbaz's design from his Spring 2003 collection.

Perry Ellis

Born Portsmouth, Virginia, 1940

Died New York City, May 30, 1986

Awards Neiman Marcus Award, 1979 · Coty American Fashion Critics' Award *"Winnie,"* 1979; *Return Award, 1980; Hall of Fame, 1981; Special Award (men's wear), 1981; Hall of Fame Citation (women's wear), 1983; Men's Wear Return Award, 1983; Hall of Fame (men's wear), 1984; Hall of Fame Citation (women's wear), 1984* · Council of Fashion Designers of America (CFDA) *Outstanding Designer in Women's Fashion, 1981; Outstanding Designer in Men's Fashion: 1982, 1983* · Cutty Sark Men's Fashion Award *Outstanding Menswear Designer: 1983, 1984* · Fashion Walk of Fame, 2002

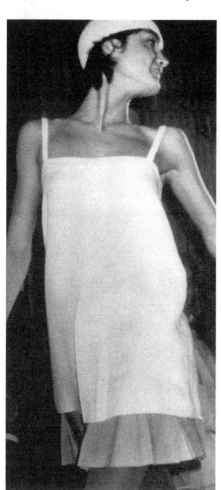

ELLis came to fashion design relatively late, having previously worked in retailing and merchandising. He took his B.A. at William and Mary College, and his M.A. in retailing from New York University. He was sportswear buyer for Miller & Rhoads in Richmond, leaving in 1967 to work as a merchandiser to John Meyer of Norwich, a conservative sportswear firm. There he acquired three important design tools—sketching, pattern making, and fabric selection. In 1974 he joined the Vera Companies as merchandiser, and the next year became designer for the Portfolio division of Vera.

Perry Ellis Sportswear, Inc., was established in 1978 with Ellis as designer and president; men's wear followed in 1980. Then came furs, shearling coats for both men and women, cloth coats, and for Japan, a complete sportswear line. There were shoes, legwear, scarves, Vogue patterns, and sheets, towels, and blankets. A fragrance collection was launched in 1985.

From the beginning, the clothes were distinguished by a young, adventurous spirit and the use of natural fibers: cotton, silk, linen, and pure wool. Hand knitted sweaters of cotton, silk, and cashmere became a trademark. This use of fine fabrics and handwork soon drove the collection up into a higher price bracket. Hence, in 1984, the Portfolio name was revived for a moderately priced collection with much the same relaxed classic look as the original.

Ellis believed that people should not take fashion too seriously or be overly concerned with what they wear, and, following his own dictates, usually dressed informally for his rare public appearances. He was active in the Council of Fashion Designers of America and served two terms as president. He was elected to a third term the week before his death. In his honor, the organization established the Perry Ellis Award, to be given annually "for the greatest impact on an emerging new talent." David Cameron was the first recipient in 1986.

The company has continued in business under the direction of a number of designers. MARC JACOBS took over in 1989 and after several unprofitable seasons was dropped by the company in February 1993, when the designer and bridge sportswear collections were discontinued. The Perry Ellis name continues to be licensed in both the United States and Europe.

Perry Ellis and design from 1979 (left). *Also see Color Plate 6.*

E

Elizabeth Emanuel

Born London, England, 1953

ELizabeth and David Emanuel gained international attention for their wedding dress for Diana, Princess of Wales. They attended Harrow School of Art and together took a postgraduate course in fashion at the Royal College of Art, the only married couple to be accepted there. They opened their own ready-to-wear firm in 1977, switching to custom-made in 1979. In June 1990 they closed their business and announced the end of their marriage.

The Emanuels' fantasy ball gowns and wedding dresses, afloat in lace, taffeta, organza, and tulle, evoked a romantic, bygone, never-never time. Licenses included bed linens, sunglasses, and perfume.

Lady Diana Spencer arriving at St. Paul's Cathedral for her wedding to Prince Charles, July 29, 1981.

F

Alberto Fabiani

Nicole Farhi

Jacques Fath

Fendi

Salvatore Ferragamo

Gianfranco Ferré

Alberta Ferretti

Anne Fogarty

Fontana

Tom Ford

Mariano Fortuny

Alberto Fabiani

Born Tivoli, Italy

Fabiani was introduced to fashion in Paris at the age of eighteen by a family friend, an Italian tailor. After three years' apprenticeship, he returned to Italy to work in his family business and in 1952 emerged as a designer with his own distinctively Italian viewpoint, lively and elegant. A part of the burst of fashion creativity that occurred in Italy in the 1950s, he was married to SIMONETTA, also a designer. Together they moved to Paris, opening their couture house in 1961. After a successful beginning, the business failed and Fabiani returned alone to Rome where he rebuilt his business successfully with clients from Italy, Europe, and the United States. He has since retired.

Nicole Farhi

Born France, July 25, 1946
Awards British Fashion Award *"British Classics,"* 1989 · *"Contemporary Collections,"* 1995, 1996, 1997

During 1965 and 1966, Farhi studied design at Studio Berçot, a Paris hotbed of creativity and independent thinking. She went on to freelance work, designing for women, men, and children, and creating accessories, textiles, knits, and underwear for Pierre D'Alby and the Italian fabric house Bianchini Ferrier, among others. She also did illustrations for the magazines *Elle* and *Marie Claire.*

In 1973, Farhi began a freelance association in London with Stephen Marks, designing for both the Stephen Marks and French Connection labels. In 1983, the Stephen Marks label was changed to Nicole Farhi to coincide with the opening of a Nicole Farhi boutique at Harvey Nichols, London. There have been freestanding shops in London and New York since 1984, and more recently in Oslo and Tokyo.

A complete professional, Farhi excels in well-cut separates, with simple, sexy dresses, strong coats, and outerwear. She sees her female customer as the "classic working woman."

Jacques Fath

Born Lafitte, France, September 12, 1912
Died Paris, France, November 14, 1954
Awards Neiman Marcus Award, 1949

Left, Fath and model, 1951. Right, from 1947.

Robe créa imprimé

T. Fath

9

Fαth's clothes were flattering, feminine, and sexy without slipping into vulgarity. They followed the lines of the body with hourglass shapes and swathed hips, and often had full, pleated skirts and plunging necklines. He did not sew or sketch but draped material while his assistants made sketches.

Son of an Alsatian businessman, grandson of a painter, and great-grandson of a dressmaker, Fath attended both business school and drama school, acting briefly in films. He showed his design talent early on in costumes for the theater and films, opened his first couture house in Paris in 1937 with a small collection of 20 models. He went into

the Army in 1940, was captured, and on his release reopened his house, which he managed to keep open during the war. After Liberation, he became enormously successful, eventually expanding his salon from the single wartime workroom with one fitter to an establishment with 600 employees. In 1948 he signed with a U.S. manufacturer to produce two collections a year, one of the first French couturiers to venture into ready-to-wear. The Fath name also went into perfume, scarves, stockings, and millinery.

Handsome and personable, Fath had a flair for publicity and showmanship and became one of the most popular designers of his time. He loved parties and with his wife, actress Genevieve de Bruyere, gave elaborate entertainments at their Corbeville chateau. He was also an excellent businessman. After his death from leukemia at the age of forty-two, his wife continued the business for a few years, closing it in 1957.

In early 2002 the name was bought by a newly-formed conglomerate, France Luxury Group, and Lizzy Disney, a young Brit who graduated from Central St. Martins the same year as STELLA McCARTNEY, was hired as designer.

Fendi

Founded 1918

specializing in furs, handbags, luggage, and sportswear, Fendi was founded in 1918 by Adele Fendi. After her husband's death in 1954, Signora Fendi called on her five daughters for help—Paola, Anna, Franca, Carla, and Alda were at that time aged fourteen to twenty-four. Working as a team, the sisters, with their husbands, have built the business and expanded the Fendi business, continuing to explore new areas. Their daughters, in turn, have also come into the firm. Adele Fendi died March 19, 1978, at the age of eighty-one.

In 1962 the Fendis hired KARL LAGER-FELD to design their furs, backing him with a dazzling array of new, unusual, or neglected pelts and the most inventive techniques. Their mother had made coats out of squirrel and had made it fashionable; the Fendis today still use squirrel, as well as badger, Persian lamb, fox, and sundry unpedigreed furs, often several in one garment. They are noted for such innovations as furs woven in strips and coats left unlined for lightness—the furs are always light-hearted and fun. Fendi styles have glamour, but their success is based on an understanding of what women need and want. The Fendi double F initials, designed by Lagerfeld, have become an international status symbol.

Left, Carla Fendi and right, from 2001.

In addition to furs, there are Fendi accessories and ready-to-wear for women and men. Lagerfeld continues to be responsible for the women's ready-to-wear, the avant-garde men's collection is designed by Silvia Fendi. Previously entirely a family business, the firm is now part of the LVMH empire.

Salvatore Ferragamo

Born Bonito, Italy, June 1898
Died Fiumetto, Italy, August 7, 1960
Awards Neiman Marcus Award, 1947

Ferragamo began working as a shoemaker in Bonito when he was thirteen, emigrated to the United States in 1923. He studied mass shoemaking techniques then opened a shop in Hollywood, designing shoes and making them by hand for such film stars as Dolores Del Rio, Pola Negri, and Gloria Swanson. He also maintained a successful business in ready-made shoes.

He returned to Italy and in 1936 opened a business in Florence. By the time of his death in 1960 he had ten factories in Italy and Great Britain. After his death the business was carried on by his wife and daughters Fiamma and Giovanna, and his son Ferruccio. In addition to shoes, the Ferragamo name appears on handbags, scarves, and luxury ready-to-wear sold in freestanding boutiques and in major specialty stores.

Early Ferragamo designs are fantasies of shape, color, and fabric. He is said to have originated the wedge heel and the platform sole, also the Lucite heel. While still elegant, the emphasis for many years shifted to ladylike, conservative styling and comfortable fit but in the age of the stiletto, the house has shown more extreme styles and proved itself very much in step with the times.

Salvatore Ferragamo with Paulette Goddard in 1959.

Gianfranco Ferré

Born Legnano, Italy, ca. 1945

Ferré's day clothes have a strong sculptural quality, yet they are fluid, clean-lined, and comfortable. A fine tailor and leading exponent of architectural design. Ferré originally intended to be an architect—he studied in Milan and qualified in 1967. After a period working for a furniture maker and time off for travel, he began designing jewelry, and by 1970 had made a name for himself as an accessories designer. He sold his shoes, scarves, and handbags to other designers, including LAGERFELD, and designed striped T-shirts for Fiorucci. As a freelancer he began designing sportswear and raincoats and by 1974 was showing under his own name.

In 1989 he joined CHRISTIAN DIOR, replacing MARC BOHAN as design director. At Dior his clothes were marked by lush extravagance in the traditional couture

mode. He was replaced at Dior by JOHN GALLIANO in 1996. Ferré continues to produce his signature ready-to-wear collection in Italy with what is considered the most accomplished workroom in Milan.

Left, Gianfranco Ferré. Right, from 2003.

Alberta Ferretti

Born Gradara near Riccione, Italy, May 2, 1950

To the business born, Alberta Ferretti began at an early age to collaborate with her mother, who owned an atelier, and by the age of eighteen had her own boutique. Her first collection appeared in 1974. From 1981, when she presented her first *prêt-à-porter* collection, her business has grown to include the signature couture collection, diffusion sportswear, and a Japanese operation with boutiques in Tokyo, Osaka, and Yokohama. She is owner and managing director of AEFFE, which produces and distributes her clothes. It also produces MOSCHINO Cheap & Chic, Ultra OZBEK, and NARCISO RODRIGUEZ.

Ferretti's approach is feminine and elegant—soft, traditional shapes tweaked to make them contemporary and interpreted in the finest Italian fabrics. It's a look that's both witty and sexy. Her other projects have included glassware, ceramics, and a perfume, *Femina*.

Anne Fogarty

Born Pittsburgh, Pennsylvania, February 2, 1919

Died New York City, January 15, 1981

Awards Coty American Fashion Critics' Award *Special Award (dresses)*, 1951 · Neiman Marcus Award, 1952 · International Silk Association Award, 1955 · National Cotton Fashion Award, 1957

Anne Fogarty wears white cotton pique from her summer 1957 collection to accept National Cotton Fashion Award.

Fogarty is best known for her "paper doll" silhouette, for crinoline petticoats under full-skirted shirtdresses with tiny waists, for the camise, a chemise gathered onto a high yoke, and for lounging coveralls. In the early 1970s she showed a peasant look with ruffled shirts and hot pants under long quilted skirts. She also designed lingerie, jewelry, shoes, hats, coats, and suits.

After study at Carnegie Tech, Fogarty moved to New York, where she worked as a model and stylist. Between 1948 and 1957 she designed junior-size dresses for Youth Guild and Margot, Inc., next spent five years at Saks Fifth Avenue. She established Anne Fogarty Inc. in 1962, and closed it 12 years later. At the time of her death she had completed a collection of spring-summer dresses and sportswear for a Seventh Avenue firm.

In 1940 she married Tom Fogarty, with whom she had two children. They later divorced and she married twice again: Richard Kolmar who died in 1971, and Wade O'Hara, from whom she was divorced.

Fontana

Founded Parma, Italy, 1907

originally a small dressmaking establishment founded in Parma by Amabile Fontana, the business was taken over by her three daughters, Micol and Zoe as designers, Giovanna in charge of sales. In 1936 they moved to Rome and after World War II made a name for themselves in the emerging Italian haute couture as *Sorelle Fontana* (Fontana Sisters). Their designs were marked by asymmetric lines and interesting necklines, and were noteworthy for delicate handwork. They were particularly admired for their evening gowns.

Fontana created Ava Gardner's costumes for *The Barefoot Contessa*, Margaret Truman's wedding gown, also clothes for Jacqueline Kennedy. The house was at its peak in the 1950s, when it contributed largely to Italian fashion.

Tom Ford

Born Texas, 1962
Awards Council of Fashion Designers of America (CFDA) *Designer of the Year*, 2000

Ford grew up in Santa Fe, New Mexico, where his parents had a business in real estate development, and even as a child was intensely focused and confident of success. He moved to New York in 1979 to attend NYU and be an actor, and soon was working successfully in TV commercials while honing his fashion instincts at the then celebrity hangout Studio 54. After a hair stylist predicted that he would lose his hair, he left acting and enrolled at Parsons School of Design, studying fashion and interior design. In 1990, following jobs with PERRY ELLIS and Cathy Hardwick, Ford moved to Gucci. The firm was then known mainly for luggage and leathers and for the Gucci

Right, Tom Ford on the runway. Left, from the Gucci Spring 2002 collection.

moccasin with a horse's bit across the instep, certainly not known for fashion.

In 1994, while continuing in his role as designer, Ford was made Creative Director for the company and also Communications Director for their ready-to-wear business. When Gucci acquired Yves Saint Laurent in 1999 Ford also became Design Director for Yves Saint Laurent Rive Gauche and YSL cosmetics.

—————————————————

Gold shirtdress from YSL Women Spring 2003 Paris collection.

As Creative Director for both Gucci and YSL, Ford is responsible not only for the design of shoes, watches, luggage, and ready-to-wear for women and men, but is also involved in product development, in deciding which designers Gucci should back, and in the companies' advertising campaigns. With his rare combination of commercial ability and keen sense of fashion he has been given credit for revitalizing a fading brand and for moving a great fashion name into the new century.

Mariano Fortuny

Born Granada, Spain, 1871
Died Venice, Italy, 1949

Fortuny's father was a well-known painter who died when his son was only three years old. After art studies—painting, drawing, and sculpture—Fortuny became interested in chemistry and dyes, which he studied in Germany. At the turn of the 20th century he moved to Venice, where he experimented with every aspect of design, from dyeing and printing silks by methods and in patterns of his own invention, to shaping clothes to his own aesthetic standards.

His silk tea gowns in rich and subtle colors have been widely collected, both by museums and by women who treasure the rare and beautiful. The most famous design is the *Delphos* gown, which first appeared in 1907 and which he patented. This is a simple column of many narrow, irregular, vertical pleats permanently set in the silk by a secret process. Slipped over the head and tied at the waist by thin silk cords, it clings to the figure and spills over the feet. It may have sleeves or be sleeveless. There is also a two-piece version called *Peplos,* with a hip-length overblouse or longer, unpleated tunic. These dresses are both beautiful and amazingly practical. For storage, each is simply twisted into a rope and coiled into a figure eight, then slipped into its own small box. Status symbols at the time they were made, the dresses have become so once again, bringing such high prices at auction they are almost too costly to wear. He also designed tunics, capes, scarves and kimono-shaped wraps to be worn over the *Delphos.*

Fortuny invented a process for printing color and metals on fabric to achieve an effect of brocade or tapestry. Velvets were dyed in many layers and sometimes printed with metallics, gold, or silver. Fortuny fabrics are still used in interior design, still manufactured in Venice.

Painter, photographer, set and lighting designer, inventor, Fortuny has in recent years been recognized again for his originality and wide-ranging creativity. An exhibition of more than 100 examples of his work, including dresses, robes, textiles, and clocks, opened in Lyon, France, in May 1980. From there it travelled to New York's Fashion Institute of Technology and on to the Art Institute of Chicago. Fortuny designs are regularly included in costume exhibitions at museums and design schools.

For an evening cape designed by Fortuny see Color Plate 10.

G

James Galanos

Irene Galitzine

John Galliano

Jean-Paul Gaultier

Rudi Gernreich

Nicolas Ghesquière

Romeo Gigli

Marithé & François Girbaud

Hubert de Givenchy

Alix Grès

James Galanos

Born Philadelphia, Pennsylvania, September 20, 1925
Awards Neiman Marcus Award, 1954 · Coty American Fashion Critics' Award
"*Winnie,*" 1954; *Return Award,* 1956; *Hall of Fame,* 1959 · National Cotton
Fashion Award, 1958 · Council of Fashion Designers of America (CFDA) *Lifetime
Achievement Award,* 1984 · *Fashion Walk of Fame,* 2001

one of the greatest, most independent designers working in America during the last half century, Galanos has been widely considered the equal of the great European couturiers. His ready-to-wear became a symbol of luxury both for its extraordinary quality and for stratospheric prices comparable to those of the couture.

The son of Greek immigrants, Galanos left Philadelphia for New York to study at Traphagen School of Fashion and after only a few months began selling sketches to manufacturers. He worked for HATTIE CARNEGIE in 1944, and went to Paris where he worked with ROBERT PIGUET (1947-1948). He returned to New York and designed for Davidow, moved to Los Angeles, and worked at Columbia Pictures as assistant to JEAN LOUIS. In 1951, with two assistants and a $500 loan from Jean Louis, he started his own business; he gave his first New York showing in 1952 in a private apartment.

In an age where hems were left unfinished, linings banished, and seams worn inside-out, Galanos still believed that a garment should be as luxurious inside as out and insisted on lining his clothes. Intricate construction, flawless workmanship, and magnificent imported fabrics were his hallmarks, as well as detailing rarely found in ready-to-wear. Impeccably precise matching of plaids

James Galanos (right) and design from 1962 (left).

and the delicate cross pleating of his legendary chiffons are just two examples. Long admired by connoisseurs of fashion, he achieved wider recognition as one of Nancy Reagan's favorite designers. She chose a white satin Galanos gown for the first Inaugural Ball in 1981 and, for the second in 1985, a slim, jeweled dress with bolero top.

Because he likes the climate and relaxed living style, Galanos chose to live and work in Los Angeles, where he assembled a workroom of near-miraculous proficiency and skill. He did not give large public showings, preferring to exhibit his clothes to the press and retailers in the more intimate settings of hotel suites. In 1976, New York's Fashion Institute of Technology presented "Galanos—25 Years," a special fashion show and exhibition celebrating his 25th year in business. He retired and closed his business in January 1998.

Princess Irene Galitzine

Born Tiflis, Russia, ca. 1916

GaLitzine made her name in the 1960s with silk palazzo pajamas as a sophisticated evening look. Cut with wide legs from fluid silks, often fringed with beads, sometimes with attached necklaces, they were an instant sensation. She was also known for at-home togas, evening suits, tunic-top dresses, and evening gowns with bare backs or open sides.

Raised in Rome after her family fled the Russian Revolution, Galitzine studied art and design in Rome, where she worked three years for the FONTANA sisters. She opened an import business in Rome in 1948, first showed her own designs in 1949. She closed her business in 1968, continuing to design for various companies—cosmetics, furs, household linens. She revived her couture house in 1970 and showed sporadically for several years.

John Galliano

Born Gibraltar, 1960
Awards British Fashion Council *Designer of the Year*, 1987 · Council of Fashion Designers of America (CFDA) *International Award*, 1997

From the Spring 2003 Christian Dior collection.

The son of a spanish mother and an English father, Galliano was not permitted by his parents to study art until he reached college. At London's prestigious St. Martin's College of Art and Design, he studied textiles, learning about fabric, color, and the way cloth drapes, before switching to design. His graduation collection was called "Les Incroyables" after the group of young French dandies of the Directoire period who went by that name.

Galliano started his career as part of the wildly uninhibited avant-garde London design scene. His designs were twisted and artfully torn, weird and also beautiful. By the end of the 1980s, his style had evolved and matured into a smoother, more sophisticated manner based on flawless technique and complete command of craft, a synthesis of the original and the salable. In 1990 he joined the Paris ready-to-wear showings and has also shown in New York. His work is worldly and assured, in the forefront of fashion.

In July 1995 he was named to succeed

G

HUBERT DE GIVENCHY as designer of both Givenchy couture and ready-to-wear, and in 1996 moved to Christian Dior, another LVMH holding. There, in collection after collection, Galliano has proceeded to deconstruct Dior's bourgeois image, sometimes to critical outrage, and in the process has helped return the house to profitability. He has also continued to show his signature collection in London.

— — — — — — — — — — — —

Gown from his 1994 collection. *Also see Color Plate 18.*

Jean-Paul Gaultier

Born Paris, France, 1952
Awards Council of Fashion Designers of America (CFDA) *International Designer of the Year, 2000*

AT age fourteen Gaultier was presenting mini collections of clothes to his mother and grandmother, and at fifteen had invented a coat with book-bag closures, an idea he was to use in a later collection. When he was seventeen he sent some design sketches to CARDIN, for whom he worked as a design assistant for two years. Other stints followed at Esterel and PATOU, after which he turned to freelancing in 1976.

Once on his own Gaultier rejected the attitudes of his couture training, reflecting much more the spirit of London street dressing. He became the bad boy of Parisian fashion, using his considerable dressmaking and tailoring skills to produce irreverent send-ups of the fashion establishment. His juxtapositions of fabrics, scale, and shapes are unexpected and often witty, such as gray lace layered over voluminous gray wool knits, and overscaled coats over tiny vests cropped above the waist. Madonna has worn his designs—the notorious cone bra, for example—and modeled in his showings. His perfume, in a corseted bottle packaged in a beverage can, was introduced in 1994.

Gaultier in 1993 and design from Spring 2002 couture collection.

Hermès acquired a 35 percent share of the company in 1997, enabling Gaultier to open shops internationally and enter the couture arena. The fashion world has since watched, astonished, as its one-time *enfant terrible* uses his creativity and awesome technical ability in the service of French classicism. In May 2003 he was named the replacement for MARTIN MARGIELA at Hermès, with his first collection for Fall/Winter 2004.

Rudi Gernreich

Born Vienna, Austria, August 8, 1922
Died Los Angeles, California, April 21, 1985
Awards Coty American Fashion Critics' Award *Special Award (innovative body clothes),* 1960; *"Winnie,"* 1963; *Return Award,* 1966; *Hall of Fame,* 1967 · Knitted Textile Association *Crystal Ball Award,* 1975 · Council of Fashion Designers of America (CFDA) *Special Tribute,* 1985 · *Fashion Walk of Fame,* 2000

Probably the most original and prophetic American designer of the 1950s and 1960s, Gernreich was the only child of an Austrian hosiery manufacturer who died when his son was eight years old. He was first exposed to fashion in his aunt's couture salon, where he made sketches and learned about fabrics and dressmaking. In 1938 he left Austria with his mother and settled in Los Angeles where he attended Los Angeles City College and Art Center School. In 1942 he joined the Lester Horton Modern Dance Theater as dancer and costume designer. He became a U.S. citizen in 1943.

After five years with the Horton company, Gernreich decided he was not sufficiently talented as a dancer and left. For the next few years he sold fabrics. When he designed a series of dresses to demonstrate his wares the dresses aroused so much interest that in 1951 he formed a partnership with William Bass, a young Los Angeles garment manufacturer, and began developing his personal view of fashion. He established his own firm in 1959, and in addition, designed a collection for Harmon Knitwear, a Wisconsin manufacturer.

Gernreich specialized in dramatic sport clothes of stark cut, enriched by bold graphic patterns and striking color combinations. Always interested in liberating the body, he introduced a knit maillot without an inner bra in 1954, the era of constructed bathing suits. He favored halter necklines and cut-back shoulders to allow free movement, designed the soft "no-bra" bra in skin-toned nylon net, as well as "Swiss cheese" swimsuits with multiple cutouts, see-through blouses, knee-high hosiery patterned to match tunic tops and tights. His favorite shifts kept getting shorter until they were little more than tunics, which he showed over tights in bright colors or strong patterns.

Gernreich's innovations often caused a commotion, the see-through blouse, for example, and the topless bathing suit he showed in 1964. He was never interested in looking back, disdaining revivals of past eras. In 1968, at the height of his career, he announced he was taking a sabbatical from fashion. He never again worked at it full time, although he did return in 1971 with predictions for a future of bald heads, bare bosoms with pasties, and unisex caftans. He also freelanced in the fields of furniture, ballet costume, and professional dance and exercise clothes.

Quiet and cultivated in his tastes, Gernreich lived in a Hollywood Hills house furnished with modern classics by Charles Eames and Mies van der Rohe.

Rudi Gernreich with his model, Peggy Moffitt, 1968. *Also see Color Plate 3.*

Nicolas Ghesquière

Born Loudon, France, 1972

Awards Council of Fashion Designers of America *International Designer of the Year*, 2001

Unlike many of his designing contemporaries, Ghesquière never formally studied dress design, instead, had part-time internships starting at the age of fourteen with such working designers as AGNES B. and Corinne Cobson. He grew up in Central France, with a Belgian father who managed golf courses and a French mother with a liking for fashion. As a child, he was in love with *Star Wars* and sports, particularly riding, swimming, and fencing.

After completing school he worked from 1990 to 1992 with JEAN-PAUL GAULTIER, designing knits and working on Gaultier's junior line, a period he considers his true fashion education. He was at Balenciaga designing uniforms and funeral clothes for a Japanese licensee when head designer Joseph Thimister left, and in 1997 the young designer was given a chance at the top job. He was so completely unknown that no one came to his first show, but word soon got out and he is now considered one who must be watched, a leader of the avant-garde. The clothes may range from elaborate patchwork minis to rugged leather jackets, and he has developed a devoted following of young fashionables, particularly for his fitted trousers.

Ghesquière has switched the emphasis at Balenciaga Le Dix from evening under Thimister to day clothes, in which some viewers find subtle references to Balenciaga styles of the 1940s and 1950s. In July 2001, when Balenciaga was acquired by Gucci, Ghesquière was given a nine percent share in the house, and as creative director, extensive responsibility for "the brand's creative direction and image."

Nicolas Ghesquière (left) and (right), from Spring 2001.

G

Romeo Gigli

Born Italy, 1950

Gigli's father and grandfather were antiquarian booksellers, and he grew up in an aura of antiquity. This background is in some contrast to the simplicity and modernity of his clothing designs, which nevertheless have something about them romantically rich and strange. Trained as an architect, he began designing in 1979, giving his first show in March 1982, with his first success in 1986.

Since then his style has become more pronounced—a close, gentle fit, soft draping, and a liking for asymmetry—over all, a sense of fluidity and graceful movement. The pieces mean little on the hanger but take shape on the body. Using rich and luxurious fabrics in sun-dried colors, he achieves a kind of throwaway chic, and except for the romanticism of his designs could be considered one of the minimalists.

Following a 1991 rupture with his partners, he restructured his company and moved his showings from Milan to Paris, where he has continued to show with typically quiet success.

Romeo Gigli (center) and designs from 1987 (left) and Spring/Summer 2003 (above).

Marithé & François Girbaud

Born Marithé; Lyon, France, 1942
François; Mazamet, France, 1945

champions of relaxed sportswear, the Girbauds established their business in 1965. The clothes, for both men and women, seem totally unconstructed but are more complex than they appear, and entirely functional.

Jackets are often double, with one layer that buttons on for warmth; sweaters may be wool on the outside, cotton inside. This same thinking goes into their clothes for children. In the United States they are best known for their

jeans and fatigue pants of soft, stonewashed denim. In April 2001 they were commissioned to design uniforms for Air France.

Hubert de Givenchy

Born Beauvais, France, February 20, 1927

Givenchy studied at L'école des Beaux Arts in Paris, and at age seventeen went to work in the couture at LELONG. He later worked at PIGUET and FATH, and spent four years at SCHIAPARELLI, where he designed for the boutique. In February 1952 he opened his own house near BALENCIAGA, whom he admired greatly and by whom he was much influenced.

His youthful separates brought early recognition, especially the "Bettina" blouse, a peasant shape named for the famous French model who worked with him when he first opened. When Balenciaga closed his house, Givenchy took over many of the workroom people, assuming much of the older designer's reputation for super-refined couture, with clothes noted for masterly cut, exceptional workmanship, and beautiful fabrics. Those for day remained within a framework of quiet elegance while the late-day and evening segments of the collection were more exuberantly glam-

orous to fit the lives of his conservative clientele.

In 1988 Givenchy sold his business to LVMH Moët Hennessy Louis Vuitton, with a seven-year contract to remain as

designer. He announced his retirement in July 1995, following the presentation of his final haute couture collections. The British designer, JOHN GALLIANO, was named to replace him, followed by

Givenchy (above) and design from 1994 (left).

G

ALEXANDER McQUEEN when Galliano moved to Dior in 1996. McQueen left in early 2001, ending a stormy relationship with LVMH, and was replaced in March of that year by the Welsh designer, JULIEN MACDONALD.

_____

Givenchy couture 1979.

In addition to couture, Givenchy interests include Nouvelle Boutique ready-to-wear, perfumes, and men's toiletries. Licensing commitments have extended from men's and women's sportswear and shirts to small leathers, hosiery, furs, eyeglasses, and home furnishings.

Alix Grès

_____

Born Paris, France, November 30, 1903
Died November 24, 1993
Awards *Légion d'Honneur*, 1947 · Chambre Syndicale de la couture Parisienne
Golden Thimble Award, 1976

considered one of the most talented, imaginative, and independent designers of the couture, Madame Grès is ranked by many with VIONNET, although very different. She was born Germaine Emilie Krebs and first wanted to be a sculptor, but the combination of family disapproval and lack of money turned her to dressmaking. Under the name Germaine Barton she apprenticed at the House of Premet and in the early 1930s was making and selling muslin toiles, copied from the couture. In 1933, with anonymous financial backing, she opened a salon, Alix, where she was not

a principal but a salaried employee, obtaining a half interest in the house in 1938. As Grès refused to take German clients and had a tendency to defy Nazi edicts, the house closed in 1940. A few years later, having lost the right to the name Alix, she reopened briefly as Grès, the first name of her artist husband, Serge Czerefkow, spelled backward, but was forced to close after only six months. After the war she reopened under the same name.

Her background as a sculptor showed in her mastery of draping, especially in the evening dresses of chiffon or the

fine, silk jersey (called Alix after her use of it) she had encouraged the mills to make. Working directly with the fabric on a live model, Grès molded it to the figure, often baring some portion of the midriff; a gown could take two to three months to complete. These dresses, so fluid in feeling, were actually intricate marvels of construction. Other recurring themes were jersey day dresses with cowl necklines, deep-cut or dolman sleeves, kimono-shaped coats, asymmetric draping. She travelled widely and brought back ideas that inspired her in her own work. Her influence has

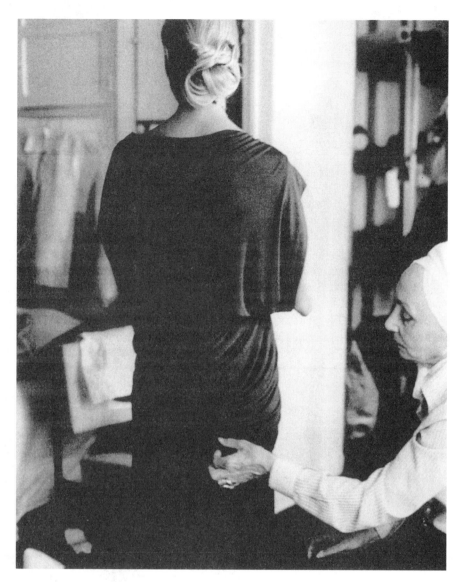

Above, Mme Grès in 1979 and right, Grès design from 1974.

the Metropolitan Museum of Art in 1994. On December 13, 1994 the fashion world was shocked to learn from a story in the French newspaper, *Le Monde*, that Madame Grès was dead, indeed had died more than a year before in a retirement home in the Var region of France. The fact had been kept secret by her daughter, who as recently as a month prior to the appearance of the article had replied to queries with quotations in her mother's name.

Madame Grès sold her house to a French industrialist in 1984; it was resold in 1986, went bankrupt and closed in 1987. In 1988 the name was sold to a Japanese company and the business continued, primarily in Japan in *prêt-à-porter* and with numerous licenses in France and overseas.

been felt by many designers and continues into the present time.

Small, serious, and intensely private, Madame Grès was always shy of publicity and details of her life are scarce. It is known that her husband was a painter and sculptor who left Paris for Tahiti soon after the birth of their one daughter, Anne, in 1939. Professionally, she went her own way; she resisted doing ready-to-wear until 1980, the last of the couture designers to make the move. Perhaps symbolically, her perfume is named *Cabochard,* which means an obstinate or pigheaded person. She was elected chairman of the Chambre Syndicale de la Haute Couture in 1973, and continued as honorary president throughout the 1980s. A retrospective exhibition of her work was mounted by

G

H

Halston

Katharine Hamnett

Holly Harp

Norman Hartnell

Edith Head

Jacques Heim

Joan Helpern

Stan Herman

Carolina Herrera

Tommy Hilfiger

Halston

Born Roy Halston Frowick, Des Moines, Iowa, April 23, 1932
Died San Francisco, California, March 26, 1990
Awards Coty American Fashion Critics' Award *Special Award (millinery):* 1962,
1969; *"Winnie,"* 1971; *Return Award,* 1972; *Hall of Fame,* 1974 · *Fashion Walk of
Fame,* 2000

Halston grew up in Evansville, Indiana, and attended Indiana University and the Chicago Art Institute. While still in school he designed and sold hats. He moved to New York in 1957, worked for Lilly Daché, and in 1959 joined Bergdorf Goodman as a milliner. There he gained a name and a fashionable clientele. His fashion influence was immediate: he originated the scarf hat and designed the pillbox hat Jacqueline Kennedy wore for her husband's inaugural. In the late 1960s he started designing ready-to-wear.

In 1968 Halston opened his own firm for private clients and immediately established himself with a pure, ungimmicky, all-American look. His clothes were elegant and well made, with the casual appeal of sportswear. His formula of luxurious fabrics in extremely simple, classic shapes made him one of the top status designers of the 1970s. He has been quoted as saying, "I calmed fashion down!"

Among his successes were the long cashmere dress with a sweater tied over the shoulders, the combination of wrap skirt and turtleneck, evening caftans, and long, slinky, haltered jerseys. He pioneered in the use of Ultrasuede®. Halston worked closely with Elsa Peretti, first using her as a model then showing her accessories and jewelry with his

clothes. She also designed the containers for his immensely successful signature fragrance.

Halston expanded into knitwear and accessories in 1970, then into ready-to-wear. In 1973 he sold the business to a conglomerate. In 1983 when he signed with J.C. Penney for a cheaper line, a number of his accounts decided to drop

his regular line. He attempted to regain ownership of his custom business and designer ready-to-wear in late 1984 but was unable to do so and went out of business.

The name was revived in 1997, first with Randolph Duke, and later by a succession of other designers.

Halston with models in his showroom, 1982.

Katharine Hamnett

Born Gravesend, Kent, England, 1948

Awards *Cotton Designer of the Year, 1982 · British Designer of the Year, 1984*

As both a feminist and a supporter of the peace movement, Hamnett has often carried her political concerns into her work. Her 1983 "Choose Life" T-shirt collection, for example, displayed such slogans as "Worldwide Nuclear Ban Now," "Stop Acid Rain," and "Preserve the Rainforests."

She was born into a diplomatic family, educated at Cheltenham Ladies College, studied art in Stockholm before enrolling at St. Martin's College of Art and Design in London to study fashion. While still in school she worked as a freelance designer and after graduation in 1969 opened a sportswear firm, Tuttabankem, with a school friend. After its demise, she designed for a number of firms in England, France, Italy, and Hong Kong before establishing Katharine Hamnett Ltd. in 1979.

Her clothes are relaxed and easygoing classics with a witty attitude, and are often based on work clothes. Men's wear with the same feeling as her women's clothes appeared in 1982. The

Katharine Hamnett (above) and from her 1994 collection (right).

clothes have been sold through high-end specialty stores and in her own free-standing shops; she has had her own accessory, shoe, tie, and eyewear lines.

True to Hamnett's beliefs, her company emphasizes environmentally sound practices, with a minimum use of packaging and a maximum use of natural fibers such as cotton and wool, plus those, like Tencel®, considered environmentally friendly. In late 2001,

financial problems forced her to shut down part of her business, shrinking it "back to the core."

Holly Harp

Born Buffalo, New York, October 24, 1939
Died Los Angeles, California, April 24, 1995

The daughter of a machinery designer, Harp dropped out of Radcliffe in her sophomore year and went to Acapulco, where she designed sandals and clothes to go with them. She returned to school at North Texas State University to study art and fashion design, married Jim Harp, an English instructor and later moved to Los Angeles. In 1968, with a loan from her father, she opened a boutique on Sunset Strip, which she called Holly's Harp. Henri Bendel gave her a boutique in 1972; she started her wholesale line in 1973, and her clothes were soon sold in fine specialty stores around the United States. Other design commitments included Simplicity Patterns and Fieldcrest bed linens.

Holly Harp's early designs were offbeat evening clothes, popular with entertainment figures and rock stars. She soon switched from feathers and fringe to subtler, sophisticated cuts, often on the bias, usually two-piece and in one size. Essentially very simple and wearable, the clothes were elegantly conceived in matte jersey or chiffon, frequently decorated with hand-painted or airbrushed designs. They were also imaginative, unconventional, and expensive, making her customer a free-thinking woman with money. Harp's design philosophy leaned to risk-taking: "Whenever I'm trying to make an aesthetic decision, I always go in the direction of taking chances."

The firm continued for several years after her death but has since shut down. There was a showing of her designs in April 2002 at Decades, the Los Angeles shop specializing in vintage designer clothing.

Norman Hartnell

Born London, England, June 12, 1901
Died Windsor, England, June 8, 1979
Awards Neiman Marcus Award, 1947

EDUCATED AT CAMBRIDGE UNIVERSITY, WHERE he designed costumes and performed in undergraduate plays, Hartnell was expected to become an architect but instead turned to dress design. After working briefly for a court designer and selling sketches to LUCILE, he opened a business with his sister in 1923. At the time a French name or reputation was indispensable to success in London so in 1927 he took his collection to Paris. In 1930 he again showed in Paris, resulting in many orders, particularly from American and Canadian buyers. The Hartnell couture house became the largest in London. He was dressmaker by appointment to H.M. the Queen, whose coronation gown he designed, and to H.M. the Queen Mother. He was knighted in 1977.

Hartnell is most identified with elaborate evening gowns, lavishly embroidered and sprinkled with sequins, particularly the bouffant gowns designed for the Queen Mother and for Queen Elizabeth II. He also made well-tailored suits and coats in British and French woolens and tweeds. By the 1970s he was making clothes in leather, designing furs and men's fashions. In September 1990, the house was revived with MARC BOHAN as fashion director. The first collections were couture; ready-to-wear followed in fall 1991. The firm has since gone out of business.

Norman Hartnell and models, 1954.

Edith Head

Born San Bernardino, California, 1907
Died Los Angeles, California, 1981
Awards Motion Picture Academy Awards: *The Heiress*, 1949; *Samson and Delilah*, 1950; *All About Eve*, 1950; *A Place in the Sun*, 1951; *Roman Holiday*, 1953; *Sabrina*, 1954; *The Facts of Life*, 1969; *The Sting*, 1973

Edith Head had a long and illustrious career of over 50 years, starting at Paramount Pictures where she was chief designer for 29 years. Hired as a junior designer by Howard Greer sometime in the 1920s, she became the studio's number one designer in 1938 when the then department head, TRAVIS BANTON, left Paramount for Universal Studios.

The dates are somewhat ambiguous but she graduated from the University of California at Berkeley where she majored in languages, and went on to Stanford for a master's degree in French. She taught French at private schools for girls, studied art at night at Otis and Chouinard, married and divorced, before answering a want ad for an artist, which led to her first job at Paramount.

When Greer left Paramount to open his own salon, he was succeeded by Banton, who made Head his assistant.

As Banton's assistant and later as head designer, she designed for stars as diverse as Mae West, Dorothy Lamour (the sarong!), Barbara Stanwyck, and Audrey Hepburn, and for every type of film from Westerns to drawing room comedies, from musical comedies to monster movies. Given the variety of movies and the sheer quantity of her production, it is not surprising that she did not establish an "Edith Head look." When Paramount was acquired by Gulf+Western in 1966, Head was out of a job but soon moved to Universal to become resident costume designer. Over the years, she won eight Oscars for her work, starting in 1949 with *The Heiress,* and received 33 nominations. She also freelanced at MGM, Warner Brothers, Columbia, and Fox.

In addition to her film work, she did opera costumes, women's uniforms for the Coast Guard and Pan American Airlines, and designed printed fabrics. She also taught a course at UCLA, wrote articles and books, appeared on television and radio talk shows, and lectured to clubs around the country. Unlike many of her colleagues, she did not do custom work and was not interested in dressing women for the world outside of movies.

Above, Grace Kelly in *TO CATCH A THIEF*, 1955; and (left) Paul Newman and Robert Redford in *THE STING*, 1973.

Jacques Heim

Born Paris, France, 1899
Died Paris, France, January 8, 1967

Although not now a household name, Jacques Heim was in his time an important and influential designer. He introduced cotton beachwear to the haute couture in 1937, was the first to recognize the younger customer with his Heim Jeunes Filles collection. He helped popularize the bikini, and beginning in 1946, opened his own chain of boutiques. He was President of the Chambre Syndicale de la Couture from 1958 to 1962.

Heim's parents were fashionable furriers and it was in their firm that he started his design career when he was twenty-six. Sometime in the 1930s he opened his own salon in the avenue Matignon with his wife as *directrice*. His clothes were elegant and refined, very much in the haute couture tradition. After his death, direction of the firm was taken over by his son, Philippe.

Joan Helpern

Born New York, New York
Awards Coty American Fashion Critics' Award *Special Award (footwear)*, 1978 · Cutty Sark Men's Fashion Award *Men's Footwear Design*, 1986 · Fairchild Publications and *Footwear News Footwear Designer Award*, 1988; *Hall of Fame*, 1990 · *Golden Slipper*, Florence, 1988 · *Scarpe d'Oro*, "The Golden Shoe Award" in Italy, 1989 · Fashion Footwear Association of New York, "Ffany Award," 1990 · Silver Trophy, Florence, 1992 · Italian Trade Commission *Michelangelo Award for design* (first designer award to an American for footwear), 1993

Joan and David, the family firm established in 1967 by David and Joan Helpern, is primarily known for imaginative, fashionable shoes for women and men. The firm has been involved in every aspect of the shoemaking process—designing, manufacturing in Italy, distribution, and retailing. Starting in 1986, other fashion categories were added: bags, belts, socks, scarves, sportswear, knitwear, jewelry, sunglasses, shawls, umbrellas, and hats.

Joan Helpern, the design half of the team, believed that the design of a product should be relevant to its use. In

Joan and David Helpern, 1994.

approaching her work she matched a fresh, inventive approach to the desires and needs of her customer, whom she saw as highly intelligent and motivated, with a clear sense of self and personal style.

Ms. Helpern has been widely recognized for her accomplishments, both in her own field with citations from industry publications, and by such magazines as *Savvy* and *Working Woman* for her business success. She is a member of the Council of Fashion Designers

of America and of the Committee of 200, an international organization of leading businesswomen.

The firm was sold in October 2000.

Stan Herman

Born New York, New York, September 17, 1930
Awards Coty American Fashion Critics Award *Special Award (young contemporaries design)*, 1965; *"Winnie,"* 1969; *Special Award (loungewear)*, 1975 · Store Awards: Burdine's, 1965; Hess, 1967; Joseph Horne, 1968

Hard working and versatile, Herman has turned his designing hand variously to hats, dresses, sportswear, lingerie and loungewear, and uniforms. He has also done a stint as a nightclub entertainer. After earning a B.A. from the University of Cincinnati, he worked in the New York garment industry while attending Traphagen School of Fashion. By 1954 he was designing hats at John Frederics. He went on to work at a number of firms before arriving at Mr. Mort in 1961, leaving in 1971. He has continued to design for many other companies, often concurrently, including Henri Bendel, Youthcraft-Charmfit, Slumbertogs, and multiple uniform houses, always in the affordable range, and appeared with great success on QVC.

Herman believes that fashion is one of life's nourishments, which, like all good food, must be grown each season to remain fresh. That is why he prefers to freelance. He recharges his creative energies through painting, singing, sailing, tennis, opera, and community activism. A member of the Council of Fashion Designers of America since 1967, he served as Vice President from 1982, and since 1991 as President.

Carolina Herrera

Born Caracas, Venezuela, January 8, 1939
Awards Dallas Fashion Award *Fashion Excellence Award*

Herrera came to fashion from a background where couture clothes and private dressmakers were the norm—she grew up in Caracas among women who appreciated and wore beautiful clothes. In 1980 she moved to New York with her husband and family, and encouraged by DIANA VREELAND among others, established her own firm in April 1981 with the backing of a South American publisher. Going into the dress business seemed a natural step as she had worked closely with her Caracas couturiers, often designing her clothes herself. She

Designer Caroline Herrara and an evening gown from Spring 2003.

quickly made a name and developed a following.

Best known for her designer ready-to-wear—elegant clothes with a couture feeling and feminine details—she also makes clothes to order for private clients, many of whom are her friends. Estée Lauder, the late Jacqueline Onassis, and Nancy Reagan have all worn her designs and she made Caroline Kennedy's wedding dress. She has had licensing agreements in Japan and designed furs for Revillon; a lower-priced line of ready-to-wear called CH was introduced in 1986.

Herrera recognizes BALENCIAGA as her greatest influence. His example can be seen in her emphasis on a clear, dramatic line and her insistence that women can be feminine, chic, elegant, and, at the same time, comfortable.

Tommy Hilfiger

Born Elmira, New York, 1952
Awards Council of Fashion Designers of America (CFDA) *Men's Wear Designer of the Year,* 1995 · Parsons School of Design *Designer of the Year Award 1998*

Hilfiger was something of a fashion boy wonder, starting out by selling hippy chic to New York college kids, and with a string of ten specialty stores named People's Place in upstate New York by the time he was twenty-six. He moved to New York City and into designing in 1979; his first collection under his own label appeared in 1984,

preceded by an advertising campaign that pronounced him the new leader in men's fashion.

His first customers were predominantly middle-class, middle-American, white males, but in the early 1990s when gangsta rapper Snoop Doggy Dog wore one of his shirts on Saturday Night Live, sales took off and he immediately moved to exploit this new market. Designs moved toward the street with baggier pants, and more casual styles.

Hilfiger has proved himself a gifted marketer and an astute businessman. In addition to his core men's business, he has added sportswear and intimate apparel for women and juniors, clothes for children, and plus sizes. There are also multiple accessories and fragrances for both men and women and a Web site.

Actively involved in a number of charities, Hilfiger serves on the board of directors for The Fresh Air Fund and the Race to Erase MS (Multiple Sclerosis).

Designer Tommy Hilfiger and sketches from Fall 2002.

I–J

Irene

Betty Jackson

Marc Jacobs

Charles James

Eric Javits

Mr. John

Betsey Johnson

Stephen Jones

Irene

Born Irene Lentz; Brookings, South Dakota, 1901
Died Los Angeles, California, 1962

Irene designed in two worlds, one the world of film and the other of real women. She started by dressing many of Hollywood's brightest stars for their private lives and was more and more often commissioned to design their on-screen wardrobes. Her first screen credit was at RKO in 1932 and was shared with Howard Greer; in 1942 she became executive designer at MGM when Adrian left. Her MGM years were not happy—she had to deal with other executives, producers, directors, cameramen, and publicity people, and was more involved with administrative duties than with design—but she stayed out her seven-year contract. After she left, while she continued to design personal wardrobes for a number of stars, she rarely designed again for the screen.

Accomplished in custom and ready-to-wear as well as film, Irene came to design after a brief fling at acting. She studied music at the University of California at Los Angeles, then draping, drawing, and fashion design at the Wolfe School of Design. Around 1928, newly married and at the urging of her husband and friends, she opened a small dress shop on the UCLA campus. This quickly became a success, attracting affluent students and eventually, movie stars Lupe Velez and Dolores Del Rio. When her husband died suddenly, she closed her shop and spent some time touring England and the Continent, living for several months in Paris. This period, which exposed her to the Paris couture, had a lasting influence on her work.

On her return from Europe, Irene reopened her salon, soon moved to larger quarters, and in 1936 was persuaded to become designer and head of the Custom Salon at Bullock's Wilshire. Her clothes were not only beautiful but very expensive, even more so than comparable Paris creations, marking their wearers as women of means as well as taste. Shortly before her contract with MGM expired, Irene was granted permission to design for a wholesale concern, a venture financed by 25 leading department stores who held exclusive rights to the designs. The project was a success from coast to coast.

Irene's personal life was often unhappy: her first husband died only two years after they were married, her second marriage was stormy, and she suffered from a perceived lack of success in films as compared to her commercial work. Overwhelmed by personal problems, she committed suicide in 1962.

Betty Jackson

Born Bacup, Lancashire, England, 1949

After a three-year fashion course at Birmingham College of Art, Jackson worked in London as a free-lance illustrator for two years, in 1973 joined WENDY DAGWORTHY as an assistant designer. She moved to another firm in 1975, stayed four years then spent two years at still another. In 1981 she opened under her own name.

Jackson is well known for her imaginative use of prints. Her clothes are young, classic in feeling but updated with a fresh sense of scale. They have sold well in America and Italy. Her first men's wear appeared for fall 1986.

Marc Jacobs

Born New York City, 1964

Awards Council of Fashion Designers of America (CFDA) *Perry Ellis Award for New Fashion Talent, 1987; Women's Wear Designer of the Year, 1992, 1997; Accessory Designer of the Year, 1998–1999 · Fashion Walk of Fame, 2002.*

whiLe STiLL a STudenT aT Parsons School of Design, Jacobs was designing sweaters and also working as a stock boy at one of New York's Charivari stores. He was hailed as a "hot talent" on his graduation and was building a reputation as an original designer of young fashion with a flair for light-hearted, individualistic clothes when the firm he was working for went out of business in October 1985.

He reopened on his own for Fall 1986, in 1988 moved to Perry Ellis International to design their women's collection. While often well received by retailers and press, the collection was never profitable and was dropped in February 1993, leaving Jacobs without a backer. After freelancing as a design consultant he showed a small collection under his own name for Fall 1994, backed partly by the Perry Ellis organization. The clothes were characteristically spirited and were favorably received.

In 1997 Jacobs sold the company to LVMH and became the designer at Louis Vuitton for both women and men. He moved to Paris but has continued to show in New York—his men's collection and his two women's lines, Marc Jacobs and the lower-priced Marc.

From Spring/Summer 2003 Marc collection.

Designer Marc Jacobs.

Charles James

Born Sandhurst, England, July 18, 1906
Died New York City, September 23, 1978
Awards Coty American Fashion Critics' Award *"Winnie,"* 1950; *Special Award (innovative cut),* 1954 · Neiman Marcus Award, 1953 · *Fashion Walk of Fame,* 2001

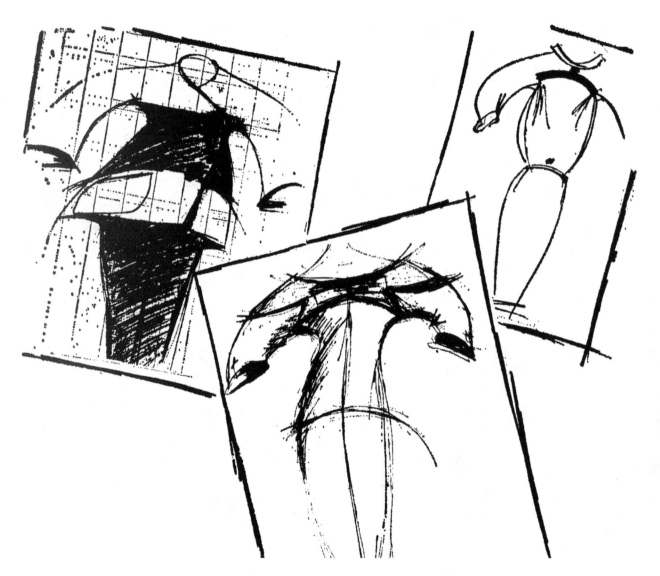

Charles James sketches for *Women's Wear Daily,* 1960. *Also See Color Plate 13.*

STORMY AND UNPREDICTABLE, FIERCELY INDEPENDENT, James is considered by many students of fashion to be a genius, one of the greatest designers, ranking with BALENCIAGA. His father was a colonel in the British Army, his mother an American from a prominent Chicago family; Charles was educated in England and America. After a brief stay at the University of Bordeaux, he moved to Chicago where he began making hats. He moved to New York in 1928, went on to London where he produced a small dress collection, which he brought back to New York. He then traveled back and forth between the two cities before moving to Paris around 1934 to open his own couture business.

In Paris, James formed close friendships with many legendary couture figures, including PAUL POIRET and

CHRISTIAN DIOR, whose obituary he wrote for *The New York Post.* His exceptional ability was recognized and acknowledged by his design peers. While he admired SCHIAPARELLI in her unadorned period, MADAME GRÈS was his favorite designer because she thought as he did in terms of shape and sculptural movement.

He returned to New York around 1939 and established his custom house, Charles James, Inc. He worked exclusively for Elizabeth Arden until 1945, continued to operate in New York and sometimes London until 1958, when he retired from couture to devote himself to painting and sculpture.

During the 1960s James conducted seminars and lectured at the Rhode Island School of Design and Pratt Institute. He designed a mass-produced line for E.J. Korvette in 1962, invented new techniques for dress patterns, created a dress form, jewelry designs, and even furniture, occupied himself with preparing his archives. For five years, usually at night, he worked with the illustrator ANTONIO, who made drawings of all his work to be kept as a permanent record.

James was a daring innovator, a sculptor with cloth. Each design began with a certain "shape," and hours were spent on the exact placement of a seam. Bold and imaginative, his designs depend on intricate cut and precise seaming rather than on trim. He was noted for his handling of heavy silks and fine cloths, for his batwing, oval cape coat, for bouffant ball gowns, for dolman wraps and asymmetrical shapes. In 1937, when his short, white satin evening coat filled with eiderdown appeared on the cover of *Harper's Bazaar,* Salvador Dalì called it "the first soft sculpture."

Since he considered his designs works of art, it is only appropriate that they are in the costume collections of many museums, including the Metropolitan Museum of Art, the Brooklyn Museum, the Smithsonian Institution, the Fashion Institute of Technology, and London's Victoria and Albert. His ideas are still influential today.

Eric Javits

Born New York, New York, May 24, 1956

From 2002.

IT COULD BE SAID THAT Eric Javits came to hat design through a combination of genes and childhood influences—his grandmother, Lily Javits, was a milliner and painter and he used to watch her at work in her studio. Eric attended a succession of private schools and the Rhode Island School of Design, where he studied painting, sculpture, drawing, and photography, and made hats in his spare time. He graduated in 1978 with a degree in fine arts and with Eliot Whittall founded Whittall and Javits, Inc., producing hats in the bridge and better price ranges. He was bought out in 1985, then founded Eric Javits, Inc., specializing in women's hats, often with coordinated handbags.

His hats are romantic and flattering and have been worn in films, used in advertising promotions, shown in designers' runway presentations and on the covers of fashion magazines. He also has a large and diverse international clientele. Javits promotes his business with television guest appearances and is active in professional organizations; he is a member of the Council of Fashion Designers of America (CFDA) and the Millinery Institute of America. Outside of business, he pursues his interest in painting and is involved in community service and charitable activities.

Mr. John

Born Germany, March 13, or 14, ca. 1902
Died New York City, June 25, 1993
Awards Coty Fashion Critics Award *Special Award (millinery)*, 1943

Gloria Swanson, the Duchess of Windsor, Rosalind Russell—those are just a few of the fashionable women who wore Mr. John's hats in the 1940s and 1950s—and Greta Garbo, Marlene Dietrich, and Marilyn Monroe were just a few of the stars who wore them on screen. An original and prolific designer, he made every style from close-fitting cloches to picture hats, relying on shape when other milliners were loading hats with flowers and plumes. Wearable and flattering, his creations included such touches of wit as a face-hugging veil studded with a single rhinestone as beauty mark.

Born somewhere in Germany to Rose and Henry Harberger, Mr. John came to the United States with his parents. He worked briefly in his mother's Manhattan millinery shop then in 1928 formed a partnership with Frederic Hirst to make hats as John Frederics. He changed his name legally to John Frederics but in 1948, after breaking up with Hirst, opened the Mr. John salon on East 57th Street and again changed his name, this time to John P. John. He designed accessories, women's clothing, and furs but hats were his primary claim to fame. The business closed in 1970 although he continued to design for private clients until a year or so before his death.

Betsey Johnson

Born Wethersfield, Connecticut, 1942
Awards Coty American Fashion Critics' Award "Winnie," 1971 · Council of Fashion Designers of America (CFDA) *Special Award for her Timeless Talent*, 1998–1999 · Fashion Walk of Fame, 2002

Johnson attended Pratt Institute for one year, then went to Syracuse University, graduating cum laude and a member of Phi Beta Kappa. In her senior year she was guest editor at *Mademoiselle* magazine where the sweaters she made for editors earned her a job designing at the Paraphernalia boutiques. These collections, original and irreverent, established her at age twenty-two as a leader of the youth-oriented, anti-Seventh Avenue design movement of the 1960s.

In 1969, Johnson and two friends started the boutique Betsey Bunky Nini; she has designed for Alley Cat, Michael

Milea, and Butterick Patterns. In July 1978, with a partner, Chantal Bacon, she formed Betsey Johnson, Inc. to manufacture sportswear, bodywear, and dresses. She also operates a number of Betsey Johnson retail stores.

Johnson has always designed to please herself. Over the years, her ideas have included: the Basic Betsey, a clinging T-shirt dress in mini, midi, or maxi lengths; a clear vinyl slip-dress complete with a kit of paste-on stars, fishes, and numbers; and the Noise Dress with loose grommets at the hem. There have

Betsey Johnson, 2002.

Left, from Spring 2001 and vinyl slip dress from 1966.

been tutu skirts, bubble minis and micro-minis, pretty suits that managed to be both cheeky and wearable, and dresses that toe the line between risqué and cute. She has worked in a variety of fabrics, from cotton-and-spandex knits to rayon challis to heavyweight spandex in vibrant colors, designing her own fabrics and knits.

Johnson is unique. Imaginative and uninhibited, she designs for spirited nonconformists like herself, of whom there are enough to have kept her in business for over 30 years. She has consistently kept her clothes affordable for a younger customer, only adding a more expensive Ultra line in the late 1990s, which she says was necessary to grow the business. "The higher the price line the higher the respect level from the industry, even though it's much easier to make a great $500 dress than a great $100 dress."

Stephen Jones

Born West Kirby, England, May 31, 1957

In 1984 Stephen Jones became the first British milliner to work in Paris, designing hats for the collections of JEAN-PAUL GAULTIER, THIERRY MUGLER, and REI KAWAKUBO of Comme des Garçons. He has worked with ZANDRA RHODES, JOHN GALLIANO, and VIVIENNE WESTWOOD, among other English designers. Combining fantasy with confident style, his hats have been described as witty, outrageous, and daring; he continues to collaborate with designers around the world.

Educated at Liverpool College, Jones went on to study at St. Martin's College of Art and Design, graduating in 1979. He immediately began to make hats for his friends in the pop world including Steve Strange, Boy George, and Duran Duran. In September 1980 he opened his first salon in a store called "PX" in Covent Garden, and soon established a burgeoning custom clientele. He has been invited to represent Great Britain in fashion shows in New York, Montreal, Helsinki, and Tokyo, and his hats are in the permanent collections of the Victoria and Albert Museum in London, the Brooklyn Museum, and the Australian National Gallery in Canberra.

Other design projects have run the gamut from scarfs, handkerchiefs, and gloves, to interior design and TV commercials.

Top hat from Jones's Fall/Winter 2003 "Poseur" collection.

K

Gemma Kahng

Norma Kamali

Donna Karan

Rei Kawakubo

Kenzo

Emmanuelle Khanh

Omar Kiam

Barry Kieselstein-Cord

Anne Klein

Calvin Klein

Kōkin

Koos van den Akker

Michael Kors

Gemma Kahng

Born Masan, South Korea, ca. 1955

Gemma Kahng, 2002.

one of a number of designers with a fresh point of view to emerge in the late 1980s, Gemma Kahng made her first impression with well-tailored suits and sexy little dresses in distinctive color combinations. Suit jackets were closely fitted and fastened with oversized, ornamental buttons, which became a signature.

A graduate of the school of the Art Institute of Chicago, Kahng established her own business in New York in 1989. Specializing in designer ready-to-wear, she expresses her quirky point of view in ornaments and details. While her strength lies in simple shapes and excellent tailoring, she cannot resist embellishing them with pockets, buttons, and lace. She has also expanded into accessories—handbags, belts, and costume jewelry.

Norma Kamali

Born New York City, June 27, 1945
Awards Coty American Fashion Critics' Award *"Winnie,"* 1981; *Return Award*, 1982; *Hall of Fame*, 1983 · Council of Fashion Designers of America (CFDA) *Outstanding Women's Fashions*, 1982; *Innovative Use of Video in Presentation and Promotion of Fashion*, 1985 · Fashion Institute of Design & Merchandising (Los Angeles) *FIDM Award*, 1984 · The Fashion Group *"Night of the Stars"* Award, 1986 · Fashion Walk of Fame, 2002

of Basque and Lebanese descent, Kamali grew up on New York's Upper East Side where her stepfather owned a candy store. Her mother made most of her daughter's clothes, as well as costumes for neighborhood plays, dollhouse furniture, "anything and everything." Kamali studied fashion illustration at the Fashion Institute of Technology, graduating in 1964. Unable to find work in her field, she took an office job with an airline, using the travel opportunities to spend weekends in London.

In 1968 she married Eddie Kamali, an Iranian student. They opened a tiny basement shop in which they sold European imports, largely from England, and also Norma's own designs in the same funky spirit. In 1974 they moved to a larger, second floor space on Madison Avenue and Kamali moved away from funk, doing suits, lace dresses, and delicate things. Divorced in 1977, she established a retail boutique and wholesale firm the next year on West 56th Street naming it OMO (which stands for On My Own) Norma Kamali. In 1983 she moved her thriving business across the street into a multilevel,

ion avant-garde as Donna Summer, Diana Ross, and Barbra Streisand.

Subsequent collections have included swimsuits cut daringly high on the hip, children's clothes, lingerie, and, at one time, a moderately-priced line for the Jones Apparel Group. She has since added fragrance and beauty products, as well as eyewear and innovative active wear. In 1978, her draped and shirred jumpsuits, using parachute fabric and drawstrings, were included in the "Vanity Fair" show at the Costume Institute of the Metropolitan Museum of Art, where they are now part of the permanent collection. She has continued to include parachute designs in her work.

Starting with her *Fall Fantasy* video in 1984, she has moved into the use of technologies and direct mail for selling. Her 1996 fall collection was presented on the Internet and since 1998 it has been possible to shop on her Web site for anything Norma Kamali, from shoes to swimwear to wedding gowns.

In 1997 Kamali started working with art students at New York's Washington Irving High School, her alma mater, helping them to form a business so that while in school they might learn the importance of art and commerce in making a living. The same year, the school inducted her into their Hall of Fame, which honors alumni who have contributed to the arts.

— — — — — — — — — — — —
Left, from Fall/Winter 2000, and parachute jumpsuit, 1978.

multiangled environment finished in concrete. Here, with video monitors showing film productions of her collection, she can display everything she designs, from accessories to couture.

Kamali was first recognized for adventurous, body-conscious clothes with giant, removable shoulder pads. Definitely not for the timid, her clothes were collected by such members of the fash-

Donna Karan

Born Forest Hills, New York, October 4, 1948

Awards Coty American Fashion Critics' Award "Winnie" (with Louis Dell'Olio), 1977; *Hall of Fame (with Louis Dell'Olio)*, 1982; *Special Award (women's wear)* (with Louis Dell'Olio), 1984 · The Fashion Group *"Night of the Stars"* Award, 1986 Council of Fashion Designers of America (CFDA) *Special Award*, 1985; *Special Award*, 1986; *Womenswear Designer of the Year*, 1992, 1996 · Parsons *Fashion Critics Award for Influence in Head-to-Toe Dressing*, 1996 · *Fashion Walk of Fame*, 2001

Daughter of a fashion model and a haberdasher, Karan was steeped in fashion from childhood. After her second year at Parsons School of Design, she took a summer job with ANNE KLEIN and never returned to school. She was fired by Klein after nine months and went to work for another sportswear house, returning to Klein in 1968, becoming associate designer in 1971. When Anne Klein became ill in 1973, Karan became head designer and asked LOUIS DELL'OLIO, a school friend, to join her as co-designer. While it is impossi-

Donna Karan, 2002.

Left, from Fall/Winter 2001.

ble to separate her designs at Anne Klein from Dell'Olio's, their hallmark was always wearability—terrific blazers, well-cut pants, strong coats, sarong skirts, easy dresses—classic sportswear looks with a stylish edge and an element of tough chic.

In 1984 Karan and her late husband, the sculptor Stephan Weiss, founded Donna Karan New York with the backing of Takihyo Corporation of Japan, Anne Klein's parent company. Karan's first collection under her own label established her immediately as a new fashion star. It was based on a bodysuit over which went long or short skirts, blouses, or pants, to make a complete, integrated wardrobe. These pieces were combined with well-tailored coats and bold accessories, everything made of luxurious materials. As the clothes followed the body closely without excess detail or overt sexiness, the effect was both spare and sensuous. Her idea was to design only clothes and accessories she would wear herself—the best of everything for a woman who could be a mother, a traveller, perhaps a business owner, someone who doesn't have time to shop. The clothes are definitely in the status category.

Her company has grown into a giant with myriad divisions, including the hugely successful DKNY and its numerous offshoots. Donna Karan Men was founded in 1991, followed in 1992 by DKNY Men. Home furnishings, eyewear, accessories, and underwear are all part of the mix; fragrances and cosmetics were licensed to Estée Lauder in 1997. There are also retail stores worldwide, both company-owned and licensed. The firm went public in 1996

and in 2001 was acquired by the LVMH conglomerate.

Karan is on the boards of directors of the CFDA, the Design Industries Foundation for Aids (DIFFA), and the Parsons School of Design, where she also lectures and is a critic, and has been involved in numerous activities connected with social causes.

— — — — — — — — — — —

From Fall/Winter, 1994.

K

Rei Kawakubo

Born Tokyo, Japan, 1942
Awards The Fashion Group "*Night of the Stars*" Award, 1986 · Mainichi Newspaper
Fashion Award, 1983 · Veuve Cliquot, Paris, *Business Woman of the Year*, 1991 ·
French Ministry of Culture *Chevalier de l'Ordre des Arts et des Lettres*, 1993

The most avant of the Tokyo avant-garde, Kawakubo was a literature major at Keio University in Tokyo, graduating in 1965. She came to fashion design after two years in the advertising department of a textile firm and three years as a freelance stylist. She started designing women's clothes under the label Comme des Garçons in 1969, establishing Comme des Garçons Co., Ltd.

Designer Rei Kawakubo, 1992.

Left, from 2001.

in 1973. Her company, of which she is president, has expanded to include men's wear, knits, fragrance, home furnishings, and freestanding stores worldwide. Her collections are shown in Tokyo and Paris.

Originally, Kawakubo designed almost exclusively in tones of gray and black; she has since softened the severity of her view with subtle touches of color. She plays with asymmetrical shapes, and drapes and wraps the body with cotton, canvas, or linen fabrics, often torn and slashed. In her early

Paris showings, she emphasized the violence of her designs by making up her models with an extreme pallor and painted bruises and cuts.

She has been successful in the United States with in-store boutiques and her own freestanding shops. These are so minimalist that there is often nothing at all on display. In spring 1987, the Fashion Institute of Technology included her clothes in an exhibition entitled, "Three Women: Kawakubo, Vionnet, McCardell."

Kenzo

Born Kyoto, Japan, February 28, 1940

The son of hotelkeepers, Kenzo won top prizes in art school, and began his fashion career in Tokyo designing patterns for a magazine. He arrived in Paris in 1964, one of the first of his compatriots to make the move, and found work with a style bureau. He sold sketches to Féraud, and freelanced several collections, including Rodier.

In 1970 he opened his own boutique, decorating every inch with jungle patterns, and named it Jungle Jap. The clothes were an immediate success with models and other young fashion individualists. Money was scarce for his first ready-to-wear collection, so although designed for fall-winter, it was made entirely of cotton, much of it quilted. He showed it to the sound of rock music, using photographic mannequins rather than regular runway models. These were innovations, and like many other Kenzo ideas were the beginning of a trend.

Kenzo, 1990.

Kenzo was always a prolific originator of fresh ideas, known for spirited combinations of textures and patterns in young, wearable clothes that were often copied. His designs have been widely distributed in the United States in both his own freestanding shops and in-store boutiques. A renowned party-lover, he celebrated his 1999 retirement with a 2-hour extravaganza, presenting his final collection and a retrospective

Kenzo designs from 1980 (above).

of his 30-year career to 4,000 of his favorite party guests. The Kenzo company has continued with Frenchman Gilles Rosier as designer of the women's clothes and a succession of designers for men. It is now a part of the LVMH fashion empire.

K

Emmanuelle Khanh

Born Plain, France, September 7, 1937

Khanh started designing in 1959 with a job at Cacharel. Although she began her fashion career as a mannequin for BALENCIAGA and GIVENCHY, she rebelled against the couture in her own work and is credited with starting the young fashion movement in France. She was a revolutionary who is quoted as saying, "This is the century of sex. I want to make the sexiest clothes."

She first became known for The Droop, a very slim, soft, close-to-the-body dress, contrasting sharply with the structured couture clothes of the time. Her clothes had a lanky 1930s feeling with such signature details as dog's ear collars, droopy lapels on long, fitted jackets, dangling cufflink fastenings, and half-moon moneybag pockets. Altogether, her work reflected an individual approach symbolic of the 1960s. Khanh survived the era and for a number of years continued to produce soft and imaginative fashions. In 2002 the company was acquired by France Luxury Group, a new conglomerate that at the same time bought the JACQUES FATH name and that of Jean-Louis Scherrer.

She is married to Vietnamese engineer and furniture designer, Nyuen Manh (Quasar) Khanh, also prominent in avant-garde fashion circles of the 1960s.

Omar Kiam

Born Alexander Kiam, Monterey, Mexico, ca. 1893
Died New York City, March 28, 1954

Now known mainly for his movie work, Kiam had a solid fashion career both before he moved to Hollywood between 1934 and 1939 and after he left. His string of 23 film credits included costumes for *Wuthering Heights, Algiers, Dodsworth, Stella Dallas,* and *The Hurricane.* Janet Gaynor, Loretta Young, Ruth Chatterton, and Merle Oberon were some of the actresses he costumed.

Born in Mexico, where his American parents were hotelkeepers, Kiam was in a prep school in Poughkeepsie, New York, studying *The Rubaiyat of Omar Kiam* when his classmates began calling him Omar, and the name stuck. At eighteen, instead of college he chose to work as a stock boy for $10 a week at a St. Louis millinery manufacturer. In his spare time he began playing with wire hat frames, decorating them with straw, flowers, and ribbons, earning a promotion to the pattern department.

Eventually he became "bored with bonnets" and shortly before the first World War, moved to New York and a job as a skin sorter at a retail furrier. When he persuaded a disgruntled customer unhappy with a coat made from a standard pattern to let him design one for her, she was pleased with the result and he was soon designing suits, gowns, ensembles, and fur coats, eventually for a company of which he was half owner. His name on the label had nationwide recognition, leading to his Hollywood invitation. When he returned to New York in 1941 it was as chief designer for Ben Reig, a wholesaler of upscale dresses, suits, and coats, where he remained until his death.

Kiam believed that women dress for other women. His designs were characterized by simple shapes with intricate details and were what he called "distinctive clothes for women who would rather be smart than pretty."

Barry Kieselstein-Cord

Born New York City, November 6, 1943

Awards Art Directors Club of New York, 1967 · Illustrators Society of New York, 1969 · Coty American Fashion Critics' Award *Outstanding Jewelry Design*, 1979; *Excellence in Women's Wear Design*, 1984 · Council of Fashion Designers of America (CFDA) *Excellence in Design*, 1981

Barry Kieselstein-Cord and a selection of his designs.

KIESELSTEIN-CORD COMES FROM A family of designers and architects, including his mother, father, and both grandfathers. His formal education included study at Parsons School of Design, New York University, and the American Craft League. He first attracted the attention of the fashion world with his jewelry, which was introduced at Georg Jensen around 1972. By the end of the decade, his designs included handbags and other accessories and were sold around the United States and exported abroad.

Working mainly in gold and platinum, Kieselstein-Cord starts with a sketch, moving from there directly into metal or wax, depending on whether the design will be reproduced by hand or from a mold. Each piece is finished by hand. His jewelry has been praised for elegance, beauty, and superb craftsmanship, which is also true of his handbags and other accessories. While he aims at timeless design not tied to fashion, pieces such as the Winchester buckle and palm cuffs have been collected by fashion designers and celebrities everywhere.

In addition to his designing career, he has worked as art director/producer of commercial films at an advertising agency and as creative director for a helicopter support and maintenance company. He has served as vice president of the Council of Fashion Designers of America (CFDA) and as a director.

Anne Klein

Born Brooklyn, New York, August 3, 1923

Died New York City, March 19, 1974

Awards Coty American Fashion Critics' Award "*Winnie*," 1955; *Return Award,*
1969; *Hall of Fame,* 1971 · Neiman Marcus Award: 1959, 1969 · *Fashion Walk of
Fame, 2001*

Anne Klein was just fifteen when she got her first job on Seventh Avenue as a sketcher; the next year she joined Varden Petites as a designer; in 1948 she and her first husband, Ben Klein, formed Junior Sophisticates. She designed for Mallory leathers in 1965; operated Anne Klein Studio on West 57th Street in New York, and in 1968, with Sanford Smith and her second husband, Chip Rubenstein, formed Anne Klein & Co., wholly owned by Takihyo Corporation of Japan.

Anne Klein in her studio, 1962.

From 1971.

Early in her career, Klein became known for her pioneering work in taking junior-size clothes out of little-girl cuteness and into adult sophistication. At Junior Sophisticates there was the skimmer dress with its own jacket, long, pleated plaid skirts with blazers, and gray flannel used with white satin. At Anne Klein & Co., the emphasis was on investment sportswear, an interrelated wardrobe of blazers, skirts, pants, and sweaters, with slinky jersey dresses for evening. Klein was also a pioneer in recognizing the value of sportswear as a way of dressing uniquely suited to the American woman's way of life. In 1973, she was among five American and five French designers invited to show at the *Grand Divertissement* at the Palace of Versailles. The other Americans were BILL BLASS, STEPHEN BURROWS, HALSTON, and OSCAR DE LA RENTA.

After Anne Klein's death, the firm continued with DONNA KARAN and LOUIS DELL'OLIO as co-designers. When Karan left in 1984 to establish her own label, Dell'Olio became sole designer.

Struggling to redefine its identity, Anne Klein ran through a dizzying succession of designers, at least five, including Dell'Olio and RICHARD TYLER. In

1999 the company was acquired by
Kasper ASL Ltd., which, in February
2001, changed designers once more,
naming Charles Nolan. Nolan, formerly
with Ellen Tracy, resigned in 2003 to
work on a political campaign.

Meanwhile, after many label changes,
Anne Klein became Anne Klein New York
while Anne Klein 2 was rechristened AK
Anne Klein. Furs, swimwear, and sleepwear were added to the existing licenses,
as well as coats and accessories.

Anne Klein, Spring/Summer 1974.

Calvin Klein

Born New York City, November 19, 1942

Awards Coty American Fashion Critics' Award "Winnie," 1973; Return Award, 1974; Hall of Fame, 1975; Special Award (fur design for Alixandre), 1975; Special Award (contribution to international status of American fashion), 1979; Women's Apparel, 1981 · Council of Fashion Designers of America (CFDA) Best American Collection: 1981, 1983, 1987; Womenswear Designer of the Year, 1993; Menswear Designer of the Year, 1993 · Fashion Walk of Fame, 2000

Klein attended New York's High School of Industrial Art (now the High School of Art and Design) and the Fashion Institute of Technology, from which he graduated in 1962. He spent five years at three large firms as apprentice and designer; his first recognition came for his coats.

In 1968, with long-time friend Barry Schwartz, he formed Calvin Klein Ltd., which has developed into an extensive design empire. Besides women's ready-to-wear and sportswear, and men's wear, it has included everything from blue jeans to furs to shoes to women's underthings modeled on traditional men's undershirts and briefs; from bed linens to cosmetics, skin care, fragrances, and pantyhose. Calvin Klein Home, a luxury home furnishings collection was introduced in April 1995. He has promoted his products with provocative, sexy, often controversial advertising, notably for his jeans and for *Obsession*, the first of his women's fragrances.

Considered the foremost exponent of spare, intrinsically American style, Klein has kept his initial focus and maintained a consistent vision while remaining completely in touch with the times. He has said, "It's important not to confuse simplicity with uninteresting," and executes his simplified, refined, sportswear-based shapes in luxurious natural fibers, such as cashmere, linen, and silk, as well as leather and suede. His color preferences are for earth tones and neutrals—his hallmark is a lean, supple elegance and an offhand, understated luxury.

In June 1993, as part of a benefit in the Hollywood Bowl for AIDS Project Los Angeles, the designer presented a 20-minute showing of his collection, which also marked his 25th anniversary in his own business. The company was sold to Phillips-Van Heusen in December, 2002.

Upper left, from Spring/Summer 2003. Calvin Klein (far left) and from 1979 (left).

Kōkin

Born Buffalo, New York, August 29, 1959

Kōkin studied at the state university of New York at Buffalo, moved to New York, and in 1980 began what he planned as an acting career. For fun, he took a millinery course at Fashion Institute of Technology and in 1983 found himself in business making hats. His creative output now includes hair accessories, scarves and wraps, and of course, hats.

Early on he was strongly influenced by theater and film fashions from his growing-up years. Later, as he studied the great designers, such as CHARLES JAMES, BALENCIAGA, DIOR, and SCHIAPARELLI, they exerted a powerful effect on his thinking. His sense of theater is a continuing trait and his hats have an edge of drama and wit—they are not for

Kokin and design, 1994.

women who want to avoid notice. Kōkin has done hats for films and music videos and has been honored by his own trade organization as designer of the year in 1991, 1992, and 1994, and in 1993 by the National Kidney Foundation.

Koos

Born Koos van den Akker; Holland, ca. 1932
Awards American Printed Fabrics Council "Tommy" Award for his unique use of prints, 1983

Koos started making dresses when just eleven years old. He studied at the Netherlands Royal Academy of Art, worked in department stores in The Hague and in Paris, and whizzed through a two-year fashion program at L'École Guerre Lavigne in Paris in seven months. After an apprenticeship at CHRISTIAN DIOR, he returned to The Hague and spent six years there selling custom-made dresses in his own boutique.

In August 1968, with a portable

sewing machine and very little money, he came to New York. He first set up his "office" by the fountain at Lincoln Center, taking commissions from passersby. After this, he designed lingerie for Eve Stillman and eventually opened his own boutique. He has survived the death of his partner and severe financial problems and been reborn with a new partner, a new boutique, and a monthly show on QVC. There he has, with great success, sold his secondary

line—Chinese-made versions of his costly collages translated into printed fabrics. The boutique sells the collage originals and also his one-of-a-kind furniture pieces. Past projects have included men's wear, furs, home furnishings, and theater designs.

For his women's clothes Koos has always specialized in simple shapes in beautiful fabrics, enriched with his signature "collages" of colorful prints and lace. They are considered collectors'

items and have been on display in the Museum of Contemporary Crafts, New York. Customers have included Cher, Madeleine Kahn, Elizabeth Taylor, and Gloria Vanderbilt.

In recent years, references to his patchwork collages have showed up in the work of several younger designers, MARC JACOBS and NICOLAS GHESQUIERE, to name just two.

Koos van den Akker, 1987 (right); a signature collage-look from 1976 (left).

1 Gianni Versace's stripes for a summer evening, 1992.

2 Alexander McQueen demonstrates mastery of cut and fit. Spring 2002 Ready-to-Wear.

3 Three by Rudi Gernreich. Left to right: wool tweed mini-bloomers, 1968; patchwork-patterned wool bathing suit, ca. 1956; peacock-print, wool jersey mini-dress with peacock feather hat.

4

5

6

7

4 The genius of Yves Saint Laurent defined in color and cut. From his Ballets Russes couture collection, 1976-1977, and his farewell showing, Spring 2002.

5 Chanel evening coat of gold-brocaded silk crepe, ca. 1927.

6 Perry Ellis's spirited take on ethnic sources, 1982.

7 The pure shapes and exquisite embroideries of Callot Soeurs, ca. 1924, left, and 1926.

8 Giorgio Armani's modern evenings, sequin-encrusted jackets and weightless petal skirts, 1994.

9

9 Grandeur and glamour, Mainbocher ballgown, 1949.

10 From Mariano Fortuny, pleated silk *Delphos* gown with printed silk velvet cape, ca. early 1930s.

11 The hat's the thing—lacquered straw and feathers by Philip Treacy, from his collection shown with the Paris couture, Fall 2001.

12 By Geoffrey Beene, master of subtle color and shape, 1982.

13 Charles James ballgowns, sculptures in silk satin, 1948.

10

11

12

13

14

15

16

17

14 Audrey Hepburn in *My Fair Lady,* costumed by Cecil Beaton, 1964.

15 Paul Poiret's bold horizontals in silk faille, ca. 1922-1923.

16 Column of silk damask pleats, wrapped and tied by Claire McCardell, 1950.

17 Valentino's airy evening coverage. Spring 2003 Ready-to-Wear.

18 Ethnic references from John Galliano. Fall 2002 Ready-to-Wear.

19 Evening opulence elaborated by Christian Lacroix. 1990 couture.

20 All-American take on evening. Left to right: red wool jersey by Norman Norell for Traina-Norell, 1954; Adrian Original dinner dress, red-and-white horse print on black silk crepe, 1945; Claire McCardell's red-and-black striped velvet coat over black wool jersey, ca. 1950s.

21 Flamenco according to Balenciaga, fuchsia silk-and-linen gazar with feather underskirt, ca. 1959.

Michael Kors

Born Long Island, New York, August 9, 1959

Awards Council of Fashion Designers of America (CFDA) *Womenswear Designer of the Year, 1998/1999*

Kors attended the Fashion Institute of Technology for one semester in 1977. He then worked for three years as designer, buyer, and display director for a New York boutique before starting his own business in 1981. His first collection of 16 pieces, entirely in

Michael Kors and design from MICHAEL KORS Spring/Summer 2003.

brown and black, sold to 8 accounts. By 1986 the list had grown to over 75 specialty stores. He has also designed a secondary collection called Kors, approximately half the price of the regular collection, has done cashmere knits for

the Scottish firm of Lyle & Scott, and had licensing agreements for shoes and swimwear.

In 1977 Kors signed an agreement with Céline, a division of LVMH, as designer director for ready-to-wear, with his first collection for Fall 1998. This made him part of the group of younger American and British designers hired to re-energize aging French houses—think JOHN GALLIANO, TOM FORD, MARC JACOBS, ALEXANDER MCQUEEN, and JULIEN MACDONALD. When objections were raised that he was really an American sportswear designer, he pointed out that both CHANEL and YVES SAINT LAURENT, quintessentially French designers, had strong sportswear orientation. He has continued to present his Michael Kors and Kors by Michael Kors collections in New York.

Kors designs individual pieces, then combines them into outfits. His aim is a flexible, versatile way of dressing by which a woman can put pieces together in different ways to achieve any desired effect, from the most casual to the dressiest. The clothes are clean and understated in cut and executed in the most luxurious fibers and fabrics— cashmere, silk, leathers, fur. They fit securely into the deluxe sportswear category and are clearly meant for a sophisticated, modern woman of means who dresses to please herself.

L

Christian Lacroix

Karl Lagerfeld

Kenneth Jay Lane

Helmut Lang

Jeanne Lanvin

Guy Laroche

Ralph Lauren

Hervé Leroux

Judith Leiber

Lucien Lelong

Tina Leser

Christian Louboutin

Jean Louis

Lucile

Christian Lacroix

Born Arles, France, 1951

Awards French government *Légion d'Honneur* for services to fashion, 2002

Lacroix is given credit by some critics for revitalizing the Paris couture at a time when it had grown stale, and with his irreverent wit and sense of humor, returning an element of adventure to fashion.

A native of Provence in the South of France, he grew up surrounded by women, developing an early interest in

fashion and accessories. After studies in art history and classic Greek and Latin at Montpellier University, he went to Paris in 1972 to attend L'École du Louvre. A stint as a museum curator followed, then in 1978 Lacroix turned to fashion, first as a design assistant at Hermès, next for two years at Guy Paulin. He went to Japan for a year as an assistant to a Japanese designer, returned to Paris and joined JEAN PATOU in 1982 as chief designer of haute couture.

At Patou he produced collection after idea-filled collection of theatrical, witty clothes and fantastic accessories. Imaginative and elegant, not all were wearable by any but the most daring, but many would appeal to an adventurous woman with flair and confidence in her own style. After five years with Patou, Lacroix left in 1987 to establish his own couture house backed by LVMH, the French conglomerate that also owns Dior. The arrangement includes ready-to-wear. Under his own name, he has continued to show the same irrepressible instinct for drama, with the ready-to-wear somewhat less extreme that the couture. In 2002 he was also named creative director of Pucci, another LVMH holding.

Left to right, from Fall/Winter 2003; Christian Lacroix; Fall/Winter, 1987. *Also see Color Plate 19.*

Karl Lagerfeld

Born Hamburg, Germany, September 10, 1939
Awards Neiman Marcus Award, 1980 · Council of Fashion Designers of America (CFDA) *Special Award*, 1982; *Special Award for House of Chanel*, 1988; *Accessory Award for House of Chanel*, 1991

Lagerfeld arrived in Paris in 1953, at fourteen already determined to become a clothes designer. That year he won an award for the best coat in the same International Wool Secretariat design competition in which SAINT LAURENT won for the best dress. In 1954 he was working for BALMAIN, three and a half years later went to work for PATOU.

He left Patou, again tried school, and after two years at loose ends began freelancing. In 1963 he went to work for the upscale ready-to-wear house, Chloé, as one of a team of four designers. The team of four became two, Lagerfeld and the Italian Graziella FONTANA. They continued to design the collection together until 1972 when Lagerfeld became sole designer.

In 1982 he became design director for Chanel, but continued with Chloë until 1984 when he severed the connection to work solely for Chanel and to inaugurate his first collection under his own label. Enormously hard-working and prolific, he has had a sportswear collection under his own name designed specifically for the United States, designed gloves, and done shoes for Mario Valentino and Charles Jourdan and sweaters for Ballantyne. He does both furs and sportswear for FENDI, and resumed designing for Chloé, where he was succeeded in 1997 by STELLA MC-CARTNEY. He has a number of successful fragrances for women and men.

Lagerfeld (above) and from Lagerfeld Gallery, 2002.

Lagerfeld is an unpredictable, original designer, highly professional and a master of his craft. At his best, he mixes inventiveness and wearability, spicing the blend with a dash of wit. He likes to remove clothes from their usual contexts—he has used elaborate embroidery on cotton instead of the usual silk, made dresses that could be worn upside down, and shown *crepe de chine* dresses

with tennis shoes long before it was a styling cliché. He is credited with bringing Chanel into the present while retaining its distinctive character, although inevitably, the house has become more Lagerfeld than Mlle. Coco.

Kenneth Jay Lane

Born Detroit, Michigan, April 22, 1932
Awards Coty American Fashion Critics' Award *Special Award for "Outstanding Contribution to Fashion," 1966 · Neiman Marcus Award, 1968*

Lane attended the University of Michigan for two years, went on to the Rhode Island School of Design, from which he graduated in 1954 with a degree in advertising. He worked on the promotion art staff at *Vogue* and there met French shoe designer ROGER VIVIER. Through him, Lane became an assistant designer for Delman Shoes, then associate designer of Christian Dior Shoes, spending part of each year in Paris working with Vivier.

In 1963, still designing shoes, Lane made a few pieces of jewelry that were photographed by the fashion magazines and bought by a few stores. Working nights and weekends, he continued to design jewelry, using his initials K.J.L. By June 1964 he was able to make jewelry design a full-time career.

Like a designer of precious jewels, Lane first makes his designs in wax or by carving or twisting metal. He says, "I want to make real jewelry with not-real materials," and he sees plastic as the modern medium—lightweight, available in every color, and perfect for simulating real gems. He likes to see his jewelry intermixed with the real gems worn by

Kenneth Jay Lane pins, 1991.

his international roster of celebrity customers. This list is long and includes both Jacqueline Onassis and the Duchess of Windsor, and more recently, First Ladies Nancy Reagan, Barbara Bush, Hillary Clinton, and Laura Bush.

His jewelry is sold in fine department and specialty stores throughout the world and he has promoted it with great success on the televised home shopping channel QVC both in the United States and Japan. Lane has been recognized worldwide with awards from magazines, design schools, and his own industry. His book, *Kenneth Jay Lane, Faking It,* was published in 1996.

Helmut Lang

Born Vienna, Austria, 1956
Awards Council of Fashion Designers of America (CFDA) *International Award*, 1996;
Menswear Designer of the Year, 2000

Lang was raised in the Austrian Alps, and at eighteen moved to Vienna to study business. He worked behind a bar, became involved with artists and "night people," and was encouraged by his friends to do something creative. He got into fashion when he met someone who could make up the things he had in his mind, as at that time he had no idea how to put them together himself. His vision of fashion developed gradually until in 1984 he opened a shop in Vienna. By 1987 he had a contract with an Italian textile firm and a

Helmet Lang (above) and from Fall/ Winter 2003 (right).

licensing agreement with Mitsubishi in Japan, where he now has numerous boutiques. Lang lived in Vienna and showed in Paris until 1999 when he

sold 50 percent of his company to Prada, moved to New York to live, and began showing in the Seventh-on-Sixth shows in New York.

Variously dubbed a deconstructionist, a minimalist, a follower of the Japanese avant-garde, Helmut Lang is really none of the above but very much his own man. An anomaly simply by being Austrian, he exhibited his distinctive view of fashion and clothes fully formed with his first Paris showing in 1986, when he sent out waif-like models with scrubbed faces in simple silhouettes and somber colors. His personal stamp—experimentation with fabric technology, including PVC, nylon, Lurex®, stretch synthetics, shiny cellophane-like effects, and his rumpled looks and subtle layerings—were there from the beginning and have been enormously influential. One wing of fashion sees him as a prophet; the other sees him as the antithesis of fashion. He believes that fashion has to do with attitude, appearance, and character, and that it defines the spirit of the time. His clothes express his view of how modern men and women want to dress: without affectation and with the understanding that perfect cut, comfort, and ease of movement are among fashion's great luxuries.

Jeanne Lanvin

Born Brittany, France, 1867
Died Paris, France, July 6, 1946
Awards *Légion d'Honneur*

The eldest of a journalist's ten children, Lanvin was apprenticed to a dressmaker at the age of thirteen, and became a milliner when she was twenty-three. The dresses she designed for her young daughter, Marie-Blanche, were admired and bought by her hat customers for their children, and this business in children's clothes evolved into the couture house of Lanvin, Faubourg St. Honoré.

Lanvin's designs were noted for a youthful quality, often reflecting the influence of the costumes of her native Brittany. She collected costume books, daguerreotypes, historical plates, and drew inspiration from them, notably for the *robes de style* for which she was famous, and for her wedding gowns. She took plain fabrics and decorated them in her own workrooms, maintaining a department for machine embroidery under the direction of her brother. The house also produced women's sport clothes and furs, children's wear, and lingerie. In 1926 she opened a men's wear boutique, the first in the couture, directed by her nephew, Maurice Lanvin.

She was famous for her use of quilting and stitching, for her embroideries, for the discreet use of sequins. Fantasy evening gowns in metallic embroideries were a signature; she introduced the chemise during World War I. She was one of the first couturiers to establish a perfume business, with *Arpège* and *My Sin* among the most notable fragrances.

Mme. Lanvin was an accomplished businesswoman and was elected President of the Haute Couture committee of the Paris International Exhibition in 1937. She represented France and the couture at the 1939 New York World's Fair. After her death the House of Lanvin continued under the direction of her daughter, the Comtesse de Polignac.

The couture was designed by Antonio del Castillo from 1950 to 1963, and from 1963 until 1984 by JULES-FRANÇOIS CRAHAY. Control of the firm passed from the Lanvin family in 1989. Maryll Lanvin, who had taken over design direction of ready-to-wear, and after Crahay's retirement of the couture, was replaced by CLAUDE MONTANA for couture, Eric Bergère for ready-to-wear. The couture operation was discontinued in 1992. Since 1989 the women's ready-to-wear has been the province of a succession of designers, including Eric Bergère, Dominique Morlotti, Ocimar Versolato, and Cristina Ortiz.

The firm, which was owned by L'Oréal, was sold in July 2001 to a Taiwanese investment group. ALBER ELBAZ was named designer for women's fashion in 2001, with his first collection for Fall/Winter 2002.

Jeanne Lanvin gown, 1931.

Guy Laroche

Born La Rochelle (near Bordeaux), France, ca. 1923
Died February 16, 1990

LAROCHE arrived in Paris at age twenty-five with no immediate goals and no interest in clothes. Through a cousin working at JEAN PATOU, he toured several couture houses and fell in love with the business. He got a job as assistant to JEAN DESSÈS and stayed with him five years. From 1950 to 1955 he freelanced in New York, then returned to Paris and opened a couture establishment in his apartment. His first collection was for fall 1957. In 1961 he expanded and moved to the Avenue Montaigne, where the house is still located.

In the beginning influenced by BALEN-CIAGA, Laroche soon developed a younger, livelier, less formal look. "It was very, very conservative when I started. I gave it color . . . youth, suppleness and informality." His evening pants were worn by the most fashionable women in Paris.

Laroche had his greatest fame during the early 1960s. At the time of his death, he presided over an extensive company producing both Laroche couture and ready-to-wear and with boutiques around the world. Other licensed ready-to-wear labels in the group included Christian Aujard, Lolita Lempicka, ANGELO TARLAZZI, and a lower-priced collection by THIERRY MUGLER. The Laroche name has been on products ranging from intimate apparel, furs, luggage, sportswear, rainwear, dresses, and blouses, to sunglasses, accessories, footwear, and of course, fragrances.

Ralph Lauren

Born New York City, October 14, 1939
Awards Coty American Fashion Critics' Award *Men's Wear*, 1970; *Return Award (men's wear)*, 1973; *"Winnie,"* 1974; *Return Award*, 1976; *Hall of Fame (men's wear)*, 1976; *Hall of Fame (women's wear)*, 1977; *Men's Apparel*, 1981; *Special Award (women's wear)*, 1984 · Council of Fashion Designers of America (CFDA) *Special Award*, 1981; *Retailer of the Year*, 1986 · *Fashion Walk of Fame*, 2000

A gifted stylist, RALPH LAUREN has taken his dream of a mythic American past of athletic grace and discreet elegance and transformed it into a fashion empire. He chose the name Polo as a symbol of men who wear expensive, classic clothes, and wear them with style. He extends the same blend of classic silhouettes, superb fabrics, and fine workmanship to his women's apparel. For both women and men, the attitude is well-bred and confident, with an off-hand luxury. He has projected his romantic view in his advertising, featuring a large cast of models in upper-crust situations, and through his flagship New York stores. Definitely investment caliber, the clothes are known for excellent quality and high prices.

The son of an artist, Lauren arrived in the fashion world without formal design training. He took night courses in business while working days as a department store stock boy. After college he sold at Brooks Brothers, was variously an assistant buyer at Allied Stores, a glove company salesman, and New York representative for a Boston necktie manufacturer. He started designing neckties, and in 1967 persuaded Beau Brummel, a men's wear firm, to form the Polo neckwear division. The ties were unique, exceptionally wide, and made by hand of opulent silks. They quickly attracted attention to the designer and brought him a contract to design the

Ralph Lauren (left) and gown from 2003 (right).

Polo line of men's clothing for Norman Hilton, with whom he established Polo in 1968 as a separate company producing a total wardrobe for men. In 1971 Lauren introduced finely tailored shirts for women and the next year a complete ready-to-wear collection.

Lauren has also done film work, designing for the leading men in *The Great Gatsby* in 1973, and in 1977, the clothing for *Annie Hall.* His myriad brands include Polo Ralph Lauren, Polo Sport for active sports, and the Ralph Lauren Collection, as well as products for a total home environment introduced in 1983. There are, of course, fragrances for both men and women. In 2002 he showed his top-of-the-line Purple Label men's collection in Milan, where it was very well received.

Some collections are distributed only outside the United States in countries such as Canada and Japan, and licensing has expanded worldwide. In 1997 he took his company public on the New York Stock Exchange.

From 2003 (left) and 1978 Western-influenced separates (right).

Hervé L. Leroux

Born Hervé Léger, Bapaume (Pas de Calais), France, May 30, 1957

In his previous design incarnation as Hervé Léger, Leroux was known for his instantly-recognizable, body-enhancing banded dresses. He was forced from his own design house by investors in 1998, reemerging in 2001 with a small fall-winter collection and a new name suggested by KARL LAGERFELD, which translates as Hervé the Red.

The designer's preparation for a fashion career was an education in art history and theater. In 1975 he began designing hats and accessories for designers such as Tan Giudicelli, and two years later started his serious apprenticeship, first as assistant to Giudicelli, then assisting Karl Lagerfeld at FENDI and CHANEL. He spent two years designing for the Italian firm Cadette, then in 1985 joined LANVIN, working with Maryll Lanvin on the ready-to-wear and couture collections. Lanvin gave

him a boutique under his name in the same year. He also collaborated with DIANE VON FURSTENBERG in that year. He has designed furs for Chloé, ready-to-wear for Charles Jourdan, and costumes for theater and advertising campaigns.

His first collection under the Léger label appeared in 1992 with both couture and deluxe ready-to-wear. These were frankly sensuous clothes that wrapped the body closely with bands and tucks, at their best both seductive and beautiful. His new approach replaced bands with draping, and brash, bright colors with subtler, deeper tones—the clothes were beautiful, glamorous, and elegant. He was looking, he said, for a new way to wrap and follow the female form. Leroux acknowledges CHARLES JAMES as his major influence, followed by Lagerfeld.

Leroux design from 1994.

Judith Leiber

Born Budapest, Hungary, January 11, 1921
Awards Coty American Fashion Critics Award *Special Award* (handbags), 1973 ·
Neiman Marcus Award, 1980 · Council of Fashion Designers of America (CFDA)
Lifetime Achievement Award, 1994 · Dallas Fashion Award *Fashion Excellence
Award* · Accessories Council *Hall of Fame* award, 2001

Renowned for her fantastic jeweLed evening bags, Judith Leiber learned her craft in Budapest, starting as an apprentice at nineteen, the only woman in what was considered a man's trade. It was there she met her American husband at the end of World War II; they married and she came to the United States as a war bride in 1946. She worked in the handbag industry until 1963 gaining a diversified experience in every type of bag and every price range. Then she and her husband went into business for themselves. The company was sold to a British conglomerate in 1993, resulting in expansion of the business and the addition of a retail presence.

Leiber designed everything, from the small animal shapes encrusted with thousands of jewels to daytime bags in rare leathers, softened with pleats, braid, coins, charms, and stones. She listed her influences as the 1920s, 1930s, and oriental art, and wanted her bags to be great to hold, beautiful to look at, and practical. She also made some accessories, such as wallets, key chains, and belts, but is best known for her crystal-adorned minaudieres, which appeared in 1967, each made by hand and taking up to two weeks to complete. The bags have become collector's items for women who wear real jewelry and designer clothes.

She has been much honored with innumerable awards from trade groups, colleges and universities, and charitable organizations. In late 1994, New York's Fashion Institute of Technology marked her 30th year in business with an exhibition of her work. She announced her retirement in January 1998.

In September 2000 the company was again sold, this time to a consortium of investors known as the Pegasus Group, subsequently renamed the Leiber Group for its most productive division.

From Leiber's 1990 collection.

Lucien Lelong

Born Paris, France, October 11, 1889
Died Anglet (near Biarritz), France, May 10, 1958

LeLong made his first designs at the age of fourteen for his father, a successful dressmaker. Trained for business, he decided on a career in couture and designed his first collection; two days before its presentation in 1914, he was called into the Army. He was wounded in World War I, invalided out after a year in the hospital, and received the *Croix de Guerre.*

In 1918 he entered his father's business and took control soon after. By 1926, the year he established *Parfums Lelong,* the house was flourishing and continued to do so until World War II. A farsighted businessman, he was one of the first to have a ready-to-wear line, established in 1934. Lelong was elected president of the Chambre Syndicale de la Couture Parisienne in 1937. He held the post for ten years, including the Occupation period when the Germans wanted to move the entire French dressmaking industry to Berlin and Vienna. Lelong managed to frustrate the plan and guided the couture safely through the war years. He reopened his own house in 1941 with DIOR and BALMAIN as designers. A serious illness in 1947 caused him to close his couture house, but he continued to direct his perfume business.

Lelong was considered a director of designers rather than a creator. PIERRE BALMAIN, CHRISTIAN DIOR, and HUBERT DE GIVENCHY all worked for him, and Dior particularly praised him as a good friend and a generous employer. From 1919 to 1948, his house produced distinguished collections of beautiful, ladylike clothes for a conservative clientele. Lelong believed strongly in honest workmanship and good needlework and it was his credo that a Lelong creation would hold together until its fabric wore out. He was also an accomplished painter, sculptor, composer, and sportsman.

Lucien Lelong (left) and a coat from 1939 (above).

Tina Leser

Born Philadelphia, Pennsylvania, December 12, 1910
Died Sands Point, Long Island, January 24, 1986
Awards Neiman Marcus Award, 1945 · Coty American Fashion Critics' Award
"*Winnie*," 1945

LESER STUDIED ART IN PHILADEL-PHIA and Paris. In 1935 she opened a shop in Honolulu to sell her fashion designs; she returned to New York in 1942 after the outbreak of World War II and began to make the glamorous sportswear that became her trademark. For ten years she designed for a sportswear manufacturer, and in 1952 formed her own company, Tina Leser Inc. She retired in 1964, returned to fashion in 1966, and then quit for good in 1982.

One of the group of innovative sportswear designers that included CLAIRE MCCARDELL and TOM BRIGANCE, Leser always was distinguished by her romanticism and her use of exotic fabrics from the Orient and Hawaii. These she often enriched with embroidery and metallic threads. She used hand-painted prints and designed harem pajamas and toreador pants long before the other designers who were later credited with them. She is also thought to have been the first to make dresses from cashmere.

She was married first to Curtin Leser, from whom she was divorced, then to James J. Howley, who survived her. They had one daughter.

Tina Leser dress in exotic floral print, 1945.

Christian Louboutin

Born Paris, France, January 7, 1964

Designer Christian Louboutin.

Louboutin, whose father was an architect-designer of train interiors, fell in love with shoes at an early age when he was taken to a museum with a magnificent parquet floor. At the entrance there was a large sign like a traffic sign with the silhouette of a high-heeled pump in a red circle sliced through with a red line, and inside women were walking around shoeless. He then started sketching the design on school books, homework, and notebooks. At sixteen, he was given a book on the shoe designer Roger Vivier, and his dedication to shoes became total.

His education continued backstage at the Folies Bergère, where he learned the importance of function—shoes had to be sturdy enough to take the grind of dancing, jumping, and kicking, and not cause injuries. At eighteen, an interview at Christian Dior led to a job with Dior's shoe designer, Charles Jourdan, where he learned technique. He freelanced for Chanel, Saint Laurent, Maud Frizon, and then worked with his idol Roger Vivier on his retrospective at the Louvre. Watching and studying, Louboutin developed his own characteristic silhouette—slim and pointy-toed, reminiscent of the 1950s—and his signature red soles.

The first Louboutin shop opened in Paris in November 1991, followed by boutiques in London, New York, and Los Angeles, and in luxury stores from Tokyo to São Paulo. He has continued to collaborate with designers as varied as Yves Saint Laurent, Gaultier, and Jeremy Scott.

Jean Louis

Born Jean Louis Berthault, Paris, France, 1907
Died Palm Springs, California, April 20, 1997
Awards Motion Picture Academy Award for *The Solid Gold Cadillac*, 1956

First at Columbia, where JAMES GALANOS worked as his assistant, later at Universal, Jean Louis was head designer for major Hollywood movie studios. His 60 film credits include *Pal Joey, Ship of Fools, Born Yesterday, A Star is Born,* and *From Here to Eternity.* He made costumes for the films and fashions for the closets of many of Hollywood's brightest stars, including Lana Turner, Vivien Leigh, Joan Crawford, Rosalind Russell, Greta Garbo, Katherine Hepburn, and Judy Garland. He also designed the gowns for Loretta Young's entrances on her *Loretta Young Show,* an eight-year fixture on NBC TV.

Louis trained in Paris, came to the United States in 1936, and went to work at Hattie Carnegie, where he designed the prototype of the little Carnegie suit. With its closely-fitted jacket and straight skirt, it became the uniform of ladies who lunch. His tenure there coincided with that of both CLAIRE MCCARDELL and NORMAN NORELL.

In 1943, he left New York and private customers for Hollywood, working for the studios until the early 1960s. He then opened a salon in Beverly Hills, continuing film work on a freelance basis. Louis retired in 1988 and in 1993 married Loretta Young, who had been the best friend of his late wife.

Lucile

Born Lucy Kennedy, London, England, 1862
Died London, England, 1935

NOW known mainly for the designers who worked for her, including MOLYNEUX and TRAVIS BANTON, Lucile was the most successful London-based couturiere of her time. Her fashion career began in the 1890s when she and her mother set up as dressmakers; as they became known and their business grew, she started doing business under the name Lucile. Around the turn of the century she married Sir Cosmo Duff Gordon and as Lady Duff Gordon was soon dressing London's very grandest ladies. She opened a New York branch in 1909, a salon in Paris in 1911. Her business declined after World War I, when her floating chiffons were too exotic for the times. While her design viewpoint was romantic and theatrical, she was a tough and forward-thinking business-woman with the vision to see the potential of the North American market and the ability to succeed there.

Julien Macdonald

Bob Mackie

Mainbocher

Mariuccia Mandelli

Mary Jane Marcasiano

Martin Margiela

Vera Maxwell

Claire McCardell

Stella McCartney

Jessica McClintock

Mary McFadden

Alexander McQueen

Gene Meyer

Nicole Miller

Rosita & Ottavio Missoni

Issey Miyake

Isaac Mizrahi

Philippe Model

Captain Edward Molyneux

Claude Montana

Hanae Mori

Robert Lee Morris

Franco Moschino

Rebecca Moses

Thierry Mugler

Jean Muir

Julien Macdonald

Born Wales, 1974

When Julien Macdonald was chosen by LVMH to replace Alexander McQueen at Givenchy in 2001, he was not well known beyond fashion's inner circles but had a solid background designing knitwear for Chanel couture. His success at knits would seem natural as he grew up in a family of gifted knitters steeped in an age-old Welsh knitting tradition.

After some dance training, Macdonald enrolled for one year at Cardiff Art College where he discovered a passion for textile design. He moved on to Brighton, began experimenting with knitwear techniques, and earned a B.A. in Fashion Textiles. He then went to London to take an M.A. from the Royal College of Art. His 1996 graduate collection of finely-spun knit dresses and cobwebby crochets caught the attention of KARL LAGERFELD, who brought him to Chanel as knitwear designer.

Macdonald launched his own company in 1997 with a spectacularly experimental collection. Subsequent showings have attracted a considerable celebrity following with his combination of ethereal gossamer knits and glitzy sequined dresses featuring serious slits. The London fashion press has dubbed him "the Welsh Versace."

Eveningwear from Macdonald's Fall 2001 collection.

Bob Mackie

Born Los Angeles, California, March 24, 1940

Awards Council of Fashion Designers of America (CFDA) *Special Award for his Fashion Exuberance*, 2001

Mackie grew up in Los Angeles where he studied art and theater design. While still in art school, he worked as a sketcher for designers JEAN LOUIS and EDITH HEAD, and for Ray Aghayan, whose partner he became. The spectacular costume designs he and Aghayan, together and separately,

Cher, (left) wearing a Bob Mackie creation at the 1986 Academy Awards ceremony; evening costumes, Fall 2003 (above).

have designed for nightclub performers and stars of TV and movies have established the two in the top rank of their field. Among the celebrities they have dressed are Marlene Dietrich, Carol Burnett, Mitzi Gaynor, Barbra Streisand, Raquel Welch, Carol Channing, and notably, Cher.

Mackie's talents extend well beyond costumes—he has been successful in both couture and ready-to-wear and has also ventured into swimwear and loungewear. His work was the subject of a major show at New York's Fashion In-stitute of Technology in the fall of 1999. It covered every aspect of his work, from the designs he did for Carol Burnett's TV show and the costumes for Cher, to his own couture and ready-to-wear. There was even a series of costumes for Barbie, in which she appeared as as-sorted historical characters. What was completely evident was his technical mastery, allied with an ebullient wit and sense of fun.

Bob Mackie, 1999.

Mainbocher

Born Main Rousseau Bocher; Chicago, Illinois, October 24, 1891
Died Munich, Germany, December 26, 1976

NOTED FOR A NEARLY INFALLIBLE sense of fashion, Mainbocher created high-priced clothes of quiet good taste, simplicity, and understatement. He was the first American designer to succeed in Paris and before that had a distin-guished career as a fashion journalist.

Encouraged by his mother, he studied art at the Chicago Academy of Fine Arts and in New York, Paris, and Munich. In 1917 he went to France with an Ameri-can ambulance unit and stayed on in Paris after the war to study singing. To support himself he worked as a fashion illustrator for *Harper's Bazaar* and *Vogue.* By 1922 he had abandoned music and become a full-time fashion journal-ist, first as Paris fashion editor for *Vogue* then as editor of French *Vogue.* During his journalistic career, he in-vented the "Vogue's Eye View" column and discovered the artist, ERIC, and the photographer, HOYNINGEN-HUENE. He re-signed from the magazine in 1929 to open his own Paris salon.

With his many influential contacts and sure fashion sense he had an imme-diate success. The Duchess of Windsor, whose wedding dress he made, and Lady Mendl were among his clients. It is said that in his first year in business he in-troduced the strapless evening gown and also persuaded French textile man-ufacturers to again set up double looms and weave the wide widths not produced since before World War I. Mainbocher left Paris at the outbreak of World War II and in 1939 opened a couture house in New York. He became the designer with the most snob appeal, designing elegant and expensive clothes for elegant and expensive women, screening his clients according to his own stringent stan-dards. He also designed uniforms for the American Red Cross, the WAVES, the SPARS, and the Girl Scouts.

In his work he was greatly influenced by VIONNET and used the bias cut with

great mastery. Elegant evening clothes were his forte, from long ball gowns of lace or transparent fabrics to short evening dresses and beaded evening sweaters with jeweled buttons. He made dinner suits of tweed, combining them with blouses of delicate fabrics. Pastel gingham was a signature, accessorized with pearl chokers, short white kid gloves, and plain pumps. Mainbocher knew his own worth and insisted that fashion magazines show his designs on two facing pages, never mixed with those of other designers, no matter how great.

A skillful editor of others' work as well as a creator, Mainbocher has been ranked with MOLYNEUX, SCHIAPARELLI, and LELONG. His design philosophy, often quoted: "The responsibility and challenge . . . is to consider the design and the woman at the same time. Women should look beautiful, rather than just trendful."

Mainbocher designs from *Harper's Bazaar,* April 1931. *Also see Color Plate 9.*

Mariuccia Mandelli

Born Near Milan, Italy, ca. 1933

Krizia, the firm headed by Mariuccia Mandelli and her husband, Aldo Pinto, was founded in Milan in 1954. She took the name of the company from Plato's dialogue on the vanity of women, an example of her sense of humor. Always interested in fashion, Mandelli was teaching school when she became frustrated by the clothes available to her in shops. With a friend, she made up some of her own designs and personally carried them around Italy to sell to retail outlets. The process gave her valuable insights into customer preferences and soon her business had grown from two workers to a *premiere* and six work-

ers. The clothes were young and original with a sense of fantasy, and her first show in 1957 won favorable press response and an award. As her business blossomed, she persuaded her husband to become her business partner and to supervise her knitwear company, Kriziamaglia, which took off in the early 1970s. Further success led to boutiques, licenses, and highly successful fragrances.

A witty, fertile designer, Mandelli filled each collection with ideas, veering between classicism and craziness. Her animal sweaters—a different bird or beast for each collection—were famous

and often copied; she is also known for fantastic evening designs, such as the tiered, fan-pleated cellophane dresses that looked like the Chrysler building. Walter Albini was a design collaborator for three years and LAGERFELD has been a consultant.

An accomplished businesswoman with a sure grasp of company affairs, Mandelli has also devoted her considerable energy to various causes of the Milan design community and is considered responsible for moving the ready-to-wear showings from Florence to Milan.

Mary Jane Marcasiano

Born New Jersey, September 23, 1955
Awards Cartier *Stargazer* Award, 1981 · Wool Knit Award, 1983 · Dupont Award *Most Promising Designer*, 1984 · Cutty Sark Men's Fashion Award *Most Promising Menswear Designer*, 1984

A 1978 graduate of the Parsons School of Design, Marcasiano designed her first collection and established her label in 1979. She has at various times designed men's wear and licensed designs for shoes, jewelry, and furs. More recently, she has concentrated on women's sportswear, particularly knits and sweaters, and including outerwear. Her company is now owned by Marisa Christina, specialists in knitwear.

Working with unusual natural and technologically advanced yarns and fabrics from France and Italy, including stretch, Marcasiano likes to combine them with leather, suede, and shearling.

Her clothes belong in that desirable category that combines elegance with comfort and ease. She sees her customer as a woman without age limits, a traveller active in business who appreciates subtle, luxurious clothes that express her individuality.

Martin Margiela

Born Belgium, 1957

Margiela first burst on the Paris scene in the late 1980s, one of a group of fashion iconoclasts from unexpected venues—from Belgium in the case of Margiela, DRIES VAN NOTEN, and ANN DEMEULEMEESTER—and HELMUT LANG from Austria. Well-trained in classic techniques, they have used their considerable skills to turn accepted ideas about clothes inside-out and upside-down, dismantling conventional approaches to beauty and fashion.

From 1976 to 1980, Margiela studied at the Academy of Fine Arts in Antwerp, and in 1984 went to work in Paris as assistant to JEAN-PAUL GAULTIER. In 1988 he presented his first collection for Spring/Summer 1989. Reflecting his view of the times we live in, he has made clothes of recycled materials: turned used linings into dresses, made subway posters or broken china into waistcoats, and constructed shirts from ripped-apart socks and hosiery. He thinks "it is beautiful to make new things out of rejects or worn stuff," and when he slashes down old or new clothes, it is not to destroy them but rather to bring them back to life in a different form. For his fifth anniversary in 1993, he recreated his favorite pieces from the previous five years. Unconventional clothes have been matched by off-beat show locations: a children's playground, a parking lot, an abandoned subway station, the Salvation Army's flea market, and the cellar of the Pont Alexandre III, perhaps the most beautiful bridge in Paris. One of fashion's true originals, he became known through his press-attracting ploys, but is personally reclusive and refuses to be photographed. He is a master of classic tailoring on which his best work rests.

In addition to his own collection, Margiela has been a consultant to two Italian sportswear houses and from 1997 to 2003 was head designer for the venerable French house of Hermès, a bastion of tradition. At the end of his contract, he was replaced at Hermès by Jean Paul Gaultier, whose first collection was for Fall/Winter 2004.

From Margiela's Spring/Summer 2003 collection.

Vera Maxwell

Born New York, New York, April 22, 1903
Died Rincon, Puerto Rico, January 14, 1995
Awards Coty American Fashion Critics' *Special Award (coats and suits)*, 1951 · Neiman
Marcus Award, 1955

MAXWELL was one of a small group of American craftsmen-designers of the 1930s and 1940s, true originals such as CASHIN and McCARDELL, who worked independently of Europe. She also represents an even smaller group of women who successfully ran their own businesses.

Born Vera Huppe, she was the daughter of Viennese parents with whom she traveled to Europe and whose European values provided the core of her early education. She went to high school in Leonia, New Jersey, studied ballet, and danced with the Metropolitan Opera Ballet from 1919 until her marriage in 1924 to Raymond J. Maxwell. She was divorced from Maxwell in 1937, and a second marriage to architect Carlisle H. Johnson also ended in divorce.

Maxwell specialized in simple, timeless clothes, marked by the effortless good looks and ease of movement particularly valued by active American women. These were largely go-together separates in fine Scottish tweeds, wool jersey, raw silk, Indian embroideries, and Ultrasuede®. Among her numerous innovations were the weekend wardrobe of 1935, consisting of a collarless jacket in tweed and gray flannel, a short pleated flannel tennis skirt, a longer pleated tweed skirt, and cuffed flannel trousers. There were also a cotton coverall for war workers that could be considered the precursor of the jump-suit, print dresses with coats lined in matching print, and the Speed Dress with stretch-nylon top, full skirt of polyester knit, and print stole—no zippers, no buttons, no hooks.

She was honored in 1970 with a retrospective at the Smithsonian Institution in Washington, D.C. In 1978, a party and show were given at the Museum of the City of New York to celebrate her 75th birthday and 50th year as a designer. She continued to work until early in 1985, when she abruptly closed her business. In 1986, at age eighty-three, she went back to work with a fall collection of sportswear, dresses, and coats but soon retired again to spend most of her time working on her memoirs.

Vera Maxwell in her showroom, 1964, with some early designs.

M

Claire McCardell

Born Frederick, Maryland, May 24, 1905

Died New York City, March 23, 1958

Awards Coty American Fashion Critics' Award "Winnie," 1944; *Hall of Fame (posthumous),* 1958 · Neiman Marcus Award, 1948 · National Women's Press Club, 1950 · Parsons Medal for Distinguished Achievement, 1956 · *Fashion Walk of Fame,* 2000

cLaire McCardeLL is credited With originating the "American Look," easy and unforced and a striking contrast to structured, European-inspired fashion. She had complete understanding of the needs of the American woman with her full schedule of work and play, and designed specifically for this customer. Her philosophy was simple: clothes should be clean-lined, functional, comfortable, and appropriate to the occasion. They should fit well, flow naturally with the body and, of course, be attractive to look at. Buttons had to button, sashes were required to be long enough not only to tie, but to wrap around and around.

Her father was a banker and state senator, and McCardell grew up in comfortable circumstances. As a child, she showed her interest in clothes with paper dolls, as a teenager she designed her own clothes. She attended Hood College for Women in Maryland, studied fashion illustration at Parsons School of Design and for a year in Paris. Returning to New York, she painted lampshades for B. Altman & Co., and modeled briefly, joining Robert Turk, Inc. in 1929 as model and assistant designer. When Turk moved to Townley frocks, Inc. McCardell moved with him, taking over as designer after his death. She stayed with Townley until 1938 when she moved to HATTIE CARNEGIE, returning to

Townley in 1940, first as designer, then as designer-partner. She remained there until her death.

McCardell picked up details from men's clothing and work clothes, such as large pockets, blue-jeans topstitching, trouser pleats, rivets, and gripper fastenings. Favorite fabrics were sturdy cotton denim, ticking, gingham, and wool jersey. She used colored zippers in an ornamental way, was partial to spaghetti ties and surprise color juxtapositions. The result was sophisticated, wearable clothes, often with witty touches.

Among her many innovations were the diaper bathing suit, the monastic dress—waistless, bias-cut, dartless—the Popover, the kitchen dinner dress, and ballet slippers worn with day clothes. She also designed sunglasses, infants' and children's wear, children's shoes, and costume jewelry. Her designs were totally contemporary; the proof of her genius is that they still look contemporary. As evidence, Parsons School of Design honored her in 1994 with an exhibition, "Claire McCardell: Redefining Modernism," one of the events celebrating the school's 100th anniversary. The show also included a selection of clothes from contemporary American

----

McCardell classics from the *Women's Wear Daily* obituary, March 24, 1958.

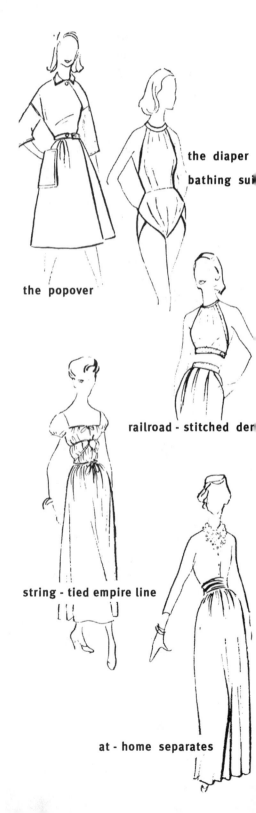

the popover

the diaper
bathing sui

railroad - stitched der

string - tied empire line

at - home separates

designers whose work might be considered in the McCardell tradition: Donna Karan, Isaac Mizrahi, Anna Sui, Adri, and Michael Kors.

Nineteen hundred and ninety-eight was a big McCardell year. Her designs were included in the show *American Ingenuity* at the Costume Institute of the Metropolitan Museum of Art; she was also honored by a show at the Maryland Historical Society in Baltimore; and in November the Fashion Institute of Technology mounted an exhibition, "Claire McCardell and the American Look."

Stanley Marcus spoke of her as ". . . the master of the line, never the slave of the sequin. She is one of the few creative designers this country has ever produced."

Claire McCardell and (right) evening dress and coat from the 1950s. *Also see Color Plates 16 and 20.*

Stella McCartney

Born England, 1972

MCCARTNEY APPEARED TO SPRING FULL-BLOWN on the fashion scene in 1995 when she graduated from London's Central St. Martins College of Art and Design with her famous parents, Paul and Linda McCartney, in the front row. She had, however, loved fashion from childhood and started her fashion apprenticeship at the age of fifteen working with CHRISTIAN LACROIX on his first couture collection. She then apprenticed herself for a time to a Savile Row tailor to improve her knowledge of her craft. Her entire graduation collection was bought by a trendy London boutique and in the same year she established her own business.

In 1997 she went to Chloé as chief designer, succeeding KARL LAGERFELD. While her name undoubtedly opened doors, it took McCartney just three years to prove herself. She understands

From Stella McCartney's Spring 2002 collection.

the needs and viewpoint of those in her own age group and designs clothes to fit their lives, combining romantic sensuality with a contemporary edge. An innate flair for marketing doesn't hurt. By the time she left Chloé, their customer base had become younger and hipper and sales had skyrocketed; they were, in fact, the best in the 35-year history of the house.

McCartney left Chloé in 2001 to open her own house with the financial backing of the fashion conglomerate, Gucci. The Gucci business was founded on leather and the arrangement with McCartney was delayed by her refusal to use fur or leather; the final contract included that proviso.

Jessica McClintock

Born ca. 1931
Awards American Printed Fabrics Council "*Tommy*" Award, 1968 · Dallas Fashion
Award: 1987, 1988, 1990, 1993

MCCLiNTOCK was raised in Maine by her mother, and as a child designed her own clothes and made patterns. Her training came from her grandmother, who was a pattern maker and seamstress. She married at nineteen, moved to California, and after her husband's death in an automobile accident in 1963, remarried, divorced, and taught school. In 1969, she invested $5,000 in a tiny California company called Gunne Sax. From this small beginning she has built a multi-faceted company operation internationally, and carved a niche in the market with her highly personal blend of prettiness and old-fashioned allure.

A formidable businesswoman, McClintock has, from time to time, added various divisions, extending her romantic viewpoint to bridal fashion and children's wear, plus licensing for accessories, china, and home furnishings. There are numerous fragrances and company-owned boutiques. She has received awards from a wide range of business, charitable, and educational organizations and is a member of the Council of Fashion Designers of America (CFDA).

Mary McFadden

Born New York City, October 1, 1938
Awards Coty American Fashion Critics' Award "*Winnie*," 1976; *Return Award*, 1978;
Hall of Fame, 1979 · American Printed Fabrics Council "*Tommy*" Award, 1984

UNTiL she was ten, McFadden lived on a cotton plantation near Memphis, Tennessee, where her father was a cotton broker; after his death she returned north with her mother. She attended Foxcroft School in Virginia, Traphagen School of Fashion in New York, École Lubec in Paris; she studied sociology at Columbia University and the New School for Social Research.

From 1962 to 1964, McFadden was director of public relations for Christian Dior-New York. She married an executive of the DeBeers diamond firm and moved to Africa in 1964. There she became editor of *Vogue* South Africa; when it closed she continued to contribute to both the French and American editions. She also wrote weekly columns on social and political life for *The Rand Daily Mail.* She divorced, remarried in 1968, and moved to Rhodesia, where she founded Vokutu, a sculpture workshop for native artists.

McFadden returned to New York in 1970 with her daughter, Justine, and went to work for *Vogue* as Special Projects Editor. While there she designed three tunics using unusual Chinese and African silks she had collected on her travels; these were shown in the magazine as a new direction and were bought by Henri Bendel, New York. The silks were handpainted using various resist techniques; the colorings were oriental in feeling with a use of calligraphy and negative spacing that became hallmarks of her future style. Mary McFadden, Inc. was established in 1976.

Exotic colorings, extensive use of fine pleating and quilting, and ropes wrapping the figure have all been recurring themes. Her poetic evening designs are best known but all her work shares the same original viewpoint, refined and sophisticated. In addition to the very high-priced luxury collection, design projects have ranged from lingerie and at-home wear to furs, bed-and-bath, and upholstery fabrics. She is a past president of the Council of Fashion Designers of America (CFDA).

Mary McFadden, 1994 (left); signature pleating from 1976 (right).

Alexander McQueen

Born London, 1970

Awards *Best British Designer of the Year, 1996, 1997 (shared with JOHN GALLIANO)*

From McQueen's Spring/Summer 2002 collection. *Also see Color Plate 2.*

MCQUEEN HAS CULTIVATED HIS IMAGE as a bad boy of fashion with presentations and designs, such as his low-cut "bumsters," which attract headlines and disguise their exquisite craftsmanship with in-your-face outrageousness. He was born in East London, the son of a taxi driver, graduated from Central St. Martins College of Art and Design, and was immediately awarded an apprenticeship with a firm of prestigious Savile Row tailors. He then worked for ROMEO GIGLI and Koji Tatsuo before opening his own East London studio.

In 1996, citing his "creative brilliance and technical mastery," LVMH named him to succeed JOHN GALLIANO as chief designer at Givenchy. He produced four collections at the house before making an arrangement with LVMH rival, Gucci, to back him in his own business, whereupon he was replaced at Givenchy by JULIEN MACDONALD.

McQueen was among the designers featured in the "London Fashion" exhibit at New York's Fashion Institute of Technology in 2001 and the same year in the "Extreme Fashion" exhibit at the Metropolitan Museum of Art.

Gene Meyer

Born Louisville, Kentucky, May 2, 1954
Awards Council of Fashion Designers of America (CFDA) *Men's Accessory Award, 1994*

Interested from boyhood in drawing and fashion, Gene Meyer studied for one year at the Louisville School of Art, and from 1974 to 1976 at Parsons School of Design in New York. While in school, he earned the J.C. Penney's Children's Design Award and two Golden Thimble Awards. It was at Parsons that he became aware of the designers who were to influence him—the great figures of the French couture of the 1940s, 1950s, and 1960s, as well as Americans such as CLAIRE MCCARDELL, HALSTON, and MAINBOCHER. After Parsons, Meyer worked as assistant designer at Anne Klein Studio, and from 1978 to 1989 for GEOFFREY BEENE, where he designed everything from evening gowns to shoes. He has taught shoe design at Parsons, and is a member of the CFDA.

When Meyer opened his own business in late 1989, he chose to join the small handful of designers specializing in made-to-order, which not only required less money up front than ready-to-wear but also gave him, he felt, greater control over quality. In 1991 he turned away from making clothes and began designing scarves. This led to necktie designs and eventually to other men's furnishings such as pocket squares and boxer shorts, and to men's ready-to-wear and accessories. His print patterns have a freehand quality although the designs are made by cutting out colored paper. Familiar motifs—stripes, circles, plaids—are given new proportions; colors are offbeat, bright, and cheerful. His designs have also been licensed for dinnerware and floor and wall tiles.

Nicole Miller

Born ca. 1952

NICOLE MILLER was raised in Lenox, Massachusetts, the child of an American father and French mother. She attended the Rhode Island School of Design, and as a sophomore took a year off to study dress cutting in Paris. She was designing coats at Rain Cheetahs in 1975 when she was hired as head dress designer at P.J. Walsh; in 1982 the company was renamed Nicole Miller.

She first gained attention for the prints she designed for scarves, which when transferred to men's ties became an immediate hit. Boxer shorts followed and men's wear with the inimitable prints used as linings. The prints—representing everything from comic book characters to magazine covers to wine labels to brand logos—are in bold graphics and brilliant colors.

In addition to the prints, there is also ready-to-wear, in the mid-priced range, young and sexy. Miller is now also known particularly for her festive special occasion clothes, including a sophisticated bridesmaid collection she says is "for brides who want to keep their friends." She has an extensive list of licenses—handbags, shoes, eyewear, fragrance—and more recently, cosmetics and skin care. A collection of fine and costume jewelry—"to incorporate the whimsical feeling and colorfulness of my ready-to-wear collection"—was launched on QVC in August 2002.

Nicole Miller (above) and design from Spring/Summer 2003 (left).

Rosita & Ottavio Missoni

Born Ottavio (Tai); Yugoslavia, 1921
Rosita; Golasecca, Varese, Italy, November 20, 1931
Awards Neiman Marcus Award, 1973

THE MISSONIS MET IN 1948 in London where Rosita was studying English and Tai was competing with the Italian Olympic track team. He was a manufacturer of track suits, a business he had begun in 1946 after his release from a prisoner-of-war camp, and his suits were part of the official Italian team uniform. She had worked for her parents in their small bedspread manufacturing company. They married in 1953, and the same year went into business together, starting with four knitting machines. Their first efforts appeared anonymously in department stores or under the names of other designers. Looking for more adventurous styling, they hired Paris designers, first EMMANUELLE KHANH and later Christiane Bailly. After a few seasons Rosita took over design of the clothes, while Ottavio created the knits.

The Missonis made their first fashion splash at the Florence showings in 1967. Ottavio's geometric and abstract patterns were so removed from the prevailing idea of knits as basics that they were already setting off fashion waves, then Rosita had the models remove their bras so they wouldn't show through the knits and the stage lighting caused the clothes to appear transparent. In those more innocent times this caused such a scandal in the Italian press that the Missonis were not invited back to Florence. They thereupon decided to show in Milan, which was also nearer home.

The collections were conceived as a joint effort with Ottavio creating the distinctive patterns and stitches on graph paper and working out the colorings, then collaborating with Rosita on the line. She, in turn, working with an assistant, draped directly on the model. Shapes were kept simple to set off the knit designs—each collection built around a few classics: pants, skirts, long cardigan jackets, sweaters, capes, and dresses. Production was limited and the clothes were expensive. In addition to the women's styles, there have been designs for men and children, licenses for bed and bath linens, and interior decorating textiles.

In April 1978, the Missonis gave a party to celebrate the 25th anniversary of their business and their marriage. First at an art gallery in Milan and again at the Whitney Museum in New York, their designs were shown as works of art. Live mannequins in new styles posed next to dummies displaying designs from previous years, arranged without regard to chronological order. Except for miniskirts and hot pants it was nearly impossible to date the designs, effectively demonstrating their timeless character.

The three Missoni children have all been in the family business: Vittorio in charge of administration, Luca helping his father in the creation of new patterns, and Angela in public relations. In 1993, Angela went into business on her own, but has since taken over design duties for Missoni from her mother. Luca was named creative director in early 2003.

Rosita and Ottavio Missoni wearing their creations and celebrating their 25 years in fashion. *Women's Wear Daily,* 1978.

Issey Miyake

Born Hiroshima, Japan, April 22, 1938
Awards Mainichi Newspaper Fashion Award: 1976, 1984 · Council of Fashion Designers of America (CFDA) *Special Award,* 1983 · Neiman Marcus Award, 1984

FROM his first coLLection in 1971, Issey Miyake has been one of the most innovative and influential designers of his time, his imagination ranging far beyond the business of fashion to a fascination with the human body, the space that surrounds it and the movement that reveals it. He has, in fact, preferred to be regarded simply as a designer and a maker of clothes, rather than as a fashion designer per se. His clothes have long been favorites of women with a strong sense of fashion and of their own style.

A 1964 graduate of Tama Art University in Tokyo, Miyake moved to Paris in 1965 to study at L'École de la Chambre Syndicale. Starting in 1966, he spent two years as assistant designer at GUY LAROCHE, went to GIVENCHY in the same

From left, Issey Miyake, 2000 and separates from 1994. Far right, from Spring/Summer 2003 by Naoki Takizawa.

capacity, and in 1969 and 1970 was in New York with GEOFFREY BEENE. In 1970 he returned to Tokyo and formed Miyake Design Studio, showing his first collection in 1971 in Tokyo and New York.

One of the earliest Japanese to make the move to Europe, Miyake has shown regularly at the Paris *prêt-à-porter* collections since 1973. Previously the 1968 Paris student revolution shook up his thinking, leading him to question traditional views of fashion as applied to the modern woman. At that time he began to use wrapping and layering, combining Japanese attitudes toward clothes with exotic fabrics of his own design.

He developed steadily, going his own way as a designer, and has exerted a considerable influence on younger iconoclasts. His design credo is, "the shape of the clothing should be determined by the shape of the body of the wearer, and clothing should enhance, not restrict, freedom of the body." He is known for innovative fabrics, brilliant use of textures, and mastery of proportion. Licenses have ranged from home furnishings and hosiery to bicycles and luggage; a fragrance, *eau d'Issey,* appeared in 1994.

"Issey Miyake Making Things," a ten-year retrospective of the designer's work, opened in Paris at the Cartier Foundation for Contemporary Art in October 1998 and was restaged at the Ace Gallery in downtown New York in November 1999. The exhibition, an exhilarating mating of architecture, space, and movement—clothes floated up in the air and descended, appeared as flat abstractions that turned into three dimensional dresses, and generally explored the outer possibilities of clothing the human form—illustrated the designer's radical approach to clothing, combining respect for tradition with the most unfettered technological experimentation. He turned over design of both the men's and women's collections to Naoki Takizawa in October 1999.

Isaac Mizrahi

Born New York City, October 14, 1961

Awards Council of Fashion Designers of America (CFDA) *Perry Ellis Award for New Fashion Talent,* 1988; *Designer of the Year:* 1989, 1991; *Special Award* (with Douglas Keeve) for *Unzipped,* 1995 · Dallas Fashion Award *Fashion Excellence Award*

when Isaac Mizrahi opened his own company he was twenty-six years old, having already worked on Seventh Avenue for six years. He grew up in Brooklyn, the son of a children's wear manufacturer and of a fashionable mother whose clothes came from BALEN-CIAGA and NORELL. He attended the Yeshiva of Flatbush, the High School of Performing Arts, and Parsons School of Design. At Parsons he received the Chester Weinberg Golden Thimble Award and a Claire McCardell scholarship. Starting in 1981, his last year at Parsons, Mizrahi worked at Perry Ellis Sportswear, staying there until 1983, when he went to Jeffrey Banks, and from there to CALVIN KLEIN. In 1987 he left Klein to form his own business. Ten years later he lost his financial backing and closed his company. He has continued with collections of shoes, coats, and fine jewelry, but in the main has moved on to other pursuits.

Mizrahi's chosen category was luxury sportswear, running the gamut from raincoats to evening wear. His work was notable for a constant flow of

Isaac Mizrahi, 1994.

new ideas and for audacity—playing it safe was not his way. The clothes were young and inventive in the CLAIRE MC-CARDELL idiom, in unexpected colors and fabrics—with their ease and pared-down glamour they appealed to sophisticates with a sense of adventure and an appreciation of quality.

He has designed costumes for movies, theater, dance, and opera, in collaboration with Mark Morris, Twyla Tharp, Bill T. Jones, and Mikhail Baryshnikov. The documentary, *Unzipped,* which recorded the travails of producing his 1994 collection, was made with his friend Douglas Keeve for an AIDS benefit, then shown at the Sundance Film Festival where it won the 1995 Audience Award for Documentaries. It was later released commercially. He has also written a series of comic books, *The Adventures of Sandee the Supermodel.*

After essentially leaving the fashion business Mizrahi has kept busy. He's indulged his theater ambitions with an off-Broadway show and cabaret act, *LES MIZrahi,* plus a TV talk show. His numerous design projects have included sets and costumes for theater and dance, as well as interiors. In early 2003, he introduced MIZ, a modestly-priced collection for Target, and announced plans for "IM to Order," a small made-to-order collection.

— — — — — — — — — —

From Mizrahi for Fall 1997.

Philippe Model

Born Sens, France, 1956

Best known in this country for his shoes, Philippe Model also designs knitwear, bags, gloves, scarves, and hats. He embarked on a fashion career in 1974 with a bachelor's degree in science and an award as "best French artisan in hatmaking." Following a three-year period styling for himself and for such designers as GAULTIER, MUGLER, and MONTANA, he established his own company in 1981. By 1993 his designs were distributed to over 200 stores throughout the world, including three shops of his own in Paris. He also freelances for other shoe companies. Model's designs are elegant and refined, not strident, but still meant to be noticed. They could be called accessory haute couture. Additional projects include men's knitwear, perfume, interior design, and costumes and shoes for opera, which is one of his passions.

Captain Edward Molyneux

Born Hampstead, England, September 5, 1891
Died Monte Carlo, March 23, 1974

Molyneux is remembered for fluid, elegant clothes with a pure, uncluttered line—well-bred and timeless. These included printed silk suits with pleated skirts, softly tailored navy-blue suits, coats, and capes with accents of bright Gauguin pink and *bois de rose.* He used zippers in 1937 to mold the figure, and was partial to handkerchief-point skirts and ostrich trims. His distinguished clientele included Princess Marina of Greece, whose wedding dress he made when she married the Duke of Kent, the Duchess of Windsor, and such stage and film personalities as Lynn Fontanne, Gertrude Lawrence, and Merle Oberon.

Molyneux evening gown, *Harper's Bazaar,* June 1931.

Of French descent and Anglo-Irish birth, Molyneux got his start in fashion in 1911 when he won a competition sponsored by the London couturiere, LUCILE, and was engaged to sketch for her. When she opened branches in New York and Chicago, he went with her to the United States, remaining until the outbreak of World War I. He joined the British army in 1914, earned the rank of captain and was wounded three times, resulting in the loss of one eye. He was twice awarded the Military Cross for Bravery.

In 1919 he opened his own couture house in Paris, eventually adding branches in Monte Carlo, Cannes, and London. He enjoyed a flamboyant social life, assembled a fine collection of 18th century and Impressionist paintings, opened two successful nightclubs, and was a personal friend of many of his clients. At the outbreak of World War II he escaped from France by fishing boat from Bordeaux and during the war worked out of his London house, turning over profits to national defense. He established international canteens in London and was one of the original members of the Incorporated Society of London Fashion Designers.

In 1946 he returned to Paris and reopened his couture house, adding furs, lingerie, millinery, and perfumes. Because of ill health and threatened blindness in his remaining eye, he closed his London house in 1949, and in 1950 turned over the Paris operation to Jacques Griffe. He retired to Montego Bay in Jamaica, devoting himself to painting and travel. Persuaded by the financial interests behind his perfumes to reopen in Paris as Studio Molyneux, he brought his first ready-to-wear collection to the United States in 1965. The project was not a success; Molyneux's elegant, lady-like designs were totally out of step with the youth-obsessed 1960s. He soon retired again, this time to Biot, near Antibes.

Art lover, war hero, bon vivant, sportsman, Molyneux gave generously of his personal resources—money, time, and energy. He worked with the British Government during World War II and later financed dressmaking schools for French workers.

Claude Montana

Born Paris, France, 1949

Montana began designing in 1971 on a trip to London. To make money, he concocted papier-maché jewelry encrusted with rhinestones, which were featured in fashion magazines and earned him enough money to stay on for a year. On his return to Paris, he went to work for MacDouglas, a French leather firm. Montana has also designed knitwear for the Spanish firm Ferrer y Sentis, and collections for various Italian companies including Complice. His reputation grew throughout the 1970s and 1980s and in 1989, he joined LANVIN to design their couture collection, while continuing his own ready-to-wear business. His couture designs were very well received by the press and praised for their elegance and modernity, but he and Lanvin parted company in 1992 and the Lanvin couture operation was discontinued.

Beyond the biker's leathers that made his name, Montana developed into one of the more interesting of the contemporary French designers, with an exacting eye for proportion, cut, and detail. He is a perfectionist, with the finesse of a true couturier and a leaning toward operatic fantasy. His clothes feature strong, uncompromising silhouettes and a well-defined sense of drama. They have been sold in fine stores in the United States, Italy, Germany, and England, and under license in Japan.

From Spring 1993.

M

Hanae Mori

Born Tokyo, Japan, January 8, 1926
Awards Neiman Marcus Award, 1973

Actively engaged in fashion for over 40 years, Hanae Mori was a quiet phenomenon—a Japanese woman, working wife, and mother, who made an extraordinary success in what is in her country a man's world. She graduated from Tokyo Christian Women's College with a degree in Japanese literature then after marrying Ken Mori, heir to a textile firm, went back to school to study sewing, sketching, and design. In 1955 she opened a small boutique in the Shimjuku section of Tokyo where her clothes attracted the attention of the burgeoning Japanese movie industry. After designing costumes for innumerable films, she opened a shop on the Ginza, Tokyo's famous shopping street.

With her husband, Mori developed a multi-million-dollar business with some 20 affiliated companies. Her ready-to-wear was sold at fine stores worldwide and in her own boutiques in Japan, Paris, and the United States, along with accessories, sportswear, and children's clothes. Fabric designs were licensed for bed and bath linens. There were hair salons and TV shows; a publishing division, headed by Akira Mori, the elder of her two sons, editing the Japanese edition of *Women's Wear Daily,* among other titles. The younger son, Kei, directed the firm's European operations. In June 1978 she consolidated her business offices, couture operation, and boutiques in a glass-and-steel headquarters building designed by noted Japanese architect Kenzo Tange.

In January 1977 Hanae Mori brought her couture collection to Paris and continued to show there each season. She was the first Japanese designer to be admitted to the Chambre Syndicale de la Haute Couture Parisienne.

While her design approach was the most international of her compatriots, Mori made extensive use of her Japanese background in her fabrics, which were woven, printed, and dyed especially for her. She utilized the vivid colors and bold linear patterns of Hiroshige prints, while butterflies and flowers, the Japanese symbols of femininity, showed up frequently in her prints, which she has used to great advantage in cocktail and evening dresses, meticulously executed in Eastern-flavored patterns with Western styling and fit. Her clients included film celebrities and the wives of affluent Japanese politicians; she designed the ivory satin gown for Masako Owada's 1993 wedding to Japan's Crown Prince Naruhito.

In late December 2001 the company announced the sale of most of its ready-to-wear, licensed apparel business, and directly-owned shops to a Japanese-British investment group. Mrs. Mori was expected to continue with the couture. A few months later, buffeted by the long-term Japanese recession, the company filed for bankruptcy.

A hand-screened print by Hanae Mori, 1975.

Robert Lee Morris

Born Nuremberg, Germany, 1947

Awards Coty American Fashion Critics' Award *Jewelry Design* (for Calvin Klein), 1981 · Council of Fashion Designers of America (CFDA) *Special Award (for founding Artwear and for jewelry design)*, 1985; *Women's Accessory Award*, 1994 · International Gold Award, 1987 · Platinum International Contest, *Grand Prize*, 1999 · Tahitian Pearl North America Contest, *Grand Prize*, 2000

Robert Lee Morris taught himself the basics of jewelry-making in a commune he set up in a Wisconsin farmhouse after graduation from Beloit College in 1969. The house burned down while he was visiting Vermont and there he decided to stay. His work was discovered and first exhibited by Sculpture to Wear, a gallery in the Plaza Hotel in New York City, which showed the jewelry of recognized artists, including Picasso, Arp, and Miro. After Sculpture to Wear closed, he opened Artwear in 1977 in New York's Soho district, a gallery devoted solely to exhibiting and selling the work of jewelry artists, including his own. He closed the gallery in 1993.

In 1995 Morris was honored by a 25-year retrospective at the Museum of the Fashion Institute of Technology in New York. In 1998, he formed a partnership with a major diamond firm, which allowed him to break into fine jewelry design. He has also promoted his designs successfully with his own RLM Studio show on QVC.

Working in metals ranging from brass and bronze to silver and gold, Morris pioneered in the use of organic, sculptural

Robert Lee Morris and jewelry from Classic 18 Karat gold collection.

shapes, alluding in his designs to ancient history, religion, myth, and legend. He translates timeless symbols such as crosses, daggers, keys, and fertility symbols into modern forms; there is a strong anthropological influence in his work. He has experimented with new patinas and iodized finishes, and has designed accessories for the runway shows of GEOFFREY BEENE, DONNA KARAN, and CALVIN KLEIN. Other design projects include handbags, belts, dinnerware, fragrance, pet accessories, and cosmetic containers for Elizabeth Arden.

Franco Moschino

Born Abbiategrasse, Italy, ca. 1950
Died Lake Annone, Italy, September 18, 1994

Moschino's father, the owner of an iron foundry, died when his son was four. As a child, Franco amused himself by drawing; at eighteen he ran off to Milan to study art at the Accademia di Belle Arti, supporting himself by work as a waiter and a model. In the early 1970s, the fashion drawings he was making for various magazines attracted the attention of GIANNI VERSACE, who used his work in a publicity campaign. He worked as a sketcher for GIORGIO ARMANI on collections for Beged'Or and Genny, and for 11 years designed for Cadette. In 1983 he launched his own company.

Moschino became known, if not universally admired, for his irreverent send-ups of conventional fashion thinking. He sent pairs of models out on the runway in the same outfit, one wearing it as it would appear in a serious fashion presentation, the other as it might be worn on the street. He distributed fresh tomatoes to the audience so they could let fly at any styles they disliked. He incorporated statements such as "Ready to Where?" and "Waist of Money" into jackets, shirts, and belts. These pieces and others of the same kind became best sellers, in part because of the gags but also because the clothes were carefully tailored and of fine quality.

He believed that fashion should be fun and that people should take clothes and wear them with their own particular style. His motto was *"De gustibus non est disputandum"*–"Who's to say what is good taste?" The paradox was, that as much as he made fun of the fashion establishment, he was in the end so successful that he became part of the very thing that he was ridiculing.

At the time of Moschino's death there was, in addition to the signature collection, a secondary line called Cheap & Chic, men's wear, children's wear, jeans, accessories, perfumes, and two Milan shops. His last collection was shown after he died and was well received. With a design staff of about a dozen and licenses ranging from swimwear and lingerie to perfume and sunglasses, the firm has continued in business without its founder.

Rebecca Moses

Born Circa 1956

Moses graduated from the Fashion Institute of Technology in 1977 in the same class as Andrea Jovine, receiving the ILGWU Designer of the Year award. For three years she designed coats and suits for Gallant International, then decided the times called for sportswear and went into business for herself, starting with a huge, 200-piece collection. Her company closed in June 1982, and in August of the same year Moses went into business with Victor Coopersmith. Her first offering was a small, tightly edited group of mixable sports separates. At the time she said "You learn fast that fashion is not just pretty clothes. It's a business and if you don't understand it you go out of business, fast." She left Coopersmith in October 1986, reopened doing business as R. M. Pearlman, her married name. The Moses Collection appeared in March 1988 and included everything from sportswear to suits and blouses, from evening coats to accessories. In 1992 she broke with her Italian backers and began designing on a consultant basis for others including the Italian firm Genny. She has in recent years successfully shown her assured, polished collections in Milan under her own name.

Thierry Mugler

Born Strasbourg, France, 1946

The son of a doctor, Mugler started making his own clothes while in his teens. He was part of a Strasbourg ballet company, dressed windows in a Paris boutique, moved to London in 1968. After two years he moved on to Amsterdam, then back to Paris. His first collection appeared in 1971 under the label Café de Paris; by 1973 he was making clothes under his own name.

Inventive and individual, Mugler came into prominence in the late 1970s with high-priced separates and dresses marked by broad-shouldered, defined-waistline silhouettes. While he claimed to admire Madame Grès, his clothing appeared to be descended more from

Thierry Mugler, 1996 and designs from 1979 (left) and Fall 2001 Paris Fashion collection (above).

the structured chic of Jacques Fath. His tendency toward histrionic, often outrageous presentations tended to obscure what he was trying to say but he cut a sexy, saucy suit as well or better than anybody, and his collections were known for a sunny freshness and gaiety. As shown, the clothes were apt to appear aggressive and tough. Close up, they proved to be simple, well-cut, body-fitted, not overly detailed, the ready-to-wear more accessible than the couture.

Mugler retired from fashion in 1999 to concentrate on perfume. His firm, owned by Clarins, closed in December 2002, with the perfume business continuing.

M

Jean Muir

Born London, England, ca. 1929
Died London, England, May 28, 1995
Awards Maison Blanche "*Rex*" Award, New Orleans: 1967, 1968, 1974, 1976 · Fellow of the Royal Society of Arts, 1973 · Neiman Marcus Award, 1973 · Commander of British Empire, 1983 · British Fashion Council Hall of Fame, 1994

Jean Muir in her studio (left) and a knit design, 1984 (above).

of scottish descent, muir began her career in 1950 in the stockroom at Liberty. She then sold lingerie, became a sketcher in Liberty's made-to-measure department, and in 1956 joined Jaeger and soon became responsible for designing the major dress and knitwear collections. Starting in 1961, she designed under her own label which she established in partnership with her husband, Harry Leuckert, a former actor, but which they did not own. In 1966 the two founded their own company, Jean Muir, Inc.

Muir was one of the breed of anti-couture, anti-establishment designers who came on the scene in the late 1950s and early 1960s. While others have disappeared, she not only survived but flourished, her clothes treasured by women looking for a low-profile way of dressing and quality of a very high order. She created a signature look of gentle, pretty clothes in the luxury investment category, flattering, and elegant, usually in the finest English and Scottish wools, cashmeres, and suedes. She was especially admired for her leathers, which she treated like jersey, and for her jerseys in tailored shapes that are completely soft and feminine, distinguished by the most refined details—the slight bell cut of a cuff, the subtle flare of a jacket.

Hard working and demanding, Muir believed in technical training as the only serious foundation for a designer; she encouraged and worked with British art students, urging more emphasis on craft, less on art. Following her death, the company has continued with a design team that had worked with Muir.

N-O

Josie Natori

Norman Norell

Bruce Oldfield

Todd Oldham

Frank Olive

Rifat Ozbek

Josie Natori

Born Josefina Aloneda Cruz, Manila, Philippines, May 9, 1947

Before she became known for sophisticated, sensuous lingerie, Josie Natori had already established herself in the world of finance, the first woman vice-president at Merrill Lynch. As a child she studied music in Manila, but with business genes in her blood (both her mother and grandmother were successful businesswomen), she moved to New York at age seventeen to study economics at Manhattanville College. After

Josie Natori (left) and design from the Josie collection, 2001 (right).

her marriage and the birth of her son, Natori began casting around for something more creative to do, her own business. "I was really looking for something that would allow me to take advantage of being Filipino and a woman." She found her niche when a friend back home sent her some hand-embroidered blouses and a Bloomingdale's buyer suggested that she lengthen them into nightshirts.

Natori designs rely on simple, sexy shapes in luxurious fabrics, usually with the signature Philippine embroideries and appliqués, lace, and feminine detailing. In addition to the sleepwear, made in the Philippines in her own factory, there are robes, bras, and panties, and more recently, accessories such as shawls of piña fabric, a pineapple derivative, and evening handbags of exotic skins or antique silks. There is also a hipper, more affordable Josie line.

Mrs. Natori has received much recognition for her achievements, the Galleon Award from her native country among numerous others. She is a member of many business groups, including the Council of Fashion Designers of America and the Fashion Group International, and is involved in a number of cultural institutions, the Asia Society, for one. She is also active in the Philippines on behalf of women and fashion.

Norman Norell

Born Noblesville, Indiana, 1900

Died New York City, October 25, 1972

Awards Coty American Fashion Critics' Award First "Winnie," 1943; First *Return Award,*
1951; First to be elected to *Hall of Fame,* 1958 · Neiman Marcus Award, 1942 ·
Parsons Medal for Distinguished Achievement, 1956 · City of New York Bronze Medal-
lion, 1972 · Pratt Institute, Brooklyn, Honorary Degree of Doctor of Fine Arts,
1962, conferred upon him in recognition of his influence on American design and
taste, and for his valuable counseling and guidance to students of design, the first
designer so honored.

NORELL and HATTIE CARNEGIE could be said to be the parents of American high fashion, setting standards of taste, knowledge, and talent, and opening the way for the creators of today.

As a young child, Norell moved with his family to Indianapolis, where his father opened a haberdashery. From early boyhood his ambition was to be an artist and in 1919 he moved to New York to study painting at Parsons School of Design. He switched to costume design, and in 1921 graduated from Pratt Institute. His first costume assignment was for *The Sainted Devil,* a Rudolph Valentino picture. He did Gloria Swanson's costumes for *Zaza,* and then joined the staff of the Brooks Costume Company.

In 1924, in a move from costume to dress design, he went to work for dress manufacturer Charles Armour, remaining until 1928 when he joined Hattie Carnegie. He stayed with Carnegie until 1940, not only absorbing her knowledge and sense of fashion, but traveling with her to Europe where he was exposed to the best design of the day. In 1941 he teamed with manufacturer Anthony Traina to form Traina-Norell. The association lasted nineteen years, at which time Norell left to become president of his own firm, Norman Norell, Inc. The first collection was presented in June 1960.

From his very first collection under the Traina-Norell label, the designer

Norman Norell at the Coty Fashion Critics' Award rehearsal. Dress uses countless yards of silk net, topped by a spangled white satin bodice.

established himself as a major talent, quickly becoming known for a lithe, cleanly proportioned silhouette, an audacious use of rich fabrics, for faultless workmanship, precise tailoring, and purity of line. Over the years he maintained his leadership, setting numerous trends that have become part of the fashion vocabulary and are taken for granted today. He was first to show long evening skirts topped with sweaters, initiated cloth coats lined with fur for day and evening, spangled them with sequins. He revived the chemise, introduced the smoking robe, and perfected jumpers and pantsuits. His long, shimmering, sequined dresses were so simple they never went out of date, worn as long as their owners could fit into them and treasured even longer. *Norell* perfume, made in America, was a major success.

He was a founder and president of the Council of Fashion Designers of America (CFDA). On October 15, 1972, the eve of his retrospective show at the Metropolitan Museum of Art, Norell suffered a stroke; he died ten days later. His company continued for a brief period with Gustave Tassell as designer.

Jacket and pants from 1972. Also see Color Plate 20.

Bruce Oldfield

Born London, England, 1950

OLdfieLd was educated as a teacher and taught English and art before turning to fashion. He attended Ravensbourne College of Art from 1968 to 1971 and St. Martin's School of Art from 1972 to 1973. He freelanced in London, designed a line for Henri Bendel, New York, and sold sketches to other designers. His first collection under his own name appeared in 1975.

Oldfield opened a London shop in 1984 as the only outlet for his ready-to-wear, previously sold in the United States to such stores as Saks Fifth Avenue, Bergdorf Goodman, and Henri Bendel. He has a considerable custom business and is especially recognized for his eveningwear, worn by British royalty and aristocracy as well as by entertainment personalities.

Todd Oldham

Born Corpus Christi, Texas, November 22, 1961

Awards Council of Fashion Designers of America (CFDA) *Perry Ellis Award for New Fashion Talent*, 1991 · Dallas Fashion Award *Rising Star*, 1992; *Fashion Excellence Award*, 1993

Todd Oldham first appeared as designer-as-showman. His desire to be a film director found an outlet in the bravura of his showings, attended by celebrity friends and with such features as rap music and drag performers on the runway. By his own account, Oldham barely made it through high school, never went to design school, and taught himself pattern making. His first fashion experience was in the alterations department of a Polo/Ralph Lauren boutique.

He started in business in Dallas in 1985, two years later moved to New York. There he started Times Seven, making women's shirts in basic styles

Separates from 1994.

fastened with the uninhibited buttons that became a trademark: some were antique, many designed by his brother, Brad. In 1989 he signed with a Japanese company for a designer collection; his first formal presentation was for fall 1990, attracting considerable attention from the press and orders from stores. Oldham has been design consultant for the German firm Escada and worked successfully with MTV. His last runway collection was in Fall 1998, and he has since sold his trademark to Jones Apparel group, which produces and markets Todd Oldham Jeans.

Aside from the Times Seven line, sold only in Japan, Oldham has concentrated on other interests, which are varied. He has designed hotel interiors, worked successfully as a photographer, and designed home furnishings for Target. He has also been active in a wide range of social causes, from AIDS to environmental conservation to child abuse to the humane treatment of animals.

Taking simple shapes, Oldham added

Todd Oldham, 1994.

unconventional prints or beading and embroidery done in India, sometimes quirky and whimsical, sometimes lavish. A mixture of the commercial with the offbeat, the clothes were very well made and sold in such bastions of the establishment as Bergdorf Goodman and Saks Fifth Avenue.

Frank Olive

Born Milwaukee, Wisconsin, 1929
Died New York, December 14, 1995

oLive studied art and fashion in Milwaukee and Chicago before going to California to try costume design. He worked in San Francisco for a dance company and came to New York in the early 1950s hoping to design for the stage. His sketches were seen by NORELL, who persuaded Olive to try his hand at hats. He apprenticed with Chanda, sold fabrics, worked in the Tatiana custom hat department at Saks Fifth Avenue and then for Emme.

His first boutique was in Greenwich Village on MacDougal Street, where he designed hats and clothes. Even through the 1960s when hat makers "had everything going against them," Olive worked with Seventh Avenue designers on hats for their collections and also had fashionable private customers who considered a hat a necessary part of their total appearance. With the revival of interest in hats, he worked with designers for their showings and con-

tinued to produce his sophisticated, original creations for fine stores and a wide-ranging list of celebrities and other fashionable women. His hats were not only seductive and beautiful, but also notable for the quality of the materials and the meticulous crafts-manship. The business continued after his death.

Rifat Ozbek

Born Turkey, 1954

ozbek arrived in EngLand in 1970. He studied architecture for two years at the University of Liverpool then switched to fashion, studying at St. Martin's School of Art. After graduation in 1977, he worked in Italy for Walter Albini and an Italian manufacturer before returning to London and a stint designing for Monsoon, a made-in-India line. He presented his first collection under his own label in October 1984, showing out of his apartment; by his third collection he had a stylish new studio off Bond Street. In 1991 he moved his business to Milan, where he showed his collections until 1994 when he began showing in Paris.

The influence of London street fashion was evident in Ozbek's early work but translated with refinement and understatement. He has also been inspired by the way African natives mix tradi-

Ozbek (above) and from Fall 1995 RTW (right).

tional and Western elements in their dress and by the Italian and French movies he saw when growing up. He admires the fashion greats: BALENCIAGA for cut, SCHIAPARELLI for her sense of humor, CHANEL for timelessness, and YVES SAINT LAURENT for classicism. From his first collections and whatever the inspira-

tion, his clothes have been sophisticated and controlled, without the rough-edged wackiness associated with much of London fashion.

P-Q

Paquin
Mollie Parnis
Emeric Partos
Jean Patou
Sylvia Pedlar
Elsa Peretti
Phoebe Philo
Paloma Picasso
Robert Piguet
Gérard Pipart
Walter Plunkett
Paul Poiret
Zac Posen
Clare Potter
Miuccia Prada
Proenza Schouler
Emilio Pucci
Mary Quant

Paquin

Founded Paris, France, 1891
Closed 1956

one of the couture's great artists, Mme. Paquin trained at Maison Rouff and opened her couture house with backing from her husband Isidore, a banker and businessman. The house of Paquin developed into a major couture force, becoming synonymous with elegance during the first decade of the 20th century.

The Paquin reputation for beautiful designs was enhanced by the decor of the establishment and the lavishness of its showings, as well as by the Paquins' extensive social life. Management of the house and its relations with its employees were excellent, some workers remaining for more than 40 years; department heads were women. The Paquin standards were so high that there was always a demand from other couture houses for any employees deciding to leave.

Mme. Paquin was the first woman to achieve importance in haute couture. She was chairman of the fashion section of the 1900 Paris Exposition and President of the Chambre Syndicale from 1917 to 1919. Hers was the first couture house to open foreign branches—in London, Madrid, and Buenos Aires. She was the first to take mannequins to the opera and the races, as many as ten in the same costume. The house was credited with being the first to make fur garments that were soft and supple.

She was a gifted colorist, a talent especially evident in her glamorous and romantic evening dresses. Other specialties were fur-trimmed tailored suits and coats, furs, lingerie, and blue serge suits with gold braid and buttons; accessories were made in-house. She claimed not to make any two dresses exactly alike, individualizing each model to the woman for whom it was made. Customers included queens of Belgium, Portugal, and Spain, as well as the actresses and courtesans of the era. Mme. Paquin retired and sold her house to an English firm in 1920. She died in 1936.

Mollie Parnis

Born New York City, March 18, 1905
Died New York City, July 18, 1992

Mollie Parnis produced flattering, feminine dresses and ensembles for the well-to-do woman over thirty, emphasizing becomingness in beautiful fabrics, a conservative interpretation of current trends. She felt that good design did not mean dresses that had to be thrown away each year or that went out of date. The boutique collection followed the same principles but with a moderate price tag and the Studio collection, started in 1979, aimed at a younger woman.

The eldest of five children of Austrian immigrants, Parnis always knew she'd have to work for whatever she got. After leaving high school, she went to work in a blouse showroom as an assistant saleswoman and was soon designing. In 1933 she and her husband Leon Livingston, a textile designer, opened a ready-to-wear firm, Parnis-Livingston.

From there she went on to become one of the most successful businesswomen on Seventh Avenue, heading a firm which grew into a multimillion dollar enterprise, Mollie Parnis Inc. She closed her business briefly in 1962 when her husband died, but reopened it again three months later. She shut down again in 1984 but became bored and went back to work full time at Chevette Lingerie, owned by her nephew, Neal Hochman. Her first loungewear collection was for Fall 1985.

A formidable organizer, Parnis routinely managed to administer her business, plan and edit collections with her design staff; supervise selling, advertising, and promotion; and follow through on her civic interests—all in a day that began at 10 a.m. and seldom went beyond 5 p.m. She collected art and was also a noted hostess with a special affinity for journalists and politicians.

Parnis was well known as a philanthropist. She contributed scholarships to fashion schools and gave vest-pocket parks to New York City and Jerusalem, both of which honored her for her outstanding contributions. She was a founder of the Council of Fashion Designers of America and served on the Board of Directors.

Emeric Partos

Born Budapest, Hungary, March 18, 1905
Died New York City, December 2, 1975
Awards Coty American Fashion Critics' Award *Special Award (furs),* 1957

Sealskin coat, 1975.

Partos studied art in Budapest and Paris, and jewelry design in Switzerland. He served in the French Army during World War II and in the underground movement, where he met Alex Maguy, a couturier who also designed for the theater. After the war, Partos joined Maguy, designing coats and also ballet costumes.

In 1947 he went to work for his friend CHRISTIAN DIOR, whom he considered the greatest living designer. He stayed with Dior for three years creating coats and suits, was wooed away in 1950 to be design consultant for Maximilian Furs. He designed furs for Maximilian for 5 years before moving to Bergdorf Goodman to head their fur department, remaining there until his death 20 years later.

At Bergdorf's, Partos was given a free hand with the most expensive pelts available. He showed a sense of fantasy and fun with intarsia furs such as a white mink jacket inlaid with colored mink flowers, and mink worked in two-tone stripes or box shapes. He designed coats that could be shortened or lengthened by zipping sections off or on, further innovated with silk or cotton raincoats used as slipcovers for mink coats. In addition, he was noted for subtle, beautifully cut classics in fine minks, sables, and broadtail. One of the first to treat furs as ready-to-wear, Partos was a prolific source of ideas, noted for his theatrics but also as a master of construction and detail. He was a favorite with conservative customers as well as with personalities such as Barbra Streisand.

P

Jean Patou

Born Normandy, France, 1887
Died Paris, France, March 1936

Patou's first couture venture was a small house called Parry, which opened in 1914, just in time for World War I to cancel his first major showing. After four years in the army as a captain of Zouaves, he reopened under his own name in 1919. The house was an immediate success with private clients; the clothes had simplicity and elegance and looked as if they were intended to be worn by real women, not just by mannequins.

An admirer of American business methods, Patou introduced daily staff meetings, a profit-sharing plan for executives, and a bonus system for mannequins. He was also an excellent showman: he brought six American models to Paris in 1925, using them alongside his French mannequins; he instituted gala champagne evening openings, had a cocktail bar in his shop, chose exquisite bottles for his perfumes. These included *Moment Suprême* and *Joy,* promoted as the world's most expensive perfume. He was among the first couturiers to have colors and fabrics produced especially for him, is given credit for being the first in 1929 to return the waistline to its normal position and to lengthen skirts, which he dropped dramatically to the ankle.

One of many on Chanel's hate list, he returned her dislike with interest, on occasion complaining to fashion magazines of what he considered their favoritism toward her in covering collections. After Patou's death, the house remained open under the direction of his brother-in-law, Raymond Barbas, with a series of resident designers including: MARC BOHAN (1953-1957), KARL LAGERFELD (1958-1963), Michel Goma (1963-1974), ANGELO TARLAZZI (1973-1976), Roy Gonzalez (1976-1981), and CHRISTIAN LACROIX (1981-1987).

Patou's chiffon evening gowns (near right) and day dress with longer skirt (far right), all with waistlines at the normal location, 1929.

Sylvia Pedlar

Born New York City, 1901
Died New York City, February 26, 1972
Awards Coty American Fashion Critics' Award *Special Award (lingerie)*, 1951; *Return Special Award (lingerie)*, 1964 · Neiman Marcus Award, 1960

PEDLAR STUDIED AT COOPER UNION and the Art Students League, intending to become a fashion illustrator. Instead, she took a design job and discovered her true direction; in 1929, she founded her own firm, Iris Lingerie.

Pedlar was a gifted designer working in a field where the temptation for vulgarity is strong. She specialized in soft, pure shapes that a woman of any age could wear, and to her, comfort was the most important consideration. Among her more famous creations were sleep togas, the bed-and-breakfast look, and the bedside nightdress for the woman who sleeps in the nude but wants a little something decorative to wake up to. Iris Lingerie was known for exquisite fabrics and laces and perfectionist workmanship, as well as for the originality and beauty of the designs. Its uniqueness was recognized internationally and European designers such as DIOR, GIVENCHY, and PUCCI would visit Iris to buy Pedlar models. Pedlar closed her firm after 41 years because "the fun has gone out of our work now." She was married to William A. Pedlar, whom she survived by one year.

Elsa Peretti

Born Florence, Italy, May 1, 1940
Awards Coty American Fashion Critics' Award *Special Award* (jewelry), 1971 · Award for Outstanding Contribution to the Cultured Pearl Industry of America and Japan, 1978 · The Fashion Group *Night of the Stars Award,* 1986

THE DAUGHTER OF A WELL-TO-DO Roman family, Peretti earned a diploma in interior design and worked briefly for a Milanese architect. In 1961 she went to Switzerland, then moved on to London and started modeling. She was seen by models' agent Wilhelmina, who suggested that Peretti come to New York. In New York she worked for a handful of top houses, including HALSTON and OSCAR DE LA RENTA.

In 1969 Peretti designed a few pieces of silver jewelry, which Halston and GIORGIO SANT'ANGELO showed with their collections. These witty objects—a

heart-shaped buckle, pendants in the form of small vases, a silver urn pendant that holds a fresh flower—were soon joined by a horseshoe-shaped silver buckle on a long leather belt and other designs in horn, ebony, and ivory. She also designed the containers for Halston's fragrance and cosmetic lines. In 1974 she began working with Tiffany & Co., the first time in 25 years the company had carried silver jewelry. Among her much-copied designs are a small, open, slightly lopsided heart pendant

Elsa Peretti.

P

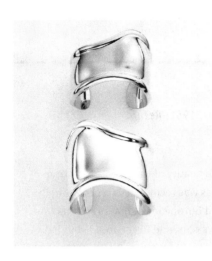

Peretti silver cuff bracelets.

that slides on a chain, and Diamonds-by-the-Yard, diamonds spaced at intervals on a fine gold chain. Her perfume, a costly scent in a refillable rock crystal bottle, is carried by Tiffany, and she has also designed desk and table accessories for the firm.

Peretti is influenced in her work by a love of nature and inspired by Japanese designs. She works in Spain and New York, and has travelled to the Orient to study semiprecious stones. Prototypes for the silver and ivory designs are made by artisans in Barcelona, the crystal pieces are produced in Germany. As a celebration of her fiftieth birthday and 15-year association with Tiffany, Peretti was honored by the Fashion Institute of Technology in April 1990 with a retrospective exhibit of her work. It was called "Fifteen of My Fifty with Tiffany."

Phoebe Philo

Born Paris, France, 1973

From Philo's Spring/Summer 2002 collection for Chloé.

PHILO GREW UP IN ENGLAND in a London suburb and entered Central St. Martin's College of Art and Design in 1993, graduating three years later. In 1997 she joined the French ready-to-wear firm Chloé, as assistant to her friend STELLA MCCARTNEY who had just been made creative director. When McCartney left Chloé in 2001 to form her own business, Philo moved into her position.

In her first collection she immediately established her own style—cool and sexy, yet romantic and luxurious, with a modern edge appealing to the new, younger customer, attracted to the label under McCartney's tenure. With Philo, new fashion categories were planned for the house, including accessories, swimwear, and a less expensive collection called See by Chloé.

Paloma Picasso

Born Paris, France, April 19, 1949

NOT ONLY is she the daughter of two artists, one of them a monumental figure in 20th-century art, Paloma Picasso is also a successful designer in her own right. She is at the center of a

burgeoning business, involved in everything from jewelry to perfume and cosmetics to home design. Her first jewelry collection was in 1971 for the Greek firm, Zolotas. In 1972 she met Rafael Lopez-Cambil, an Argentine-born playwright, for whose plays she designed sets and costumes. After their marriage in 1978, Picasso's husband devised a strategy aimed at establishing her name and work in the world of design. In 1980, Paloma Picasso joined Tiffany & Co. with a collection of gold jewelry set with precious and semi-precious stones. Her style is marked by bold, sensuous shapes, sometimes inspired by urban graffiti, sometimes of a Renaissance opulence. In addition to cosmetics and perfume, her other U.S. design projects have included top-of-the-line handbags and a less expensive, more

Paloma Picasso, 2000 and jewelry.

casual accessories collection, as well as eyewear, tablewear, fabrics, and wall coverings.

P

Robert Piguet

Born Yverdon, Switzerland, 1901
Died Lausanne, Switzerland, February 22, 1953

Piguet was the son of a Swiss banker and was expected to follow his father's profession. Instead, he went to Paris in 1918 to study design. He trained with the conservative Redfern and the brilliant POIRET, then opened his own house on the rue du Cirque. In 1933 he moved his salon to the Rond Point where he designed little himself, relying largely on the work of freelance designers. A number of designers, including DIOR and GIVENCHY, worked for him at the outset of their careers; JAMES GALANOS spent three months there working without salary. Dior said, "Robert Piguet taught me the virtues of simplicity . . . how to suppress!" Piguet's clothes appealed to a younger customer: perfectly cut, tailored suits with vests, black-and-white dresses of refined simplicity, afternoon dresses, fur-trimmed coats especially styled for petite women. He had a flair for dramatic effects, which he used to advantage in his extensive work for the theater. In the United States his influence was greater on manufacturers than on custom design.

An aristocratic, solitary man, Piguet was super-sensitive and changeable, with a love of intrigue. Elegant and charming, he was a connoisseur of painting, literature, and music. He suffered from ill health throughout his life, retiring to seclusion after each showing to recuperate from the strain of his profession. He closed his house in 1951.

Gérard Pipart

Born Rueil-Malmaison, near Paris, France, November 25, 1933
Awards Chambre Syndicale de la Couture Parisienne *Golden Thimble,* 1987

Pipart started in fashion at the age of sixteen, selling sketches to PIERRE BALMAIN and JACQUES FATH, and working for both for brief periods. He sketched for GIVENCHY, was assistant to BOHAN when at PATOU and during the short time he had his own house. After completing his two-year army service, he freelanced in ready-to-wear, produced an unsuccessful couture collection in 1963, and returned to ready-to-wear with great success. In 1963 he succeeded JULES-FRANÇOIS CRAHAY as chief designer at NINA RICCI, where he remained until 1998 when the house was sold.

Pipart never learned to cut or sew, working from detailed sketches and making corrections directly on the *toiles.* Preferring simplicity and detesting gimmicks, he was known for young, spirited, elegant clothes, a very Parisian sophistication. He has been compared to JACQUES FATH, whom he considered "the most wonderful personality I ever knew or saw." Among other designers, he greatly admired GIVENCHY and BALENCIAGA.

Gérard Pipart's summer separates for Nina Ricci, 1994.

Walter Plunkett

Born Oakland, California, 1902
Died Santa Monica, California, March 8, 1982

WALTER PLUNKETT WAS BEST KNOWN for period costumes, and particularly for *Gone With the Wind.* In the mid 1920s, after law studies and an attempt at an acting career, he took a job in the wardrobe department at FBO Studios, then specializing in Westerns. Within a few months, the studio changed its name to RKO and Plunkett, without formal training, became its costume designer. He was soon put in charge of setting up a design department. In 1931, after designing for a series of potboilers, he got his first important assignment, *Cimarron,* starring Irene Dunne. In 1933, he did *Flying Down to Rio,* the first film in which Fred Astaire danced with Ginger Rogers, and in 1935 costumed Katharine Hepburn in *Alice Adams,* the beginning of a long collaboration with the actress.

In addition to his design duties, Plunkett was manager of the RKO wardrobe department, and was in charge of payroll, budget, hiring, and firing. Underpaid and overworked, he quit RKO in 1935, returning the next year at Katharine Hepburn's request to do her costumes for *Mary of Scotland.* From then until his retirement in 1966, he worked on his own terms as a freelance designer, dressing some of the greatest stars in some of Hollywood's most ambitious productions, sometimes sharing design duties with other designers such as TRAVIS BANTON and IRENE SHARAFF.

Paul Poiret

Born Paris, France, April 20, 1879
Died Paris, France, April 28, 1944

FASCINATED BY THE THEATER AND the arts, Pioret was himself a flamboyant and theatrical figure, shrewd and egotistical, spending fortunes on fetes, pageants, and costume balls, and on decorating his homes. He designed costumes for actresses such as Réjane and Sarah Bernhardt; his friends included Diaghilev, Leon Bakst, Raoul Dufy, ERTÉ, and Iribe.

As a youth, while apprenticed to an umbrella maker, Poiret taught himself costume sketching. He sold his first sketches to Mme. Cheruit at Raudnitz

Soeurs, joined Jacques Doucet in 1896, and spent four years working for WORTH before opening his own house in 1904.

Considered by many to be one of the greatest originators of feminine fashion, Poiret was extravagantly talented, with a penchant for the bizarre and dramatic. While his forte was costume, the modern silhouette was to a great extent his invention. He freed women from corsets and petticoats and introduced the first, modern, straight-line dress. Yet he also invented the harem and hobble skirts, so narrow at the hem that walking was almost impossible. His minaret skirt, inspired by and named after a play he costumed, spread world-

Poiret consults with Joan Crawford on his designs for her MGM film, our Modern Maidens, 1929.

wide. Influenced by Diaghilev's Ballets Russes, he designed a Russian tunic coat, straight in line and belted, made from sumptuous materials. His taste for orientalism showed up in little turbans and tall aigrettes with which he adorned his models, and he scandalized society in 1911 by taking mannequins to the Auteuil races dressed in *jupes culottes,* also called Turkish trousers.

He established a crafts school where Dufy for a while designed textiles, and was the first couturier to present a perfume. In 1912 he was the first to travel to other countries to present his collection, taking along twelve mannequins. In 1914, along with WORTH, PAQUIN, Cheruit, CALLOT SŒURS, he founded the Protective Association of French dressmakers and became its first president.

Unable to adjust his style to changes brought about by World War I, Poiret went out of business in 1924. Bankrupt and penniless, he was divorced by his wife in 1929. Four years later he was offered a job designing ready-to-wear but his attitude toward money was so irresponsible that the venture failed. He took bit parts in movies, wrote his autobiography, moved to the south of France. He spent his last years in poverty and died of Parkinson's disease in a charity hospital. Poiret's extraordinary imagination and achievements flowered in the brilliant epoch of Diaghilev and Bakst. It influenced the taste of two decades.

"Sorbet," a lampshade tunic and hobble skirt, illustrated in *La Gazette Du Bon Ton,* September 1913. *See also Color Plate 15.*

Zac Posen

Born Zachary Posen, New York City, October 24, 1980
Awards Ecco Domani Fashion Foundation Award (one of five young designers), 2002

A precocious talent whose designs first showed up on the backs of celebrities who just happened to be friends or schoolmates, Posen was born into the art world, his father a successful painter. From 1996 to 1998—after school, on weekends, and holidays—he interned with Richard Martin at the

Costume Institute of the Metropolitan Museum of Art. There he developed a passion for the work of Madeleine VIONNET and was able to study her bias-cut designs up close. While at London's Central St. Martins College of Art and Design, he was one of ten students chosen to submit designs to the "Curvaceous" exhibit of Victorian underwear at the Victoria and Albert Museum (2001-2002). His contribution was a fitted, six-foot column constructed from vertical strips of glossy brown leather held together by hundreds of hooks and eyes that could be unhooked at any point. It won the V & A prize and became part of the permanent collection.

Posen's designs—dresses, blouses, coats—rely to a great extent on his favored bias cut and possess both disciplined construction and refined work-

Zac Posen and design from Fall 2002.

manship. They have a very modern femininity, sexy without vulgarity, and have been worn by models and actresses such as Naomi Campbell and Claire Danes. They have been sold at Henri Bendel in New York.

P

Clare Potter

Born Jersey City, New Jersey, 1903

Died Fort Ann, New York, January 5, 1999

Awards First Lord & Taylor Award for "distinguished designing in the field of sports clothes for women," 1938 · Neiman Marcus Award, 1939 · Coty Fashion Critics Award, 1946.

POTTER BELONGED TO THE SMALL, influential group of women designers generally considered the inventors of American sportswear—a group that included CLAIRE MCCARDELL and TINA LESER. In the 1930s they were among the first to be recognized by name.

She developed an interest in art in high school and went on to New York's Art Students League, where she took a draping course though she didn't know how to sew. She then switched to Pratt Institute in Brooklyn and after graduation found work with a dress manufacturer. In 1948 she formed a company in partnership with a former magazine editor, and by the mid-1950s was in business for herself.

Potter loved sports and designed for an active woman like herself who preferred casual clothes that were also sophisticated and discreet. Even for evening wear she stayed casual with a skirt and shirt or pants and a tunic; her evening sweaters were especially noteworthy. She simplified, got rid of ornamentation, and was admired for her use of color and uncomplicated textures. While not as adventurous as McCardell, she was equally immune to European influences and shared her understanding of how the modern American woman lived.

Miuccia Prada

Born Italy, ca. 1950

Awards Council of Fashion Designers of America (CFDA) *International Award,* 1993

Miuccia Prada came into design through her connection with her family's firm, Fratelli Prada, since 1913 maker of leather goods of the highest quality. A committed member of the Communist Party during and immediately after her university years, she resisted joining the family business until 1978 when she took over direction from her mother. Her first success was a black nylon backpack; later ones were handheld bags of the same fabric, washable, flexible, tough, and soft.

Her first ready-to-wear collection was for Fall 1989, and in 1994 Prada took part in the New York showings. Her clothes, much coveted by the more advanced fashion press, are described as supremely comfortable—nothing on the hanger but coming to life on the body. There is a younger, less expensive Miu-Miu collection, and also men's clothes and accessories.

Under the leadership of Miuccia's husband, Patrizio Bertelli, the Prada firm has become one of fashion's foremost conglomerates. Its interests include leading international design houses, fine shoemakers, and major Italian production facilities.

Designer Miuccia Prada (left) and from Fall 2003 (right).

Proenza Schouler

Born Lazaro Hernandez; Miami, Florida, 1979
Jack McCollough, New Jersey, 1979
Awards Council of Fashion Designers of America (CFDA) *Perry Ellis Award for New Talent,* 2003

The two men met in 1999 at Parsons School of Design, where they arrived after starting out on other career paths—Hernandez in medicine, McCollough in glass blowing. During his sophomore year at Parsons, Hernandez interned at Michael Kors, a spot he obtained in storybook fashion through *Vogue* editor, Anna Wintour. After discovering she was on his plane from Miami, he sent her a note mid-flight, describing himself, his love of fashion, and his admiration for her; she informed Kors that Hernandez should work for him. Meanwhile, McCollough interned at MARC JACOBS. They freelanced together at another company during their senior year and were allowed to do their senior thesis as a collaboration, producing a 15-piece collection with fabric donated by Kors. The collection was so impressive, the judges recommended the designers to Barneys' vice president for merchandising, who bought the collection for the store.

Hernandez and McCollough shun the

Jack McCollough and Lazaro Hernandez, 2002.

street-fashion aesthetic to concentrate on grown-up clothes "for women, not kids," giving a sophisticated twist to classics. Their emphasis is on spare silhouettes in fresh proportions and subdued colors, mostly black and gray, in

From Fall 2003.

deluxe fabrics such as cashmere, angora, and silk. The clothes have receive an enthusiastic response from celebrities and been embracd by both the press and retailers.

Emilio Pucci

Born Marchese di Barsento, Naples, Italy, 1914
Died Florence, Italy, November 29, 1992
Awards Neiman Marcus Award, 1954 · Council of Fashion Designers of America (CFDA)
Special Award, 1990

Descendant of Russian nobility and member of the Italian aristocracy, Pucci was educated in Italy and the United States. He was a member of his country's Olympic Ski Team in 1933–1934, and officer of the Italian Air Force during World War II, remaining in the service after the war. Even after he became involved with fashion, he retained his interest in politics and in the 1950s served two terms in the Italian Chamber of Deputies.

Pucci got into fashion by accident when ski clothes he was wearing in Switzerland caught the attention of photographer Toni Frissel. Snug and close-fitting, they were among the first made of stretch fabrics; when the Frissel photographs appeared and attracted attention, he decided to market the clothes. However, it was his simple chemises of thin silk jersey that made him a favorite of the international jet set in the 1960s. These dresses, wrinkle-resistant and packable in no space at all, were beloved by fashion professionals everywhere, and the brilliant signature prints in designs inspired by heraldic banners were copied in every price range. In 1990 there was a worldwide revival of interest in the prints. Design projects have included accessories, sportswear, underwear, fragrances for women and men, porcelain, sheets, bath linens, rugs, and airline uniforms. Since his death, the business has continued. It was bought by LVMH in 2000, and in late 2002 Christian Lacroix was brought in as designer.

Pucci beachwear, 1965.

P

Mary Quant

Born Blackheath, Kent, England, February 11, 1934
Awards O.B.E. (Order of the British Empire)

QUANT WAS A LEADING FIGURE in the youth revolution of the 1950s and 1960s—her awareness of social changes and understanding of the young customer made her a celebrity and helped put London on the fashion map. She studied at Goldsmith's College of Art in London where she met Alexander Plunket Greene, whom she later married. In 1955, with a partner, she and her husband opened a small boutique called Bazaar, the first on King's Road in London's Chelsea district. At the start they sold clothes from outside designers, but soon became frustrated by the difficulty of

Quant (right in photo) with one of the "Jolly Sailors" from her Spring 1972 collection.

getting the kind of clothes they wanted from manufacturers. Mary Quant then began to make her own designs, spirited, unconventional, and instant hits with the young, probably because they were totally unlike anything their mothers had worn, or ever would wear.

She began on a small scale, running up her designs in her own flat, but her fame grew along with that of "swinging London." By 1963 she had opened a second Bazaar, had moved into mass production with her less expensive Ginger Group, and was exporting to the United States. With her husband as business partner she had become a full-scale designer and manufacturer. She designed for J.C. Penney in the United States and for Puritan's Youthquake promotion. Her autobiography, *Quant by Quant,* was published in 1966. In the 1970s, while no longer a fashion innovator, she added to her business with licenses for jewelry, carpets, household linens, men's ties, and eyeglasses. In 1973-1974, an exhibition, "Mary Quant's London," was presented at the London Museum.

In approximately 1964 she became interested in makeup, and in 1966 launched a cosmetics line with the colors presented in a paint box and crayon kit. With Japanese partners she developed a complete body and skin-care collection as well as makeup, sold in freestanding shops in Japan. There is a showcase shop in London and shops in New York and the Far East, Australia, and New Zealand.

Quant is given credit for starting the Chelsea or Mod Look of the mid 1950s and the miniskirts of the late 1960s. Whether or not she actually originated the mini, she certainly popularized it in England and the United States. She initiated ideas that are now commonplace, using denim, colored flannel, and vinyl in clothes that only the young could wear and showing them with colored tights. For her innovative showings she used photographic mannequins rather than regular runway models and had them dance down the runway. Whatever her final stature as a designer, she was a pivotal figure in a fashion upheaval that reflected major social changes taking place around the world. The Mod Look has since made return appearances in the work of designers in both Europe and the United States. Her mini slip-dresses in bold prints reappeared under her own label in 2003.

In October 2001, New York's Fashion Institute of Technology mounted an exhibition, "London Fashion," tracing the history of the city's style contributions, from Mary Quant's mini-skirt to designs by more recent movers and shakers. These included, among others, JOHN GALLIANO, ALEXANDER MCQUEEN, HUSSEIN CHALAYAN, and VIVIENNE WESTWOOD.

R

Paco Rabanne

Tracy Reese

Zandra Rhodes

Nina Ricci

Richard Edwards

Marcel Rochas

Narciso Rodriguez

Alice Roi

Christian Francis Roth

Cynthia Rowley

Sonia Rykiel

Paco Rabanne

Born San Sebastian, Spain, 1934

Paco Rabanne's family fled to France in 1939 to escape the Spanish Civil War—at the time, his mother was head seamstress at BALENCIAGA in San Sebastian. In Paris, Rabanne studied architecture at the École Supérieure des Beaux-Arts, began designing on a freelance basis—handbags, shoes, plastic accessories, and embroideries.

In his first show in 1966, called "12 Unwearable Dresses," the dresses in question were made of plastic discs linked with metal chains, accessorized with plastic jewelry and sun goggles in primary colors. He continued the linked-disc theme in coats of fur patches and dresses of leather patches, and also used buttons and strips of aluminum laced with wire. In 1970 he was one of the first to use fake suede for dresses. He combines unlikely materials, and has designed coats of knit and fur as well as dresses made of ribbons, feathers, or tassels, linked for suppleness. His experiments have had considerable influence on other designers.

A mystic by nature, Rabanne lives monastically, unencumbered by possessions, and gives the bulk of his money to charity. Although still actively engaged in his firm, he turned over creative direction to Rosemary Rodriguez in 2000. His company is owned by the Spanish firm, Puig, which also owns NINA RICCI. At last count, there were nine fragrances for women and men.

Paco Rabanne in 1966 with long and short versions of his signature dresses made of linked plastic discs.

Tracy Reese

Born Detroit, Michigan, February 12, 1964

Tracy Reese specializes in young designer sportswear—knits, separates, and dresses for women with careers and busy, varied lives. The clothes combine a playful spirit with shape and structure.

After childhood weekends spent in art classes, Reese took a fashion design class at Cass Technical High School in Detroit. She attended New York's Parsons School of Design on scholarship, graduating in 1984, and in the same year went to work as design assistant to Martine Sitbon. In 1987, she opened her own company, which two years later fell victim to the recession, then worked at PERRY ELLIS as designer for the Portfolio division until it closed the following year. She freelanced briefly with Gordon Henderson, and from 1990 to 1995 was design director at Magaschoni for a bridge collection, Tracy Reese for Magaschoni. Reese then designed an exclusive line for The Limited and in the same year started her own company, Tracy Reese Meridian. Her designs are sold at upscale stores in the United States and in Europe and Asia.

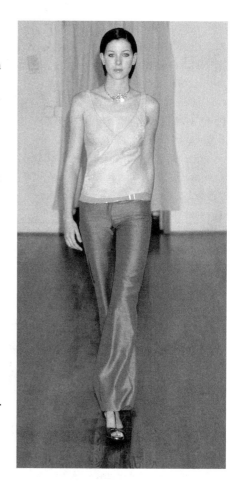

Tracy Reese (left) and a design from Spring/Summer 2002.

R

Zandra Rhodes

Born Chatham, England, 1942
Awards British Clothing Institute Designer of the Year, 1972

zandra Rhodes came into view in the late 1960s when she established her dress firm. She had planned to be a textile designer and set up her own print works and a shop to sell dresses made of her fabrics, then decided she was better able to interpret them than anyone else. She was undoubtedly right—her designs and her fabrics are of a piece, unmistakably hers, as eccentric and original as she is.

Rhodes's father was a truck driver; her mother was head fitter at WORTH in Paris before her marriage and afterward a senior lecturer in fashion at Medway College of Art. Zandra studied textile design and lithography at Medway, and then went to the Royal College of Art, graduating in 1966. By 1969 she was producing imaginative clothing, for the most part working in very soft fabrics that float and drift—chiffon, tulle, silk—handscreened in her own prints. These have included Art Deco motifs, lipsticks, squiggles, teddy bears, stars, teardrops, and big splashy patterns.

She always made news, alternately criticized and applauded. She finished edges with pinking shears and made glamorized punk designs with torn holes or edges fastened with jeweled safety pins, sleeves held on by pins or chains. Her champagne bubble dresses drawn in at the knee with elastic were acclaimed, and flounced hems finished with uneven scallops and adorned with pearls, pompoms, or braid became a signature. The clothes were beautiful and

Zandra Rhodes

romantic, a fantasy of dressing entirely distinctive and personal.

Rhodes created her own appearance as imaginatively as her clothing: hair dyed in a rainbow of colors—magenta and bright green, for example—and such makeup effects as eyebrows drawn in one continuous arc. She is considered by many to be one of the creative geniuses of "Swinging London" and has continued to thrive and take risks long after many of her contemporaries have

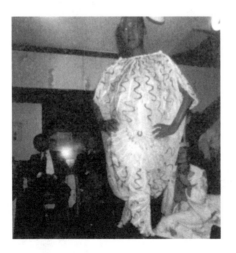

faded from the scene." Her designs were included in the 2001 "London Fashion" exhibition at the Fashion Institute of Technology.

In May 2003, her career resurgent, she opened a small Fashion and Textile Museum of her own, dedicated entirely to modern fashion and textiles. It is housed in a brilliant orange-and-pink building in South London reconstructed from a derelict warehouse.

Champagne bubble dress, 1978 (left); evening top and pants, 1994 (above).

Nina Ricci

Born Turin, Italy, 1883
Died Paris, France, November 29, 1970

Nina Ricci moved to Paris with her family when she was twelve. As a child she made hats and dresses for her dolls, and at the age of thirteen was apprenticed to a couturier. At eighteen she was the head of an atelier, and at twenty-one a premier stylist. In 1932, encouraged by her jeweler husband, Louis, she opened her own couture house.

Ricci was a skilled technician who usually designed by draping the cloth onto the mannequin, but she was not an originator of fashion ideas. The house specialized in graceful clothes for elegant women who preferred to be in fashion rather than in advance of it; trousseaux were a specialty. Typical of her attention to elegance and detail is the Ricci perfume, *L'Air du Temps,* presented in a Lalique flacon with a frosted glass bird on the stopper. She was one of the first in the couture to show lower-priced models in a boutique. After 1945 the house was managed by her son Robert. In 1951 JULES-FRANÇOIS CRAHAY became Mme. Ricci's collaborator on the collections; he took over complete design responsibility in 1959. He was succeeded in 1963 by Gérard Pipart.

Since 1998, when it was sold to the Barcelona-based beauty and fashion conglomerate Puig Group, the house has had a changing cast of designers.

Richard Edwards

Born Richard Bengtsson, Sundsvall, Sweden, February 10, 1962
Edward Pavlick, New Jersey, July 15, 1966
Awards Council of Fashion Designers of America (CFDA) *Perry Ellis Award for Menswear*
(a tie with Richard Tyler), 1995

These two men came to fashion design from totally different perspectives: Bengtsson studied fashion in Stockholm at Beckmans School of Design, designed his own collection for women before turning to men's wear, and moved to New York in 1989 to freelance for several men's sportswear companies. On the American side, Pavlick was an Industrial Design student at the University of the Arts in Philadelphia, and first worked on the design of pharmaceutical and biological research equipment. Together, they developed their first collection in 1993, which consisted of holiday shirts.

The first Richard Edwards runway presentation for men was in 1995 in New York where the business is based but since 1998 they have shown in Milan. The women's collection made its debut at the Paris showings in 2001. The Richard Edwards aesthetic for both women and men combines European and American perspectives. Precisely cut in a modern silhouette, the clothes are clean and well-structured with a quiet edge, flattering, entirely contemporary, and highly wearable.

From Spring/Summer 2001 Milan collection.

R

Marcel Rochas

Born Paris, France, 1902
Died Paris, France, March 14, 1955

Marcel Rochas, who was known for young, daring designs, opened his couture house in 1924 in the Faubourg Saint-Honoré, and moved to the avenue Matignon in 1931. According to legend, his reputation was made by the scandal that ensued when eight women wore the identical dress from his house to the same party, each having thought she had the exclusive.

Rochas generated an abundance of fantastic, original ideas, using as many as ten colors in combination and lavish quantities of lace, ribbon, and tulle. He showed a broad-shouldered military look before SCHIAPARELLI, long skirts and an hourglass silhouette several years before the New Look, and invented a waist-cincher. His perfume, *Femme,* was packaged in black lace and became a classic. He maintained a boutique for separates and accessories, also designed for films.

In 1951 he published *Twenty-five Years of Parisian Elegance, 1925-50.* Except for a licensed Japanese line the firm went out of the apparel business with the death of Rochas.

In March 1990, Parfums Rochas announced a new luxury ready-to-wear collection designed by Irishman Peter O'Brien. He was replaced by the Belgian OLIVIER THEYSKENS whose first collection was for Fall/Winter 2003.

Narciso Rodriguez

Born New Jersey, 1961
Awards Council of Fashion Designers of America (CFDA) *Perry Ellis Award* 1997

Narciso Rodriguez, the son of Cuban-American parents, studied in New York at Parsons School of Design and first became widely known in 1996 for the bias-cut wedding dress he designed for the late Carolyn Bessette Kennedy. He was, however, hardly a beginner, having worked under Donna Karan at Anne Klein immediately after his graduation from Parsons. He later worked at Calvin Klein.

He was soon recognized for his excellent tailoring and feminine, wearable designs and was hired by Cerruti to update the label; he then moved on to Madrid-based Loewe (owned by LVMH). Rodriguez turned Loewe, previously a little-known leather firm, into a major luxury goods label.

In contrast to the eccentricity of his British design peers, Rodriguez has preferred to concentrate on a less assertive look that emphasizes the woman rather than the clothes. His skillful tailoring, simple and elegant shapes in beautiful fabrics, and merchandising savvy have built his considerable reputation. His own collection, established in 1998 and shown in Milan and New York, has been an outlet for the more extreme elements of his creative imagination. In 2001, he left Loewe to concentrate on his own company, which includes shoes and handbags.

From Spring/Summer 2002 (left). Above, Narciso Rodriguez on the runway.

R

Alice Roi

Born New York City, February 6, 1976

After graduating from New York University as an art major, Alice Roi took classes in draping, illustration, and pattern making at Parsons School of Design before setting up on her own as a designer. In September 2000, she was one of three young talents chosen for the Moët & Chandon Designer Debut during Fashion Week Spring 2001. She presented her first solo show the following February. She was nominated for the Perry Ellis Award for women's wear in 2001, which she considered a high honor, but not a great deal of help when it comes to what new designers need most—a reliable backer.

Roi's clothes are lively and sassy, starting with a few simple, well-cut shapes, often with detailing that reflects her playfulness and love of parody. When she draws inspiration from the past she treats it with a refreshing cheekiness, rather than reverence. The

Designer Alice Roi (above) and from Fall 2001 (right).

clothes have been carried by forward-thinking stores in New York, Boston, London, Paris, and Hong Kong. She is a member of the Council of Fashion Designers of America (CFDA) and has contributed her time and talents to the cause of juvenile AIDS.

Christian Francis Roth

Born New York City, February 12, 1969
Awards Council of Fashion Designers of America (CFDA) *Perry Ellis Award, 1990*

The designer with the bride, Fall 1994.

A fashion prodigy, Christian Francis Roth knew when he was eleven years old that he wanted to make clothes. At sixteen, while attending the Fashion Institute of Technology at night, he served a summer apprenticeship with Koos Van Den Akker, where first as apprentice and then as a full-time employee, he learned pattern making, sewing draping, and other design skills. Working by day and going to F.I.T. at night, he finished high school in 1987. He then studied at Parsons at night for a year. In 1988 he produced his own small first collection in the Koos Van den Akker design studio. Van den Akker eventually helped him to start his own business, with his first full showing for Fall 1990.

The clothes were young and buoyant—notable for high-spirited appliqués on basic shapes and a high level of quality, which ensured that they would also be expensive. Roth has since struggled financially, been in and out of business, and has also sold a less costly line on QVC.

Twice nominated for the Mouton Cadet Young Designer Award, Roth was disqualified both times because he was not yet twenty-one. In 1989, along with Ralph Lauren, Michael Kors, and Isaac Mizrahi, he was honored by Cotton Inc. at their annual "Celebration of American Style" fashion show.

R

Cynthia Rowley

Born Highland Park, Illinois, July 29, 1958
Awards Council of Fashion Designers of America (CFDA) *Perry Ellis Award for New Fashion Talent,* 1994 (a tie with Victor Alfaro)

CYNTHIA ROWLEY WAS JUST SEVEN when she made her first dress. She was also precocious in business, selling her first eight-piece collection, a senior design project, while still at the Art Institute of Chicago. After a few seasons in Chicago, she moved to New York in 1983; five years later she incorporated her business with herself as sole owner. While truly interested in the money side of the business, she retains a creative insouciance that shows in fresh and fanciful ready-to-wear, where her greatest strength lies in dresses.

Rowley has enlarged her scope in many directions: shoes, men's wear, handbags and myriad accessories, intimate apparel, and tableware. She introduced cosmetics in 2002, has her own boutiques in the United States and Japan. In 1999, Rowley collaborated with a friend on a book, *Swell: A Girl's Guide to the Good Life,* aimed at young women—her prime customers.

Designer Cynthia Rowley (left) and dress from Spring/Summer 2003 (above).

Sonia Rykiel

Born Paris, France, 1930
Awards The Fashion Group *Night of the Stars* Award, 1986

Sonia Rykiel in 1985 (above) and (right), from Spring 2003 (right).

SONIA RYKIEL began in fashion by making her own maternity dresses, continued to design for friends after her child was born and then for her husband's firm, Laura. The first Sonia Rykiel boutique opened in 1968 in the Paris department store Galeries Lafayette, followed by her own shop on the Left Bank.

She has made her name with sweaters and sweater looks in apparently endless variations, usually cut seductively close to the body, softened with detail near the face. When her daughter became pregnant, Rykiel showed pregnant-looking mannequins in over-sized sweaters, and later added a new line of children's wear. She has continued to design for women at her own exalted fashion level and has added a men's line notable for color, joie de vivre, and wit.

R

S

Yves Saint Laurent

Fernando Sanchez

Jil Sander

Giorgio Sant'Angelo

Tanya Sarne

Arnold Scaasi

Jean-Louis Scherrer

Elsa Schiaparelli

Jean Schlumberger

Jeremy Scott

Mila Schön

Ronaldus Shamask

Irene Sharaff

Simonetta

Adele Simpson

Hedi Slimane

Paul Smith

Willi Smith

Luciano Soprani

Kate Spade

Stephen Sprouse

Lawrence Steele

Cynthia Steffe

Walter Steiger

Jay Strongwater

Anna Sui

Viola Sylbert

Yves Saint Laurent

Born Oran, Algeria, August 1, 1936
Awards Neiman Marcus Award, 1958 · Council of Fashion Designers of America (CFDA) *Special Award,* 1981

when saint laurent announced his retirement in January 2002 the story made headlines on the front pages of the world's leading newspapers, an acknowledgment of his position as a fashion giant. In an extraordinary career spanning more than 40 years, he changed the way women dressed as profoundly as CHANEL had done before him. Like her, he seemed to sense a woman's needs almost before she herself was aware of them, introducing looks that are now so accepted it's hard to remember they were once considered revolutionary or even scandalous.

The son of a well-to-do French-colonial family, Saint Laurent left Oran when he was seventeen to study art in Paris. In 1954 he shared first prize with KARL LAGERFELD in an International Wool Secretariat design competition, and a year later he was hired by CHRISTIAN DIOR as a design assistant. When Dior died suddenly in 1957, Saint Laurent succeeded him as head designer for the house, remaining until 1960 when he was called up for military service. In the Army he suffered a nervous breakdown and was discharged after just three months.

In 1961, with Pierre Bergé, his then lover and subsequent long-time partner, Saint Laurent opened his own couture house, showing the first collection in January 1962. Rive Gauche prêt-à-porter appeared in 1966 and men's wear in 1974. He also designed for film, notably for Catherine de Neuve in *Belle de Jour,* and for opera and ballet. Over the years the YSL initials were licensed for up to 167 products—everything from bed and bath linens to eyeglasses to children's clothes—and there were numerous fragrances, including *Y, Rive Gauche, Opium,* and *Paris.*

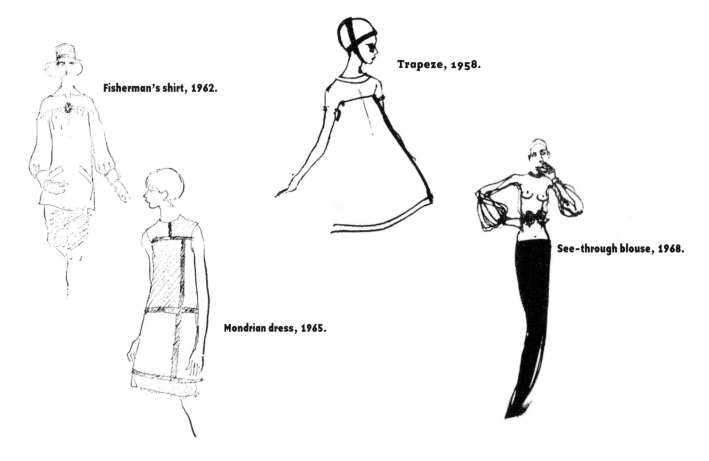

Fisherman's shirt, 1962.

Trapeze, 1958.

Mondrian dress, 1965.

See-through blouse, 1968.

Yves Saint Laurent, 1999, and evening gown, 1979. *Also see Color Plate 4.*

Within 20 years Saint Laurent reached the peak of his profession and established himself as the king of fashion, alternately taking inspiration from the street and exerting influence on it. Above all, he understood the life of the modern woman, designing simple, wearable day clothes with a slightly masculine quality in beautiful fabrics, and for evening, clothes of unabashed luxury and sensuousness, enriched with fantasy and drama.

In 1983 the Costume Institute of the Metropolitan Museum of Art mounted a 25-year retrospective of his work, the first time a living designer had been so honored. In it could be seen many of the highlights of his career, from the 1958 Trapeze dress from his first Dior collection, to such classics as the pea coat, the Safari jacket, and the Smoking jacket, and the fantasy of the rich peasants. It was possible to track his increasing mastery and polish, and the blending of vision and rigorous dedication that led to his preeminence.

In 1993 YSL was sold for $650 million to Sanofi, which in 1999 was acquired by Gucci. The American Tom Ford—already in charge of the Gucci fashion operation—was made creative director for both the women's and men's YSL Rive Gauche collections. Saint Laurent continued to create the couture line until he retired, remaining dedicated to the ideal of haute couture and the art of dressing women sensibly yet with a feeling of poetry. In his parting statement he said, "In many ways I feel that I have created the wardrobe of the modern woman . . . I am extremely proud that women the world over today wear pantsuits, smoking suits, pea coats, and trench coats."

Fernando Sanchez

Born Spain, 1930s

Awards Coty American Fashion Critics' Award *Special Award (lingerie): 1974, 1977, 1981; Special Award (fur design for Revillon), 1975 ·* Council of Fashion Designers of America (CFDA) *Special Award, 1981*

His mother was Belgian, his father Spanish, and Sanchez received his design education in France, making him a complete international. As a designer he has been at home in both Europe and America and in fields as disparate as lingerie and furs. Sanchez studied at L'École Chambre Syndicale de la Couture Parisienne in Paris and was a prize winner in the same International Wool Secretariat competition in which SAINT LAURENT won an award. He interned at NINA RICCI before joining Saint Laurent at CHRISTIAN DIOR, where Sanchez designed lingerie, accessories, and sweaters for the Dior European boutiques.

He first came to New York to do the Dior American lingerie line, and for several years commuted between Paris and New York. At the same time he began designing furs for Revillon, working for them for 12 years and becoming known for such unconventional treatments as his hide-out mink coats with the fur on the inside. He opened his own lingerie company in 1973, re-signed with Revillon in 1984 to produce a collection for the United States.

Sanchez's first successes for his own firm were glamorous lace-trimmed silk gowns, followed by camisole tops, boxer shorts, and bikini pants. He went on to develop lingerie on the separates principle, mixing colors, lengths, and fabrics to make a modern look. In 1983 he extended the same ideas into the men's market. Seductive, luxurious, trend-setting, and expensive, his lingerie has been given credit for reviving interest in extravagant underthings.

Fernando Sanchez and sleepwear, 1994.

Jil Sander

Born Wesselburen, Germany, November 27, 1943

Before becoming a major international fashion force, Jil Sander studied textile design, spent two years in the United States, and worked as a fashion journalist. She started designing in 1968, opened a boutique in Hamburg-Poseldorf, and worked as a fashion designer for a major fabric manufacturer. Her first collection under her own label appeared in 1973. Cosmetics were added in 1979, leathers and eyewear in 1984; boutiques were established in Europe, Japan, Hong Kong, and the United States; the flagship store opened in Paris in 1993.

When she began, the only German with an international design reputation was KARL LAGERFELD, and he was working in Paris. From the start, her objective was clear—design without decoration, proportions refined to perfection, with lines and cuts that were out of the ordinary. Sander brought a subtle fluidity to the most severe tailoring, her suits were extraordinary for their combination of authority and sensuality, and her dresses had a purity and sexy austerity. Her demands for the highest quality in

materials and craftsmanship were matched by her prices.

In 1999 the business was acquired by Prada; less than a year later Sander left abruptly, following a disagreement with Patrizio Bertelli, Prada's head. Design of the collection was taken over by Milan Virkmirovic, formerly buyer for Colette, the Paris boutique. Due to the terms of the sale, Sander was precluded from designing for anyone else until 2003. In May 2003 she and Bertelli made their peace and she rejoined the company she founded.

Designer Jil Sander, 1993 (below left) and designs from Spring/Summer 1998.

S

Giorgio Sant'Angelo

Born Florence, Italy, May 5, 1936
Died New York City, August 29, 1989
Awards Coty American Fashion Critics' Award *Special Award (fantasy accessories and ethnic fashions)*, 1968; *"Winnie,"* 1970 · Council of Fashion Designers of America (CFDA) *Special Award (contribution to evolution of stretch clothing),* 1987 · Fashion Walk of Fame, 2001

SANT'ANGELO spent much of his childhood in Argentina and Brazil where his family owned property. He trained as an architect and industrial designer before going to France to study art. He came to the United States in 1962. His art influences ran the gamut from high to pop, including studies with Picasso and work with Walt Disney. Moving to New York in 1963, he freelanced as a textile designer and stylist, and served as design consultant on various environmental projects. For the DuPont Company, his experiments with Lucite® as a material for fashion accessories were a sensation and received extensive press coverage.

While Sant'Angelo's initial success was with accessories, his first clothing collection of gypsy dresses and modern patchwork clothes was extremely influential. He went on to break more ground with ethnic-inspired clothing, especially a collection dedicated to the American Indian. Always very much an individualist, he was interested in new uses for materials such as stretch fabrics incorporating spandex. His designs were for those who liked their clothes a bit out of the ordinary and he maintained a couture operation for a roster of celebrity customers. He also did film costumes.

By Sant'Angelo from 1977 (left) and 1984 (above).

His many businesses included ready-to-wear and separates, as well as extensive licenses—from swimwear and active sportswear to furs to men's wear to environmental fragrances and home furnishings. After his death, the business went on for several years; the licensing operation continues.

216

Tanya Sarne

Born Tanya Gordon; England, ca. 1948
Awards British Export Award, Women's Wear, 1993

when Tanya Sarne founded Ghost in 1984, her aim was to make unstructured, comfortable, feminine clothes that a woman could wear and adapt to please herself. Multi-functional and easy the result was fashion in a moderate price range for an independent, free-spirited women who didn't want to look like everyone else.

Sarne attended the University of Sussex, where she took her B.A. with honors in History and Social Psychology. After her marriage broke up she was sales manager for Entrepais, an ethnic fashion company (1976-1978), she was then chairman and a designer for both Miz (1979-1984) and Ghost Ltd (from 1984). The company has prospered and expanded with freestanding Ghost stores in France and the United States; there are also several fragrances.

Tanya Sarne (above) and a design for Ghost, 1994 (right).

Responsibility for design of the collection was taken over by Amy Roberts in 2000, who has continued in the Ghost spirit with a modern version of the founder's original vision. Sarne has continued as the business head.

S

Arnold Scaasi

Born Montreal, Canada, May 8, 1931
Awards Coty American Fashion Critics' Award "Winnie," 1958
· Neiman Marcus Award, 1959 · Council of Fashion Designers of America
(CFDA) *Special Award (extravagant evening dress)*, 1987 · Dallas Fashion Award
Fashion Excellence Award

BEST known for spectacular evening wear in luxurious fabrics, Scaasi is one of the last of the true custom designers in the United States. The son of a furrier, he finished high school in his native Canada then took off for Melbourne, Australia to live with an aunt who dressed at CHANEL and SCHIAPARELLI. With her disciplined approach to dress and living, she was an important influence on Scaasi. He began art studies in Australia and then returned to Montreal to study couture. There he designed clothes for private clients and saved enough money to go to Paris to continue his fashion studies at L'École de la Chambre Syndicale de la Couture Parisienne. He then traveled in Europe for a year, returning to Paris as an apprentice to PAQUIN.

Arriving in New York in 1955, Scaasi worked as a sketcher for CHARLES JAMES, designed coats and suits for a Seventh Avenue manufacturer, and in 1957 opened his own wholesale business on a shoestring budget. In 1960, he bought and renovated a Manhattan town house for his ready-to-wear presentations, but changed his focus to couture in 1963. Another 20 years elapsed before he returned to ready-to-wear with Arnold

Evening gown, 1993, and Arnold Scaasi, 2000.

Scaasi Boutique, for cocktail and evening dresses.

With the mood of fashion moving away from flamboyance and toward minimalism, he closed the ready-to-wear business in 1994, choosing to concentrate on a handful of licenses and on made-to-order dresses for those women

who still cherished his entrance-making designs. Licenses have included costume jewelry, furs, men's ties, loungewear, bridal apparel, sportswear, and knits.

The Scaasi clients have included both socialites and celebrities such as Barbara Walters and Elizabeth Taylor, and presidents' wives—Barbara Bush wore his creations and he also designed a wardrobe, for her daughter-in-law Laura Bush.

218

Jean-Louis Scherrer

Born Paris, France, 1936

scherrer trained as a dancer at the Paris Conservatory but turned to fashion when he injured his back at the age of twenty. The sketches he made during his recuperation were shown to DIOR and he became Dior's assistant at the same time as SAINT LAURENT. It was at Dior that he learned the intricacies of cutting and draping that are the basis of his craft. After Dior's death and the choice of Saint Laurent as his successor, Scherrer left the house, found a backer, and in 1962 opened his own business. Since then he has had considerable success in both couture and ready-to-wear, with elegant clothes in the more elaborate couture tradition.

In April 1990, majority control of the company was acquired by a holding company, which in December 1992, citing heavy losses, dismissed Scherrer and replaced him as couturier and artistic director. Scherrer sued and negotiated a cash settlement and permission to resume designing, but did not recover the use of his name.

In late 2001 the house was bought by the newly-formed conglomerate France Luxury Group, with the first prêt-à-porter collection presented in March 2002.

Elsa Schiaparelli

Born Rome, Italy, September 10, 1890
Died Paris, France, November 13, 1973
Awards Neiman Marcus Award, 1940

The daughter of a professor of Oriental languages, Schiaparelli studied philosophy, also wrote poetry and articles on music. She married and moved to the United States, where she lived until the end of World War I. When her husband left her in 1920, she returned to Paris with her daughter Marisa to support and no money.

Her involvement in fashion began when a sweater she designed for herself, and had knitted by a member of the Paris Armenian colony, was seen and ordered by a store buyer. By 1929 Schiaparelli had established Pour le Sport on the rue de la Paix; by 1930 she was doing business from 26 workrooms employing 2,000 people. In 1935, she opened a boutique on the Place Vendôme for sportswear, later adding dresses and evening clothes.

Like her great rival, CHANEL, Schiaparelli was not simply a dressmaker but was also a part of the brilliant artistic life of Paris in the 1920s and 1930s. She had close friendships with artists, among them JEAN SCHLUMBERGER, who also designed jewelry for her, Salvador Dalí, with whom she worked on designs for prints and embroideries, Jean Cocteau, Kees van Dongen, and MAN RAY. Highly creative and unconventional she shocked the couture establishment by using rough "working class" materials for evening, colored plastic zippers as decorative features, huge ceramic buttons in the shape of hands or butterflies or whatever caught her fancy, and wildly imaginative accessories.

She showed little "doll hats" shaped like a lamb chop or a pink-heeled shoe, gloves that extended to the shoulders and turned into puffed sleeves. She fastened clothing with colored zippers, jeweler-designed buttons, padlocks, clips, and dog leashes. She showed witty lapel ornaments in the shape of hands, teaspoons, hearts, or angels, and amusing novelties such as glowing phosphorescent brooches and handbags that lit up or played tunes when opened. She was spectacularly successful with avant-garde sweaters worked with tattoo or skeleton motifs.

Schiaparelli changed the shape of the figure with broad, padded shoulders inspired by the London guardsman's uniform, a silhouette that lasted until the advent of the New Look. Both a genius at publicity and a trailblazer, she commissioned a fabric patterned with her press clippings then used the material in scarves, blouses, and beachwear, and she pioneered in the use of synthetic fabrics. Her signature color was the brilliant pink she called "shocking," the

Schiaparelli during the 1940s. From *Women's Wear Daily,* the Talleyrand suit, 1945.

name she also gave to her famous fragrance in its dressmaker dummy bottle.

Following the fall of France, she came to the United States, where she waited out the war. She returned to Paris after the Liberation and reopened her house in 1945. While she continued her business until 1954, she never regained her

prewar position. She continued as a consultant to companies licensed to produce hosiery, perfume, and scarves in her name, and lived out her retirement in Tunisia and Paris. Schiaparelli's irreverence and energy could result in vulgarity but she also produced clothes of great elegance that were extremely chic. Her major contribution was her vitality and sense of mischief, a reminder not to take it all too seriously.

Jean Schlumberger

Born Mulhouse, Alsace-Lorraine, France, June 24, 1907
Died Paris, France, August 29, 1987
Awards Coty American Fashion Critics' Award *Special Award* (the first given for jewelry), 1958 · Chevalier of the National Order of Merit of France, 1977

schLumberger was the son of an Alsatian textile magnate, who sent him to the United States while still in his teens to work in a New Jersey silk factory. On his return to France, he abandoned textiles and took a job with an art publishing firm, becoming part of the inventive Paris world of fashion, art, and society. His first jewelry designs were clips made from china flowers found in the Paris flea market. These pieces attracted the attention of ELSA SCHIAPARELLI, who admired their originality and commissioned him to design costume jewelry. He progressed to gold and precious stones and developed an influential international clientele, which included the Duchess of Windsor and Millicent Rogers.

Schlumberger went into the French Army at the advent of World War II, was evacuated from Dunkirk, and eventually came to the United States. He designed clothes for Chez Ninon, opened

Schlumberger fantasy jewel for Tiffany. Bird of platinum, 18-karat gold, and pavé diamonds, perched on a citrine rock.

an office on Fifth Avenue, then joined the Free French and served in the Middle East. After the war, he returned to New York and in 1946 opened a salon on East 63rd Street. In 1956, he joined Tiffany & Co. where he had his own salon on the mezzanine, reached by a private elevator.

Schlumberger has been compared to Fabergé and Cellini. His virtuosity, imagination, and skill brought forth exuberant fantasies: a sunflower of gold, emeralds, and diamonds with a 100-carat sapphire heart planted in a clay pot and set in a gold cachepot; snowpea clips of malachite and gold; and moss-covered shells dripping with diamond dew. He revived the Renaissance technique of enamel work,

adopted the custom of mixing semi-precious stones with diamonds, and used enamel and stones as if they were paint. His work was the subject of a lecture at the Metropolitan Museum of Art and a loan exhibition of jewelry and objects at the Wildenstein Gallery, New York.

S

Jeremy Scott

Born Kansas, 1976
Awards Venus de la Mode, 1996, 1997

A fashion nonconformist who has built his reputation on controversy, Scott studied at New York's Pratt Institute, departed for Paris in 1995 "because in Paris you can show whatever you want," and after a visit to California, moved there in 2001.

In Paris he earned both headlines and fashion awards, starting in 1996 with a collection inspired by car crash victims, Band-Aids, and hospital gowns. Successive showings featured dresses made from trash bags, cloven-toed stilettos, one-legged trousers, and white dresses with pleated angel wings. Other shows dazzled with everything gold—leather dresses, ruched lamé skirts, asymmetrical mink boleros.

Scott spent the 1998–1999 season as artistic director at Trussardi on their secondary lines, at the same time moving away from trash bag couture and closer to the mainstream. While showing both imagination and skill, his work can veer wildly between the cute-and-wearable and the kitschy.

Mila Schön

Born Trau, Dalmatia, Yugoslavia

Schön's parents left Yugoslavia for Trieste, Italy to escape the Communists; she moved on to Milan where she led a privileged life until a change in financial circumstances forced her to earn a living. In 1958 she opened a small workroom to copy Paris models and in 1965 showed her own designs in Florence.

Although based in Milan, Schön showed her couture and deluxe ready-to-wear in Rome for many years. She became well known for beautifully cut suits and coats in double-faced fabrics and for exquisitely beaded evening dresses. She changed with the times to a softer, more fluid look, but always upheld the highest standards of design and workmanship. Men's wear, swimsuits, and sunglasses were later additions.

In August 1991, Schön showed her couture collection in Paris. Since selling the business in 1994, she has been honorary president of the firm and creative director of a new, young design team.

Ronaldus Shamask

Born Amsterdam, Holland, 1946
Awards Coty American Fashion Critics' Award *"Winnie,"* 1981 · Council of Fashion
Designers of America (CFDA) *Men's Wear Designer of the Year,* 1988

one of a small group of designers with a strong architectural bent, Shamask arrived in New York City in 1971 by a circuitous route—Australia, London, and Buffalo, New York. Essentially self-taught, he moved with his family to Australia when he was fourteen, worked in the display department of a large Melbourne department store, and in 1967 moved to London where he worked as a fashion illustrator and began to paint. He then came to Buffalo and spent three years designing sets and costumes for ballet, theater, and opera. Next, he moved to New York City and worked on commissioned designs from private clients for interiors and clothing.

Shamask next undertook a 20-piece collection in muslin, cut from patterns that were actually life-sized blueprints. In 1978, he and a friend, Murray Moss, formed a company called Moss and opened a pristine, all-white shop and "laboratory" on Madison Avenue. The first presentation in 1979 consisted of the original muslin collection executed in three weights of linen. The clothes, which combined strong architectural shapes with beautiful fabrics, were cut with the utmost precision and exquisitely made. They were praised for their purity of design and exceptional workmanship.

Since 1986 Shamask has been in and out of women's and men's wear, designed costumes for the modern dancer Lucinda Childs, and returned to women's wear. The clothes, primarily high-end sportswear, have been sold through a select group of fine stores, including Bergdorf Goodman and Neiman Marcus.

Irene Sharaff

Born Boston, Massachusetts, ca. 1910
Died New York City, August 16, 1993
Awards Motion Picture Academy Awards: *An American in Paris* (for scenery and costume
for ballet sequence), 1951; *The King and I,* 1956; *West Side Story,* 1961; *Cleopatra*
(with Vittorio Nino Novarese and Renie), 1963; *Who's Afraid of Virginia Woolf,* 1966

In a remarkable career that spanned more than 60 years, Irene Sharaff designed costumes for 60 stage productions and 40 films, in addition to work for ballet and television, and even fashion illustration. Her first work, in 1928 while she was still in art school, was for Eva Le Gallienne's Civic Repertory Theatre in New York; her last film costumes were for *Mommie Dearest* in 1981; the last for the stage were for *Jerome Robbins' Broadway* in 1989. Sometimes she designed sets as well as costumes. Over the years, she earned two Donaldson awards and a Tony for her stage work, and for film received five Oscars and 15 Academy Award nominations.

Sharaff studied at the New York School of Fine and Applied Arts and the Art Students League, while working part time. By 1931, she had enough money saved to spend a year in Paris where she attended the Grande Chaumière. But even more important than school was her exposure to the theatrical designs of painters CHRISTIAN BÉRARD, Pavel Tchelitchew, and André Derain, and her discovery of the French couture with its emphasis on perfection in both design and execution. All of this had a great influence on her subsequent work. For ten years after

her return she worked with great success on the New York stage, moving to Hollywood in 1942 to work on musicals at MGM. Her design work ranged from *Meet Me in St. Louis* to *Who's Afraid of Virginia Woolf,* from *Madame Curie* to *Hello Dolly* and *The Taming of the*

———————————————————

Sharaff adjusts Elizabeth Taylor's costume for *Cleopatra,* 1963.

Shrew. Most of her work was at MGM, although she designed for a number of movies at other studios.

With rare versatility, Sharaff understood theater, dance, and film, and was at home in both modern and period settings, in realism and fantasy. Her meticulous research translated into a combination of authenticity and function; the costumes were never overpowering and were exquisitely made.

Simonetta

Born Duchess Simonetta di Cesaro; Rome, Italy, 1922

ONE OF THE ITALIAN COUTURIERS who gained international acclaim after the World War II, Simonetta began designing clothes in the 1930s and became a leading dressmaker in Rome. In 1952 she married ALBERTO FABIANI, also a designer; they continued in their separate establishments before moving to

Paris in 1962 to open a joint business called Simonetta et Fabiani. Their clothes were well received critically, but the business was not a success and Fabiani moved back to Rome in 1966, with Simonetta remaining in Paris. There, she had her own boutique and for a while worked at Chloé at the same

time as KARL LAGERFELD. Her designs were in the couture tradition: graceful, elegant, and feminine.

After her divorce from Fabiani, she left Paris and the fashion business, later traveled to India on a religious pilgrimage, and set up a leper colony there before returning to Rome.

Adele Simpson

Born Adele Smithline; New York City, December 8, 1903
Died Greenwich, Connecticut, August 25, 1995
Awards Neiman Marcus Award, 1946 · Coty American Fashion Critics' Award
"Winnie," 1947 · National Cotton Fashion Award, 1953

The youngest of five daughters of an immigrant tailor, Simpson began designing at seventeen while attending Pratt Institute at night. When she was just twenty-one she replaced her older sister, Anna, as head designer for an important Seventh Avenue manufacturer and was soon earning the then staggering sum of $30,000 annually and traveling to Paris regularly for her firm. She married Wesley Simpson, a textile executive, in 1927, worked for the Mary Lee firm until 1949, when she took over the company and named it for herself.

Simpson always saw her purpose as dressing women, not just selling dresses—her clothes were pretty, feminine, and wearable and could be coordinated into complete wardrobes. They were known for excellent design and impeccable quality; intended for women of discerning taste, they were conservative but not old fashioned. When Donald Hopson took over design of the collection, a younger, more fluid look developed. The family sold the firm in 1991 and it has since gone out of business. An exhibition, "1001 Treasures of Design," included items collected by Adele and Wesley Simpson and was presented by the Fashion Institute of Technology in 1978.

Hedi Slimane

Born 1967

Hedi Slimane for Dior, 2002.

with his international heritage–Tunisian father, Italian mother, and Brazilian grandmother—Slimane could be considered the epitome of the modern, multicultural man. He studied at L'École du Louvre and worked for José Levy before going to work at Yves Saint Laurent.

When the house was sold to Gucci in 1999 and TOM FORD became creative director for the company, Slimane left as creative director for men's wear, moving to Christian Dior as designer for Dior Homme. His first showing in January 2001 was a highly successful blend of classic French taste with a younger, edgier attitude. The silhouette was narrow and precisely cut, epitomizing his own blend of classicism and modernism. Subsequent collections have confirmed his reputation as an assured tailor whose proportions are just right, mean and lean and with no allowance for extra pounds. The clothes have also been much admired and worn by fashionable young women unwilling to wait until he designed a collection exclusively for them.

Paul Smith

Born Nottingham, England, 1946

Awards CBE, 1994 (for services to the fashion industry) · Queen's Award for Export, 1995 · Knighthood, 2000

smith worked his way up in fashion from the bottom, starting out at age eighteen as a lowly gofer in a clothing warehouse. He opened his first tiny shop for men in 1970, using his own savings, staying open only on Friday and Saturday, and carrying designers such as Kenzo, not then available outside London. He studied tailoring at night and gradually added his own designs, so successfully that by 1974 the shop had moved to larger quarters and was open full time. Developing his own cool, smart style, he had his first Paris showing by 1976 and was consultant to an Italian shirt manufacturer and to the International Wool Secretariat.

The clothes, now for both men and women, rely on simplicity of style with a twist of wit and humor. They are notable for unusual, luxurious fabrics and attention to detail—hand stitching, embroidery, vivid linings—and include tailored suits, separates, and knits, plus luggage, accessories, and swimwear. While the Paul Smith enterprise has grown into a worldwide chain, Smith still manages to advise and steer each division, maintaining the personal character of both merchandise and presentation. London's Design Museum celebrated his 25th anniversary in fashion with an exhibit called "Paul Smith True Brit." His book, *You Can Find Inspiration in Everything,* was published in 2002.

From Spring/Summer 2003.

Willi Smith

Born Philadelphia, Pennsylvania, February 19, 1948
Died New York City, April 17, 1987
Awards Coty American Fashion Critics' Award *Special Award,* 1983 · Fashion Walk of
Fame, 2002

ONE OF A NUMBER OF black designers who came to the fore in the late
1960s, Smith was the son of an iron-
worker and a housewife. He originally
intended to be a painter, studied fashion illustration at the Philadelphia Museum College of Art, and in 1965, at the
age of seventeen, arrived in New York
with two scholarships to Parsons
School of Design. He got a summer job
with ARNOLD SCAASI, then spent two
years at Parsons, during which he freelanced as a sketcher. He then worked

for several manufacturers, including
Bobbie Brooks, Talbott, and Digits.

After several failed start-up attempts,
WilliWear Ltd. was established in 1976
with Laurie Mallet as president, and
Smith as designer and vice president.
His innovative, spirited clothes—
described as classics with a sense of
humor—were fun to wear as well as functional, and brought fashion verve to the
moderate price range. Collections were
consistent in feeling from one year to
another so that new pieces mixed com-
fortably with those from previous years.
Preferring natural fibers for their comfort and utility, he designed his own textiles and went to India several times a
year to supervise production of the collections. Men's wear was introduced in
1978 "to bridge the gap between jeans
and suits." Smith also designed for
Butterick Patterns, did lingerie and
loungewear, textiles for Bedford
Stuyvesant Design Works, and furniture
for Knoll International. He was a sponsor of the Brooklyn Academy of Music's
"Next Wave" festival and designed one
of the 1984 dance presentations.

Willi Smith and separates, 1978.

S

Luciano Soprani

Born Reggiolo, Italy, 1946

Born into a farming family, Soprani, studied agriculture, and farmed briefly before breaking away in 1967 to become a designer. His first job was with MaxMara, the Italian ready-to-wear firm, where he stayed for eight years, plus another two years of free-lance. He freelanced for a number of firms until 1981, when he signed his first contract with Basile to design their women's line. After a year he was given the added responsibility for the men's wear. He has also designed for Gucci. His first collection under his own name appeared in 1981; he continues to show in Milan.

Essentially, Soprani works with strong shapes, enlivened by interesting details. His clothes are original and lively and appeal to sophisticated women worldwide.

Kate Spade

Born Katherine Noel Brosnahan, Kansas City, Missouri, December 24, 1964
Awards Council of Fashion Designers of America (CFDA) *Perry Ellis Award for Accessories*, 1995; *Accessory Designer of the Year*, 1997

Kate Spade has spent most of her professional life with accessories. After graduation in 1986 from Arizona State University, where she majored in journalism, she moved to New York and a job at *Mademoiselle* magazine. When she left the magazine in 1991 she was senior fashion editor/head of accessories.

Feeling that the market lacked stylish, practical handbags, she decided to create her own. In January 1993, with her husband, Andy Spade, she launched "kate spade handbags" with six designs, simple shapes in satin-finished nylon, emphasizing utility, color, and fabric; these continue to be signature styles. Spade believes that accessories should bring color and texture to a wardrobe, expressing the wearer's own sense of style and adding personality to her dress. The criterion for new additions is always the same—if it will be out of style tomorrow, it won't be in the line today.

The Kate Spade design universe has expanded to include leather bags and accessories, evening bags, and luggage—and on into eyeglasses, shoes, home accessories, paper, and beauty products. The products are sold in fine retail stores and in the company's own freestanding boutiques.

Designer and handbags, 2000.

Stephen Sprouse

Born Ohio, 1954

sprouse burst triumphantly on the New York design scene in 1983, and at the time was considered the archetypal "downtown" designer (as opposed to Seventh Avenue). He disappeared from view just as dramatically only five seasons later. His first collection of chemises and separates was reminiscent of the 1960s, except that the pieces were printed or painted in graffiti-like designs or sequined and colored in a Day-Glo spectrum. He was particularly admired for the perfection of his coats. Since June 1987, when he resurfaced with a new backer, Sprouse has been in and out of business, sometimes working on a custom basis. Despite the brevity of his appearances, his fashion influence has been extensive, particularly the hot, wild colors of the early collections.

At the center of the rock music scene of the 1980s, Sprouse saw his designs worn by a number of rock stars, including Debbie Harry, Iggy Pop, and Mick Jagger. In 1995, in the role of costume curator, he recreated the era for the opening of the Rock-and-Roll Hall of Fame and Museum in Cleveland, Ohio.

He has since collaborated on accessory designs with other designers, including MARC JACOBS for Louis Vuitton.

Lawrence Steele

Born Hampton, Virginia, July 3, 1963

Steele grew up an air force brat, following his father from one air base to another, from Germany to Spain, and eventually back to the United States and Rantoul, Illinois, where the family still lives. He majored in fine arts at the School of the Art Institute of Chicago, found a job in Tokyo after graduation, then moved on to Milan and FRANCO MOSCHINO, "a riot to work for . . . never took anything seriously . . ." In 1990 he went to PRADA, with its minimalist focus on fabrics and texture, and in 1994 began his own business.

He has gained a reputation for sensuous, sexy, very feminine clothes for late in the day, sophisticated clothes for svelte women unafraid of attracting attention. When his wedding dress for Jennifer Aniston appeared on the cover of *People* magazine it made his name known to an audience beyond the fashion editors, models, and film stars who were already his devoted clie[n]... designs have been sold inter[n]... ally—in Europe, North and Sou[th]... ica, the Far East, Australia, Russia, and the Ukraine.

From Milan Fall 2002 collection.

Lawrence Steele, 2002.

Cynthia Steffe

Born Molville, Iowa, June 30, 1957

Steffe grew up in small-town Boyden, Iowa, came to New York and studied at Parsons School of Design (1978–1982). She won many awards during her four-year stay: the Claire McCardell Scholarship her sophomore year, an award for the most original children's wear design, and both the Donna Karan Gold Thimble Award and the 1982 Designer of the Year awards in her senior year. While still in school, she started working as a design assistant to Donna Karan at Anne Klein & Co. In 1983 she moved to Spitalnick with her name on the label as Cynthia Steffe for Spitalnick, but left in 1988 to form her own company with her husband Richard Roberts. In late 2000, in a move to expand the brand, the company was sold to the Leslie Fay Co.

There are now two labels: Cynthia by Cynthia Steffe—essentially sleek, luxury sportswear—and the smaller deluxe Cynthia Steffe black label—ready-to-wear and sportswear in leather, cashmere, suede, and fur. The difference lies mainly in the fabrics, the customer could be the same—a confident woman, young, or with a young attitude, who chooses crisp elegance for day and sexy sophistication for evening and might very well take pieces from both lines to make a look that is modern, innovative, and completely personal.

In addition to her business, Steffe is active in a number of charities and in many industry-related activities. She has served on the Board of Governors at Parsons and as a design critic there, as guest lecturer at the Fashion Institute of Technology, on the Board of Directors of the Council of Fashion Designers of America (CFDA) and as a member of the CFDA Awards Benefits Committee. She is also on the board of the Fashion Group International.

Walter Steiger

Born Geneva, Switzerland, February 7, 1942

Walter Steiger's elegant shoes for women and men are sold in fine stores internationally and in his own freestanding boutiques. Apprenticed as a shoemaker at St. Gall, Switzerland (1958–1961), he moved on to design shoes in Paris (1962) and London (1962–1967). He established his own label in 1968 and opened his first Paris shop in 1974. He has since added accessories to his design projects.

Jay Strongwater

Born Jay Feinberg, Manhasset, New York, November 14, 1960

A summer project designing jewelry for his fashion-conscious mother led Feinberg to drop out of Rhode Island School of Design after two years to start his own fashion jewelry company, Jay Feinberg, Ltd. When he sold a controlling share of the company and the arrangement collapsed shortly thereafter, he lost the right to his name and reorganized using his mother's maiden name, Strongwater, for the new company.

With his mother in charge of showroom sales and his father taking over the business end, Feinberg was free to design his characteristic bold, opulent jewelry. He loves the process of working out new techniques, color combinations, and finishes to build a collection, always staying aware of what's happening at the moment in fashion. He has collaborated with designers such as OSCAR DE LA RENTA and BILL BLASS, and his designs have been sold at Saks Fifth Avenue, Henri Bendel, and other upscale stores

Anna Sui

Born Dearborn Heights, Michigan, ca. 1955
Awards Council of Fashion Designers of America (CFDA) *Perry Ellis Award for New Fashion Talent,* 1992

Anna Sui's restless curiosity and eclectic, unconventional approach to dress made their appearance early in her work—while still in junior high she sewed many of her own clothes, even appliquéing some of the dress fabrics onto her shoes. In her teens she began to save clippings from fashion magazines in what she calls her "Genius Files" (she still refers to

them). After high school she enrolled at Parsons School of Design in New York where she became close friends with Steven Meisel, soon to be a top fashion photographer. Sui left Parsons in her second year to work for a junior sportswear company, designing everything from swimsuits to knits and moonlighting as a stylist for Meisel's fashion shoots. Torn between styling and designing, she continued to design, and after selling six of her pieces to Macy's, opened her own business. Her first runway show was in April 1991. By September 1993 Sui had moved her business out of her apartment into quarters on Seventh Avenue and opened two boutiques, one in New York's SoHo, the second in Los Angeles.

Anna Sui (right) and from Spring/Summer 2002 collection.

Described as a mixture of hip and haute, romance and raunch, the clothes are a tribute to their designer's imagination and are popular with a younger crowd, although Sui maintains that anyone with an adventurous spirit can wear them. A great deal of their effect is based on the free-wheeling way she puts them together, "It's like playing dress-up; you keep adding things and taking bits away." She works hard to maintain a moderate price structure so that her young customers will continue to be able to afford her designs and says that the most important thing she's learned is to ship the clothes on time with good quality.

Viola Sylbert

Born New York City
Died January 19, 1999
Awards Coty American Fashion Critics' Award *Special Award (fur design)*, 1975

NOW best known for her furs, Sylbert's first successes were in leathers, sportswear, and sweaters. The daughter of a dress manufacturer, she earned her B.A. and M.Sc. in retailing at New York University. Her first love was writing, her second theatrical costume design, but to earn a living she became a fashion coordinator at Ohrbach's and gradually worked into designing. Recognizing early that "I'm not a 9-to-5 person," she began to freelance, enjoying the stimulation of working with different people on different kinds of projects. She established a routine of sketching and researching at home, and also traveled to Europe and Hong Kong.

In 1970, at the suggestion of Geraldine Stutz of Henri Bendel, she began designing furs, easy and casual in feeling with a unique fit and unusual colorings. She was fascinated with textures and the visual variations of different materials. In addition to furs she designed outerwear and knitwear, as well as "trend collections" of jersey dresses and men's sweaters for the Wool Bureau. She also ventured into loungewear, children's clothes, and accessories.

T

Vivienne Tam
Angelo Tarlazzi
Gustave Tassell
Olivier Theyskens
Bill Tice
Monika Tilley
Isabel Toledo
Philip Treacy
Pauline Trigère
Richard Tyler

Vivienne Tam

Born Guanzhou, China, 1960

Tam grew up in Hong Kong when it was a British crown colony, a bicultural background fundamental to her subsequent East-meets-West design philosophy. After graduating from Hong Kong Polytechnic University she moved to New York City, where her first collection appeared in 1982 under the East Wind Code label. She showed under her own name for the first time in 1993. Her collection for Spring 1995 caused considerable controversy, with prints on T-shirts, jackets, and dresses of Chairman Mao Tse-tung wearing a pigtail or looking cross-eyed at a bee on the end of his nose.

Her stretch mesh prints—dragons, peonies, Buddhas—are especially well known, but Tam is committed to providing fashionable clothing for modern women, clothes that are well designed, of superior quality, and affordable. Since she herself is a dedicated traveler, they must also be wearable and good travelers. Her list of celebrity clients includes Julia Roberts, Drew Barrymore, and Reese Witherspoon; the clothes are sold in fine stores in the United States and internationally, and in her flagship store in New York's SoHo district. They are included in the collections of the Metropolitan Museum of Art, the Fashion Institute of Technology, and the Andy Warhol Museum. A book, *China Chic,* written with Martha Huang, a Chinese literature scholar, was published in late 2000.

Angelo Tarlazzi

Born Ascoli Piceno, Italy, 1942

While he now works and presents his ready-to-wear in Paris, Tarlazzi received his fashion initiation and education in Italy. At nineteen he went to work at Carosa in Rome, stayed five years and became chief designer. In 1966 he left for Paris and a job with Patou. After three years at Patou he went to New York but could not find work and returned to Europe. He then freelanced for Carosa, went back to Patou (1972–1977), and then established his own business. He has also designed couture for Guy Laroche and freelanced for Basile and Biagiotti.

Tarlazzi's clothes have been described as a blend of Italian fantasy and French chic. His knits, termed "suave and sexy," are produced in Italy, the remainder of his collection is French-made.

Gustave Tassell

Born Philadelphia, Pennsylvania, February 4, 1926
Awards International Silk Association Award, 1959 · Coty American Fashion Critics'
Award "*Winnie,*" 1961

TASSELL STUDIED PAINTING AT THE Pennsylvania Academy of Fine Arts. After serving in the Army, he did window displays for HATTIE CARNEGIE, where he was exposed to the designs of NORELL and was inspired to become a dress designer. He had his own small couture business in Philadelphia then returned to Carnegie as a designer, leaving in 1952 to spend two years in Paris. While there he supported himself by selling sketches to visiting Americans, including GALANOS. He returned to the United States, and in 1956, aided by Galanos, opened his own ready-to-wear business in Los Angeles. After Norell's death in 1972, Tassell took over as designer, remaining until the firm closed four years later. He then reopened his own business.

Tassell was a friend of Norell, sharing with him a sure sense of proportion, an insistence on simplicity of line and refined detail. He was known for clothes of near-couture sophistication and perfect finish.

Olivier Theyskens

Born January 4, 1977, Brussels, Belgium

THE SON OF A BELGIAN father and French mother, Theyskens is one of the fresh talents that have come out of Belgium to show in Paris and shine on the international fashion scene. He entered Brussels' l'École Nationale Supérieure des Arts Visuels de La Cambre in October 1995 at eighteen, leaving school in January 1997 (two years into a five-year curriculum) to start work on his own first collection. This was shown in August 1997 in Amsterdam and Knokke, Belgium. His first Paris showing was the following March.

In what he calls semi-couture, Theyskens creates brilliant, grown-up dresses, coats, and suits notable for assured cut, adventurous, experimental shapes, and a sophisticated color palette. Definitely not for little girls, these are clothes for confident women with a sense of drama. His customer list includes Madonna, Nicole Kidman, and Queen Rania of Jordan. In November 2002 he joined MARCEL ROCHAS as creative director.

From Paris Fall 2003 collection.

T

Bill Tice

Born Tipton, Indiana, 1942
Died Glendale, Arizona, March 9, 1995
Awards Coty American Fashion Critics' Award *Special Award (loungewear)*, 1974 ·
American Printed Fabrics Council "*Tommy*" Award: 1971, 1988

Tice majored in fashion design at the University of Cincinnati, graduating in 1964. After arriving in New York, he spent several years working in ready-to-wear, found his niche in 1968 when he became designer for Royal Robes. In 1972 he took another detour into designer ready-to-wear, moved back into the intimate apparel field in 1975 as vice president of design at Swirl. From 1986 to 1991, he was involved in various businesses, running the gamut from his own firm, Entice Ltd. for ready-to-wear and intimate apparel, to a licensing agreement for robes, loungewear, and lingerie under the Bill Tice name, to upscale private label for Victoria's Secret and others. In 1991 he retired and moved to Arizona to spend more time with family and friends, but continued to work on special projects.

Bill Tice originated many key at-home ideas, the jersey float and the quilted gypsy look among them. In his 11 years at Swirl he produced widely imitated fleece robes, as well as innovative and salable loungewear, ranging from sundresses to printed sarongs to quilted silk coats and narrow pants. Known as a perfectionist who truly loved loungewear, he designed his own prints and the accessories for his collections, as well as slippers and evening shoes. Other design projects included patterns and domestic linens.

Innovative and energetic, Tice extended his role far beyond that of designer, initiating off-shore manufacturing, supervising workrooms and production, as well as all aspects of sales promotion, including public relations and national advertising. He produced videos for store use at point of sale before anyone else, traveled tirelessly to promote his products, and was the first intimate apparel designer to have his own boutiques in major fashion stores. His book, *Enticements, How to Look Fabulous in Lingerie,* was published by Macmillan in 1985.

Tice designs, 1976.

Monika Tilley

Born Vienna, Austria, July 25, 1934

Awards Coty American Fashion Critics' Award *Special Award (swimsuits)*, 1975
· American Printed Fabrics Council "*Tommy*" Award, 1976 (twice in one year: once for beach clothes and sportswear, once for loungewear and lingerie "for her original designs and use of prints")

Tilley Swimwear, 1973.

MONIKA TILLEY made her name with swimwear. She had always been involved in sports so that her sportswear designs, while fashionable and often seductive, were thoroughly functional. She has used bias cuts, cotton madras shirred with elastic, a technique of angling the weave of a fabric so it shapes the body. While she explained her reputation as a top swimwear designer as a matter of longevity—"I've stuck to swimwear longer than anyone else has"—her success was based on fit. She was very product oriented and also worked hard at promoting new lines with trunk shows and personal appearances.

Born into a family of conservative government officials and diplomats, Tilley grew up in Austria and England. After graduation in 1956 from the Academy of Applied Arts in her native Vienna, she studied in Stockholm and Paris before leaving Europe for the United States. She worked briefly as an assistant to JOHN WEITZ, then as a freelance designer of skiwear and children's clothes. Her career began in earnest at White Stag and Cole of California. She has also held design positions at Anne Klein Studio, Mallory Leathers, and in 1968, at Elon of California. In 1970 she incorporated as Monika Tilley Ltd., a full-service studio covering color and fiber consulting, textile and print design, and designing/marketing, specializing in men's and women's sportswear, women's lingerie and loungewear. Her list of clients included the Color Association of America, Monsanto, Malden Mills, Levi Straus, Munsingwear, Vassarette, Miss Elaine, and Elon.

T

Isabel Toledo

Born Cuba, April 9, 1961

TOLEDO IS ONE OF THE designers working in a very personal way somewhat out of the main stream. She learned to sew as a child in Cuba and started making her own clothes because everything ready made was too big for her. Arriving in the United States with her family, she attended the Fashion Institute of Technology and Parsons School of Design, and studied painting and ceramics before switching to design. She worked with DIANA VREELAND at the Costume Department of the Metropolitan Museum, restoring clothes from the Museum's collection. Her fashion career began in December 1985, when at the urging of her artist husband, Ruben Toledo, she made up a few pieces, which he then took around to the stores. Patricia Field and Henri Bendel were her first customers, followed by Bergdorf Goodman, which gave her the 57th Street windows for clothes from her first full collection.

Line and shape are paramount with Toledo, who starts with a shape such as the circle and experiments to see how far she can take it. She believes in simplicity arrived at through innovation, insists that the design must not be contrived but must evolve naturally. Her clothes, which she calls classic, range from sportswear to evening, from simple to flamboyant; they derive their uniqueness from the strength of their shapes and from her eye for details. The designs transcend age categories and appeal to women with a liking for the different.

Isabel Toledo (above), dress and floating jacket, 1994 (below).

Philip Treacy

Born County Galway, Ireland, 1967

Awards British Fashion Awards *Accessory Designer of the Year,* 1996, 1997

Couture hat designs from Fall 2001 collection. *Also see Color Plate 11.*

After studies at Dublin's National College of Art and Design, Treacy moved to London in 1988 on a scholarship to the Royal College of Art. While still in school he worked for RIFAT OZBECK and JOHN GALLIANO, among others, and soon after graduating was house milliner at HARTNELL. An interview at Chanel led to collaboration with KARL LAGERFELD on the Spring/Summer 1991 couture show, and since that breakthrough he has provided hats to Chanel for both the couture and ready-to-wear collections. His creations have also appeared regularly in the collections of VALENTINO and THIERRY MUGLER. They are sold in some of the world's finest stores—Bergdorf Goodman and Saks Fifth Avenue in the United States, Harrod's and Harvey Nichols in England, and in his own London boutique.

Treacy is fascinated by surrealist themes—animal forms, insects, hands, a crown of thorns—which take shape out of stripped feathers and distressed materials in unlikely juxtapositions. GIANNI VERSACE is reputed to have said of him, "Give him a pin, he makes a sculpture; give him a rose, he makes a poem." In January 2000 he took his creations to Paris for the first showing of haute couture hats there in 70 years.

T

Pauline Trigère

Born Paris, France, November 4, 1908
Died New York City, February 13, 2002
Awards Neiman Marcus Award, 1950 · Coty American Fashion Critics' Award
"*Winnie,*" 1949; *Return Award,* 1951; *Hall of Fame,* 1959 · *Medaille de Vermeil*
of the City of Paris: 1972, 1982 · Council of Fashion Designers of America
(CFDA) *Lifetime Achievement Award,* 1993 · *Fashion Walk of Fame,* 2001 ·
French *Légion d'honneur,* December 2001

The daughter of Russian émigrés, her father a tailor, her mother a dressmaker, Trigère's first career choice was to be a surgeon. When her father opposed the idea, she got a job making muslins at a Paris couture house. In 1929 she married Lazar Radley, another Russian-Jewish tailor. Her husband became alarmed at the rising Nazi tide and in 1936, two years after her father's death, the family—Trigère, her husband, and their two sons, as well as her brother and mother—left France for Chile. Their first stop was New York, and there they stayed.

After a business partnership with her brother and husband fell apart, her husband disappeared and Trigère found work, first with manufacturer Ben Gershel then at HATTIE CARNEGIE as an assistant to TRAVIS BANTON. Fired by Carnegie at the outbreak of World War II, Trigère, with her brother's help, scraped together enough fabric for her first collection—just 11 dresses—ready in March 1942. Her brother took the samples in a suitcase and traveling around the country by bus, sold them to fine specialty shops from Los Angeles to Minneapolis to Chicago to Philadelphia, with such success that the company was able not only to survive but to grow.

Trigère cut and draped directly from the bolt—coats, capes, suits, and dresses of near-couture quality in luxurious fab-

Left, evening gowns from 1962. Top right, Trigère in her signature tinted glasses, 1985.

rics, unusual tweeds and prints. The deceptive simplicity of the clothes was based on artistic, intricate cut, especially flattering to the mature figure. She took care of the designing for her firm while her elder son, Jean-Pierre Radley, as president of Trigère Inc., was in charge of the business end. The Trigère name has appeared on scarves, jewelry, furs, men's ties, sunglasses, bedroom fashions, paperworks, servingware, and a fragrance.

Trigère closed her business in August of 1993. In 2001, she was inducted into the Fashion Walk of Fame, whose large, white-bronze plaques honoring

American designers both living and dead were to be set into the Seventh Avenue sidewalk between 35th and 41st Streets. Trigère, whose tailoring and draping skills were legendary, chose

tailoring shears as her symbol rather than a sketch. In her acceptance speech she quipped that it was the first time she'd ever allowed anyone to walk on her.

Trigère tweed coat from 1985.

Richard Tyler

Born Sunshine, Australia, 1948

Awards Council of Fashion Designers of America (CFDA) *Perry Ellis Award for New Fashion Talent, 1993; Best Designer, 1994; Womenswear Designer of the Year, 1994; Perry Ellis Award for Menswear* (a tie with Edward Pavlick and Richard Bengtsson for Richard Edwards), 1995 · Dallas Fashion Award *Fashion Excellence Award* (for Anne Klein)

WHEN RICHARD TYLER SUCCEEDED LOUIS DELL'OLIO as designer for ANNE KLEIN, he was already a highly regarded fashion name in Los Angeles, producing beautiful clothes of near-custom quality for women and men and selling them from his own boutique. His jackets are particularly admired, not only for their inventive, graceful cut, but also for their perfectionist tailoring and finish, so flawless they could be worn inside out. Their high quality places the clothes firmly in the deluxe category.

Richard Tyler, 2001.

When he was eight years old, Tyler was taught to sew by his mother, who designed costumes for the ballet. Her credo, "Don't send it out unless it's perfect," has guided him ever since. In his teen years, Tyler apprenticed with the tailor who made suits for the Australian Prime Minister; at eighteen he opened his first boutique, Zippity-doo-dah, attracting a clientele from the music industry. After touring with a music group, he landed in Los Angeles in 1977, then spent time designing in Europe, before returning to Los Angeles. In 1987, Tyler/Trafficante, a partnership

T

Coatdress from Fall 2001.
- - - - - - - - - - - - -

with his second wife, Lisa Trafficante, and her sister Michelle, was established in Los Angeles, to design, manufacture, and wholesale the clothes. The first New York showing of the women's collection was in April 1993.

In May 1993 Tyler was named as designer for Anne Klein. While the collections were well received by his peers and the press, the traditional Anne Klein customer evidently found them too advanced and in December 1994 the company announced the end of the arrangement. Tyler continues to produce his signature line and show it in New York, with his operations based in his downtown Manhattan home-studio. A new, more moderately-priced collection called Tyler was announced in March 2002.

U-V

Patricia Underwood

Emanuel Ungaro

Valentino

Dries Van Noten

John Varvatos

Joan Vass

Philippe Venet

Donatella Versace

Gianni Versace

Viktor & Rolf

Madeleine Vionnet

Roger Vivier

Diane Von Furstenberg

Patricia Underwood

Born Maidenhead, England, 1948
Awards Council of Fashion Designers of America (CFDA), 1983

UNDERWOOD WORKED IN PARIS AS an *au pair* and at Buckingham Palace as a secretary before moving to New York in 1968. She studied at the Fashion Institute of Technology and then, with a friend, went into business making hats. Her strength is in elegantly updating classic, simple shapes from the past, such as boaters, milkmaids' hats, and nuns' coifs. Her designs have been

Patricia Underwood and 1987 hat design.

bought by leading stores, featured in fashion magazines, and have frequently been chosen by ready-to-wear designers to complement their collections.

Emanuel Ungaro

Born Aix-en-Provence, France, February 13, 1933
Awards Neiman Marcus Award, 1969

UNGARO'S PARENTS WERE ITALIAN IMMIGRANTS to the south of France. He gained his initial training working with his father, a tailor, from whom he learned to cut, sew, and fit men's clothes. In 1955, at twenty-two, he left Provence for Paris and a job in a small tailoring firm. Three years later he went to work for BALENCIAGA, where he stayed until 1963, then spent two seasons with COURRÈGES.

He opened his own business in 1965. His first collections were reminiscent of Courrèges—tailored coats and suits with diagonal seaming, little girl A-line dresses, and blazers with shorts. The clothes were widely copied in the youth market. Many of his special fabrics and prints were designed by Sonja Knapp, a Swiss graphic artist.

In the 1970s he turned to softer fabrics and more flowing lines, mingling several different prints in a single outfit and piling on layers. His designs be

Emanuel Ungaro, 2001.

came increasingly seductive, evolving into a body-conscious, sensuous look, strategically draped and shirred. As it was immediately and extensively copied Ungaro himself moved on,

retaining his penchant for mixing patterns and prints. His excellent tailoring has always remained in evidence in creations as diverse as a men's wear striped jacket tossed over a slinky flowered evening dress, or daytime suits with soft trousers cut on the bias. He has added ready-to-wear, a perfume, *Diva,* and also Ungaro boutiques in Europe and the United States. Other projects have included furs and men's wear, sheets, wallcoverings, curtains, and knitwear.

Ungaro celebrated his 35th year in business with a New York party in September 2001; the next month he named his creative director Giambattista Valli as designer of ready-to-wear. Responsibility for the haute couture remained with Ungaro.

Design from Fall 2003 couture collection.

Valentino

Born Valentino Garavani; Voghera, Italy, ca. 1932
Awards Neiman Marcus Award, 1967 · Council of Fashion Designers of America (CFDA) *Lifetime Achievement Award, 2000*

vaLentino Left itaLy for paris at age seventeen to study at L'École de la Chambre Syndicale de la Couture Parisienne, having prepared himself by studying both fashion and the French language in Milan. In 1950 he went to work for Jean Dessès, stayed five years, then worked as design assistant at Guy Laroche until 1958.

In 1959, he opened his own couture house with a tiny atelier in Rome's Via Condotti; within a few years, he was successful enough to move to his present headquarters. His first major recognition came in 1962 when he showed for the first time in Florence. In 1975 he began showing his ready-to-wear collections in Paris, and has continued to do so. His couture showings are still held in Rome. His first boutique for ready-to-wear opened in Milan in 1969, followed by one in Rome and then others around the world, including Japan. Other interests include men's wear, Valentino Più for gifts and interiors, bed linens, and drapery fabrics.

Valentino's clothes are noted for refined simplicity, elegance, and all-out glamour—precisely tailored coats and suits, sophisticated sportswear, entrance-making evening dresses—always feminine and flattering. They are notable for beautiful fabrics and exquisite workmanship and have been worn by a diverse international clientele ranging from the late Jacqueline Onassis to Elizabeth Taylor to Jennifer Lopez.

With Giancarlo Giammetti, his partner and business manager, Valentino understands the grand gesture. In 1978 he introduced his signature fragrance in France, sponsoring a ballet performance in Paris with after-theater parties at Maxim's and the Palace. In 1984, he celebrated his 25th year in business and 50th couture collection with an enormous outdoor fashion show in Rome's Piazza d'Espagna. His 30th anniversary celebration was a week of lavish lunches, dinners, a ball, and two exhibitions, attended by an international assemblage of friends and clients. A Valentino retrospective was part of an Italian promotion at the Park Avenue Armory in 1992.

Valentino and suit from Spring 2003 Ready-to-Wear. *Also see Color Plate 17.*

Dries Van Noten

Born Antwerp, Belgium, May 1958

coming from three generations of tailors, Van Noten took up the family trade while still a student at the Royal Academy of Beaux Arts in Antwerp, working for Belgian and Italian men's wear labels as a free-lance designer. His first collection under his own name was in 1985; the next year he went to London with the Antwerp Six for a presentation that brought him press recognition and orders from adventurous retailers internationally, including Barney's in New York. His Antwerp boutique opened in 1989, his first Paris men's wear showing was in 1991. He has added women's wear and accessories, showrooms in Milan and Tokyo, and shops in the Far East.

The Van Noten style is a marriage of opposites—simple with sophisticated, classic with modern—both the women's and men's collections reflecting his passion for fabrics, which are usually made exclusively for him. Although he shows in Paris and his clothes are sold around the world, he continues to live and work in Antwerp.

John Varvatos

Born Dearborn, Michigan, August 8, 1954
Awards Council of Fashion Designers of America (CFDA) *Perry Ellis Award for New Menswear Designer*, 2000; *Menswear Designer of the Year*, 2001

when john varvatos presented his first collection under his own label in 1999 he was hardly a beginner, having already put in 16 years in the men's fashion industry. He attended Eastern Michigan University, studied fashion illustration and pattern making at Fashion Institute of Technology, started with Ralph Lauren in 1983. In 1990 he was wooed away by Calvin Klein to head his men's wear division and establish the cK label. Then in 1994 he went back to Polo Ralph Lauren as senior vice president and head designer of men's wear, gaining further experience in marketing, production, and financing before embarking on his own in 1998. He has designed a limited edition of athletic shoes for Converse, opened a boutique in New York's SoHo, and there are plans for future expansion in the United States and Europe.

Varvatos combines the relaxed ease of sportswear with a refined elegance of cut, luxurious materials, and meticulous craftsmanship. He believes in presenting a total wardrobe—tailored clothing, sportswear, leather accessories, footwear—for a man he visualizes as between twenty and forty-five (or older) to put together in an individual manner.

John Varvatos (left) and design from Fall 2000 (far left).

Joan Vass

Born New York City, May 19, 1925

Awards Smithsonian Institution, Washington, D.C., "*Extraordinary Women in Fashion,*" 1978 · Coty American Fashion Critics' Award *Special Award (crafted knit fashions),* 1979 · National Cotton Council *U.S. Cotton Champion Award,* 2001

vass has built her reputation on crochets and handmade or hand-loomed knits, and imaginative, functional clothes in simplified shapes and subtle colorings, usually in her preferred natural fibers. She is recognized by retailers and the press as a highly creative, original designer.

A graduate of the University of Wisconsin, she majored in philosophy, did graduate work in aesthetics, and worked as a curator at the Museum of Modern Art and an editor at art book publisher Harry N. Abrams. With no formal fashion training, she got into designing in the early 1970s when two of her concerns intersected. First, she was bothered by the plight of women with salable skills but no outlet for them—specifically, women who either could not work away from home or did not want to be shut up in an office or factory; second, she was convinced there was a market for handmade articles of good quality.

Vass, who had always knitted and

Joan Vass (above) and 1994 knit separates.

crocheted, found a number of women with superior craft skills and in 1973 began designing things for them to knit and crochet, selling the articles privately. This new enterprise took so much time that she wanted to give it up but was dissuaded by her workers. Then

came her first large order from Henri Bendel; other stores followed and she was in business. Her firm was incorporated in 1977. In addition to Joan Vass New York—better-priced clothes for men and women—there are Joan Vass boutiques, the moderately priced Joan Vass USA collection, franchises in cities as far-flung as Los Angeles, Houston, and New Orleans, and a Web site with store listings.

Philippe Venet

Born Lyons, France, May 22, 1929

Venet in his studio, 1991; right, coat from 1992.

VENET STARTED IN FASHION AT fourteen when he was apprenticed to the best couturier in Lyons. He stayed six years then moved on to Paris and at twenty-two was working at SCHIAPARELLI, where he met GIVENCHY. In 1953 he went to Givenchy as master tailor, leaving in 1962 to open his own house. In addition to couture, he has designed costumes for the Rio de Janeiro Carnival, done sumptuous furs for Maximilian, produced a ready-to-wear line and men's wear, and operated a boutique. A superb tailor, Venet has been especially admired for his coats and suits. His clothes were beautifully cut, with great elegance and ease. There are two fragrances.

Donatella Versace

Born Reggio Calabria, Italy, 1956

Donatella Versace was ten years younger than her brother but from early on served as his inspiration, even as a child wearing the clothes he designed for her. When he moved to Florence in the mid-1970s to work in knitwear design, she followed, studying Italian literature at university and visiting him in his studio on weekends. After graduation she joined him in Milan where they shared an apartment, and when he founded his own company in 1978, she continued to function as both muse and critic. He eventually gave her responsibility for her own diffusion collection, Versus.

Following Gianni's 1997 murder, Donatella managed in three months to produce a creditable ready-to-wear collection—as creative director of the house she has continued to grow, each successive ready-to-wear and couture collection showing increased confidence and a firmer grasp of her craft. Her work is very much in the Versace mode of bold prints and forthright sexiness, not for the timid but appealing strongly to

entertainment figures and others for whom understatement is a foreign word

The Versace business has always been and continues to be a family affair, with brother Santo as president, Donatella's husband, Paul Beck, as director of men's wear, and Gianni's one-

Donatella Versace (above) and a design from Spring 2002 couture (left).

time companion, Antonio D'Amico, in charge of Versace Sport. The company has continued to expand into other areas—skin care, tabletop accessories, even hotels.

Gianni Versace

Born Calabria, Italy, 1946
Died Miami, Florida, July 15, 1997

AS his mother was a dressmaker, Versace's exposure to fashion began very early, but before embarking on a fashion career he first studied architecture. He then began designing knitwear in Florence, and from there moved to Milan where he designed for several *prêt-à-porter* firms, including Genny and Callaghan. In 1979 he showed for the first time under his own name, a collection of men's wear.

Versace became one of Europe's most popular designers, offering women many options, always sensuous and sexy. His vivid and far-reaching imagination was fueled by an insatiable curiosity and appetite for knowledge, resulting in bold prints inspired by antiquities and Byzantine mosaics and in the early 1980s, a fabric of metal mesh so soft and pliable it could be sewn by machine. This he used in beautiful, slithery evening dresses worn from California to the Riviera. As a designer he was fearless, using his mistakes to improve and grow. Like Schiaparelli, he could go over the top into vulgarity, but also produced clothes of great sophistication and elegance.

He also designed for the theater, including ballet costumes for La Scala and for Béjart's Ballet of the 20th Century. "Signatures," a retrospective exhibit celebrating 15 years of his work was mounted at the Fashion Institute of Technology in November 1992.

Versace's 1997 murder snatched a vital force from the fashion world. His business empire, however, has survived and flourished through the efforts of the family team he had formed, under the creative direction of his sister Donatella. Versace boutiques around the world sell women's and men's clothing, accessories, knits, leathers, and furs; there are fragrances for both men and women.

Left, an example of suave tailoring; Versace and bride (below), 1994. Right, from 1985. *Also see Color Plate 1.*

Viktor & Rolf

Born Viktor Horsting, May 27, 1969
Rolf Snoeren, December 12, 1969

Graduates of the Academy of the Arts in Arnhem, The Netherlands, where they studied in the Fashion Department from 1988 to 1992, Horsting and Snoeren gained their first attention in 1993 as winners of the prestigious Festival of Hyères Young Designers Award (Salon Européen des Jeunes Stylistes).

In the Paris couture showings of January 1998, the first Viktor & Rolf showing featured an "atomic bomb" evening dress collection inspired by mushroom clouds and heralded the arrival of two young designers of abundant talent and a gift for attracting press attention.

From Viktor & Rolf, Spring/Summer 2002.

While equally pressworthy, subsequent showings have earned them a solid reputation for clothes that are not only imaginative but also wearable. After five couture collections, the designers decided to concentrate on ready-to-wear, which they began showing in March 2000.

Viktor & Rolf designs are sold in such avant garde stores as Barneys in New York and have been featured in museum and gallery exhibitions in cities as far flung as New York, Tokyo, Groningen, The Netherlands, Yokohama, and Paris. In April 2002 the pair, who once created a "virtual" perfume in a flacon without an opening, announced an agreement for a fragrance scheduled to appear in 2005.

Madeleine Vionnet

Born Aubervilliers, France, 1876
Died Paris, France, March 2, 1975
Awards *Légion d'honneur, 1929*

One of the towering figures of 20th century couture, Vionnet still influences us. Her bias technique, her cowl and halter necklines, and her use of pleating are part of the designer's vocabulary.

The daughter of a gendarme, she began her apprenticeship when she was twelve and at sixteen was working with a successful dressmaker called Vincent. By the age of nineteen she had married, had a child who died, and was divorced. At twenty she went to London, where she stayed five years, working first in a tailor's workroom and then for CALLOT SOEURS. She returned to Callot Soeurs in Paris, working closely with one of the sisters, Mme. Gerber, for whom she made *toiles* and whom she considered even greater than POIRET. In 1907 she moved to Doucet and in 1912 opened her own house, which closed during World War I. She reopened in 1918 on the avenue Montaigne, closed for good in 1940.

Even while working for others, Vionnet had advanced ideas not always acceptable to conservative clients. She eliminated high, boned collars from dresses and blouses, and claimed to have eliminated corsets before Poiret. One of couture's greatest technicians, she invented the modern use of the bias cut, producing dresses so supple they eliminated the need for fastenings of any kind. Without the aid of placket openings, they could be slipped on over the head to fall back into shape on the body.

Favorite Vionnet designs, sketched for *Women's Wear Daily* in 1959 by Alex Rakoff, in collaboration with the designer.

For even more suppleness, seams were often stitched with fagotting.

She did not sketch, but instead draped, cut, and pinned directly on the figure. For this purpose she used a small-scaled wooden mannequin with articulated joints. Designs were later translated into full-size *toiles*, then into the final material. Most probably she chose this method for convenience. It is doubtful she could have achieved her effects as economically or with as little physical effort by any other means.

Vionnet introduced crêpe de Chine, previously confined to linings, as a fabric suitable for fashion; she transformed Greek and medieval inspirations into completely modern clothes, graceful and sensuous. She did not allow herself to become set in her fashion ways and it is said that in 1934 she scrapped her nearly finished collection when she realized it was out of step with the new romantic mood, completing an entirely new one in two weeks to show on the scheduled date.

Many designers trained with her. Her assistant for years was Marcelle Chaumont, who later opened her own house. Others included Mad Maltezos of the house of Mad Carpentier, and Jacques Griffe. A person of complete integrity, Vionnet was the implacable enemy of copyists and style pirates. Her motto was, "To copy is to steal."

Sketches made for *Women's Wear Daily* in 1969 with Vionnet's input.

1912 1913 1918-19 1920

1931 1931 1936 1939

Roger Vivier

Born Paris, France, 1908
Died Toulouse, France, October 1, 1998
Awards Neiman Marcus Award, 1961

Roger Vivier worked at his craft for over 60 years, from the 1930s when he opened a little workshop in Paris in the Place Vendôme, until his death at age ninety. To prepare for his métier, he studied drawing and sculpture at L'École des Beaux-Arts and apprenticed at a shoe factory owned by a relative. His shoes—lighthearted and with a spirited sense of fantasy—had a strong structural foundation traceable to his training in sculpture.

Vivier's talent was first recognized by Elsa Schiaparelli in 1937, when she commissioned him to design shoes for a collection. It was at that time that he opened his first boutique, developing a devoted celebrity following that ranged from Princess Margaret and Princess Grace to Elizabeth Taylor, Josephine Baker, and the Rothschilds. He came to the United States in the late 1930s and became associated with American shoe designer Herman Delman, working with him until 1955 and again from 1992 to 1994. The shoes were sold at fine U.S. retailers such as Bergdorf Goodman and Neiman Marcus.

From 1953 through 1963, Vivier was associated with Christian Dior, with whom he developed the first ready-to-wear designer label shoes, "Christian Dior created by Roger Vivier." During his time with Dior, he produced a myriad exquisite evening shoes—always with refined, streamlined silhouettes, frequently exuberantly, extravagantly, jeweled and embroidered. After Dior's death in 1957 he collaborated for many years with Yves Saint Laurent and also worked with a number of other top couturiers, including Balenciaga, Courrèges, Ungaro, Grès, and Nina Ricci.

In 1963 he again opened a salon, this time across from Dior, where Marlene Dietrich reportedly visited nearly every day and where it was not unusual for a fitting for a pair of shoes to take two hours. In 1974 he left Paris for a castle in the Dordogne region of France, where he continued to design shoes, this time for the Japanese market.

Vivier shoes are included in collections at the Metropolitan Museum of Art in New York and in Paris at both the Musée de la Mode et du Costume and the Musée des Arts de la Mode.

Diane Von Furstenberg

Born Brussels, Belgium, December 31, 1946

Von Furstenberg has had at least three, perhaps four separate fashion careers. She started in 1971 with moderately priced dresses of lightweight jersey, had her own custom shop for a few years on Fifth Avenue, continued with the Diane Von Furstenberg Studio and direct TV selling on QVC, and in 1997 was back in the mid-range dress business with an updated version of her wrap dress.

Educated in Spain, England, and Switzerland, Von Furstenberg took a degree in economics from the University of Geneva, moved to the United States in 1969. When she saw a need for dresses that were affordable, comfortable, and fashionable, she decided to try designing. Her first patterns were cut on her dining table, shipped to a friend in Italy to be made up. In 1971, she packed her first samples in a suitcase and started showing them to store buyers. The jersey wrap dress with surplice top and long sleeves was an immediate success and made her name. This is the dress Von Furstenberg says taught her three essential F's in designing for women. "It's flattering, feminine and, above all, functional." A perfume followed, a cosmetics line and shop, home furnishings, and the usual licenses, from eyewear to luggage.

She left the moderate-price dress market in 1977, re-entered it briefly in 1985 with a collection based on her signature wrap dress. This was followed by her retailing venture and her design-and-marketing studio and involvement with televised home shopping. In 1994 she was appointed Creative Planning Director for Q2, QVC's weekend channel. Her 1997 reincarnation was in collaboration with her daughter-in-law, Alexandra Miller Von Furstenberg, resulting in a redesign of the famous wrap dress in silk jersey with a new body, shorter length, and subtler details, as part of a complete collection of modern, wearable, affordable clothes that appeal to active, vital women of any age.

Men's and women's wear by Von Furstenberg, 1974 (above); design from Spring/Summer 2003 (right).

W

Vera Wang

Junya Watanabe

Chester Weinberg

John Weitz

Stuart Weitzman

Vivienne Westwood

Matthew Williamson

Workers for Freedom

Charles Frederick Worth

Vera Wang

Born New York City, ca. 1950

After a Lifetime focused on fashion—childhood dancer, teenage skating star who designed her own competition costumes, sixteen-year *Vogue* editor, design director for accessories at RALPH LAUREN—Vera Wang discovered her vocation. She was getting married and could find nothing to wear this side of Paris couture. So in 1990 she moved into this fashion dead spot and established her own bridal business. Today

her name is practically synonymous with the words Wedding Dress.

The Wang style is sleek, modern, sophisticated—the opposite of the sugar-puff dress that makes a bride look like the figure on top of the wedding cake. She has definite ideas about what works: weightless clothes, armholes that add grace, and enough internal support to allow a woman to feel secure while being totally comfortable. Evening clothes were a logical extension of her design philosophy and her following of stylish celebrities includes Sharon Stone, Holly Hunter, Meg Ryan, and Jane Fonda.

Her business has expanded into ready-to-wear, furs, and shoes, as well as china and glassware, sheets and towels, eyewear, and, of course, fragrance. In October 2001, *Vera Wang on Weddings* appeared, a coffee-table book containing all you'd ever need to know on the practicalities of getting married.

Vera Wang (left) and evening dress from Spring 2002.

Junya Watanabe

Born Fukushima, Japan, 1961

Awards Mainichi Newspaper Award for New Designer, Tokyo, 1993; Mainichi Newspaper Award, 1999

UPON GRADUATING FROM TOKYO'S BUNKA FASHION INSTITUTE in 1984, Watanabe went to work at Comme des Garçons, first as a pattern maker, then as a designer of the knitwear, then of the men's collection. As a protégé of REI KAWAKUBO, he has gone on to design under his own name and since 1994 has shown twice a year in Paris, including both tailored clothing and sportswear for men, and blouses, dresses, outerwear, and accessories for women.

In style, he favors a mixture of dark and bright colors, natural shoulders, and such details as extra-long sleeves and whimsically placed pockets, very much in the Kawakubo tradition but with everything—layering, textures, colors—somewhat exaggerated. A master technician, he is often characterized as part of "techno couture," innovative and cutting-edge, but his clothes are far from harsh and entirely unrelated to science fiction.

Chester Weinberg

Born New York City, September 23, 1930

Died New York City, April 24, 1985

Awards Coty American Fashion Critics' Award "Winnie," 1970 · Maison Blanche "Rex" Award, New Orleans, 1972

WEINBERG BUILT HIS REPUTATION ON simple, elegant designs, sophisticated and classic, never exaggerated or overpowering. They were always marked by beautiful fabrics, which were his passion. "Fabrics set the whole mood of my collection. I cannot design a dress until I know what the fabric will be."

A 1951 graduate of Parsons School of Design, Weinberg went on to earn a B.S. degree in art education from New York University, studying at night while working as a sketcher during the day. After graduation, he worked for a number of better dress houses before opening his own business in 1966. From 1977 till 1981 his company was a division of Jones Apparel Group, and when it closed he went to work for Calvin Klein Jeans as design director. He began teaching at Parsons in 1954 and continued to do so until the year before his death.

John Weitz

Born Berlin, Germany, May 25, 1923
Died Bridgehampton, New York, October 3, 2002
Awards Coty American Fashion Critics' Award *Special Award for Men's Wear*, 1974

By John Weitz, 1994.

weitz is considered a pioneer of practical, modern clothes for sports and informal living. He introduced women's sports clothes with a men's wear look in the 1950s, showed pants for town wear, and in the 1960s presented "ready-to-wear couture," where the design could be chosen from sketches and swatches and made up to order. For men, he produced Contour Clothes inspired by jeans, cowboy jackets, and fatigue coveralls. He was one of the first U.S. designers to show both men's and women's wear, and one of the first to license his work worldwide.

Educated in England, Weitz apprenticed in Paris at MOLYNEUX. He arrived in the United States shortly before Pearl Harbor, and served in U.S. Army Intelligence. After the war he showed his designs—women's sportswear based on men's clothes—to Dorothy Shaver, President of Lord & Taylor, who helped him get started in business. He began licensing in 1954, began his men's wear business in 1964. He has also designed accessories, among them watches, scarves, and jewelry.

A man of many interests, Weitz was a licensed racing driver and designed a two-seater aluminum sports car, the X600. His portrait photographs have been shown at the Museum of the City of New York.

Stuart Weitzman

Born Long Island, New York, July 29, 1941
Awards Ernst and Young *Entrepreneur of the Year,* Footwear News *Hall of Fame,*
Footwear Plus *Designer of the Year, category Ladies Dress Shoes*

whiLe he graduated from wharton school of finance, Weitzman had shoes in his blood—his father was a shoe manufacturer—and following graduation he went into the family business. As an apprentice working beside traditional craftsmen, he learned every step of production and became a skilled patternmaker with a broad understanding of footwear engineering.

Weitzman designs range from the highest-heeled stilettos in exotic materials—lace, silk, brocade, even platinum or 24 karat gold—to shoes made of cork or bamboo, and, of course, calfskin. Boots, moccasins, and even sneakers are part of his vocabulary, in an unusually wide range of over 50 sizes. His shoes are the choice of celebrities from Calista Flockhart to Laura Bush—perhaps because he believes so strongly that "a beautiful shoe is useless unless it feels as wonderful as it looks." He has opened retail shops in selected cities across the country and in Zurich, Switzerland.

Stuart Weitzman, 2002.

W

Vivienne Westwood

Born Tintwhistle, England, 1941

westwood became involved in fashion around 1970 through her association with Malcolm McLaren of The Sex Pistols. At the time she was earning her living as a teacher, having left Harrow Art School after only one term. She went into business with McLaren and

Left, Westwood bustle dress, 1994; the designer (top); Dandy-inspired pantsuit, 1994 (bottom).

together they owned a London shop in King's Road and another in London's West End.

Westwood belongs to the anti-fashion branch of design exemplified by Comme des Garçons, although her approach is totally different. Sometimes beautiful, sometimes ridiculous, never dull, her clothes show a fierce rejection of polite standards of dress. They are often inspired by London street life with wild swings in influences—from the leather and rubber fetishism, Punk Rock, and S & M of the 1970s, to the New Romanticism and Pirate looks of the early 1980s. For Fall 1994, she showed bustles, placing fanny pillows under just about everything and proclaiming the rear to be the new erogenous zone. Despite poor finances, she has regularly shown in Paris, and her anarchic view of dressing has had a considerable influence on other designers, both in England and around the world.

She has also had a professorship in design at the University of Berlin, and in June 2001 took an exhibition of her students' work to be shown in Paris. Her designs, both the earliest and the most recent, were shown in the "London Fashion" exhibition at the Fashion Institute of Technology in 2001–2002.

Matthew Williamson

Born Manchester, England, October 23, 1971
Awards Elle Magazine *Young Designer of the Year*

After college in Manchester, Williamson attended London's Central St. Martin's College of Art and Design, graduating in 1996. Between then and 1998, he worked briefly for ZANDRA RHODES and Monsoon and traveled to India to set up his business. He showed his first collection under his own label in September 1997.

In a small, focused collection he presents modern, easy pieces, colorful and intricately detailed, appealing to an adventurous customer confident of her taste, Madonna and Sarah Jessica Parker, for example. For Spring 2002 Williamson introduced a small group of separates for men in the same spirit as his women's clothes, and a range of scented candles. His clothes and the candles can be found at specialty stores such as Henri Bendel, Barneys, and Kirna Zabête in New York. He brought his Fall/Winter 2002 collection to New York and showed during New York Fashion Week.

Workers for Freedom

Born Graham Fraser & Richard Nott; both in 1948
Awards British Fashion Council *Designer of the Year*, 1989

The partners opened their business in a tiny shop in London in 1986 with a small stake and the intention of producing modern, wearable clothes. Fraser was a merchandise manager at Liberty of London; Nott, a former assistant to VALENTINO, was a lecturer at Kingston Polytechnic, where he received his training.

They had no plans to wholesale but were immediately besieged by retailers including Henri Bendel and Saks Fifth Avenue. From the beginning they've been somewhat out of the mainstream. They were in the vanguard in the use of embroidery and with ethnic looks and continued to lead the way, evolving from the wildness of 1980s London into a more refined view of easy, softly tailored clothes that were both delicate and feminine, sexy and sophisticated. Their early designs were included in the 2001 "London Fashion" exhibition of the Fashion Institute of Technology.

Above, sexy lady look, 1990; Graham Fraser (left in photo) and Richard Nott, 1989 (right).

Charles Frederick Worth

Born Bourne, Lincolnshire, England October 13, 1825
Died Paris, France, March 10, 1895

The founder of the house that became the world's longest-running fashion dynasty got his first job when he was just eleven and worked for a number of London drapers (a dealer in cloth or clothing) before leaving for Paris in 1845. He took a job with a shop selling fabrics, shawls, and mantles, and persuaded the firm to open a department of made-up dress models, which he designed. He was the first to present clothes on live mannequins, using his young French wife as a model. In 1858 he opened his own couture house on the rue de la Paix, which closed in 1870 at the outset of the Franco-Prussian War. Reestablished in 1874, Maison Worth maintained its fashion leadership for another eighty years.

Worth was court dressmaker to Empress Eugénie of France and to Empress Elizabeth of Austria. He dressed the ladies of European courts and society women of Europe and America. A virtual fashion dictator, he required his customers, except for Eugénie and her court, to come to him instead of attending them in their homes as had been the custom. He was an excellent businessman, was the first couturier to sell models to be copied in England and America, and was also widely copied by others without his permission. He enjoyed his success and lived in the grand manner.

Worth designs were known for their opulence and lavish use of fabrics, elaborate ornamentation of frills, ribbons, lace, braid, and tassels, which can strike the modern eye as suffocating excess. He is held responsible for the collapsi-

Left, unable to draw, Worth sketched his designs on pre-drawn stock figures. Below left, Worth, ca. 1864. Above, court dress and train, circa 1888, created for the great-great-granddaughter of George Washington' sister. Sold at Doyle New York for $101,500. A world auction record for an antique dress.

ble steel frame for crinolines and then for abolishing crinolines in 1867. Whether he actually invented it or not, he certainly exploited the crinoline to the utmost, as it reached its most extravagant dimensions during the second Empire and disappeared when the Empire collapsed. Worth promoted the use of French-made textiles, and is said to have invented the princess-style dress, court mantles hung from the shoulders, and the ancestor of the tailor-made suit for women. He was influenced by the paintings of Van Dyck, Gainsborough, and Velasquez.

After his death, the House of Worth continued under the leadership of his sons, Jean-Philippe and Gaston, then of his grandson, Jean-Charles, and finally of his great-grandsons, Roger and Maurice. When Roger retired in 1952, Maurice took over and in 1954 sold the house to PAQUIN. A London wholesale house continued under the Worth name until the 1970s. Parfums Worth was established in 1900, continues today with *Je Reviens* the best-known fragrance.

In 2001, a Worth court gown with train sold at auction in New York for $101,500, a world auction record. It had been worn by Elizabeth Washington Lewis, the great-great-granddaughter of George Washington's sister.

Y-Z

Yohji Yamamoto
Yeohlee
Zang Toi
Zoran

Yohji Yamamoto

Born Yokohama, Japan, ca. 1943

yamamoto is a member of the Japanese avant-garde that includes REI KAWAKUBO and ISSEY MIYAKE. Although often called a "designers' designer," he is not as widely famous as many of his contemporaries, nor as influential, possibly because his ideas are technically complicated and hard to copy. One of the rare true originals, he experiments with technological fabrics such as neoprene, blending them with active sports looks in his own color palette and in his own dimensions. Oversize clothes and a playful diversity of textures are his signature, along with asymmetrical hems and collars, holes, and torn edges. He likes surprise details: an unexpected pocket, a lapel that turns into a long, flowing shawl, and a new placement of buttons.

A graduate of Keio University, he studied fashion at Tokyo's Bunka Fashion Institute under Chie Kolke, who had attended L'École de la Chambre Syndicale de la Couture Parisienne in Paris with SAINT LAURENT. From 1966 to 1968 he followed the standard course, studying all aspects of the clothing industry; by 1972 he had his own company. He showed his first collection in Tokyo in 1976. In 1981 he established himself in France with a boutique in Paris, and since then has shown his designs for both men and women at the Paris *prêt-à-porter* collections.

Above, Yohji Yamamoto and from Spring 2002 (right).

Yeohlee

Born Yeohlee Teng; Penang, Malaysia, ca. 1955

AT THE RIPE OLD AGE of nine, Yeohlee talked her mother into letting her enroll in a pattern making class. There was no ready-to-wear in Malaysia—clothes were made at home or by seamstresses and tailors—and she was dissatisfied with what her mother produced from English patterns. At eighteen, she went to New York to study at Parsons School of Design and two years later sold her first five-piece collection to Henri Bendel. She founded her own company in 1981.

Her work is spare, often dramatic in impact, characterized by clear lines and geometric forms. The clothes are also comfortable and flattering, cut to allow the wearer to move with easy elegance. Yeohlee designs a complete collection but is most admired for her coats, both long and short. Working in the better price range, she feels that the timeless quality of the design, combined with superior fabrics and workmanship, makes her clothes long-term investments. They have attracted a loyal following.

With their purity of form and distinct vision, Yeohlee's designs have been chosen for numerous exhibits, including shows at the Museum of the City of New York and the Massachusetts Institute of Technology, where they were featured with such designers as ARMANI, FERRÉ, MONTANA, and MIYAKE. They have also been shown at the Victoria and Albert in London and at the Museum of Fashion in Paris, and are in the permanent costume collection of the Metropolitan Museum of Art.

In 2001 she was working on a book exploring the parallels between architecture and clothing design, and in October of that year was honored by a one-woman show at New York's Fashion Institute of Technology.

Zang Toi

Born Malaysia, June 11, 1961

zang toi, the seventh child of a grocer, left Malaysia for Canada in 1980, moved on to New York City a year later intending to study painting or interior design. Instead, he switched to fashion, and while at Parsons School of Design went to work for Mary Jane Marcasiano. He graduated from Parsons in 1983 and stayed on with Marcasiano for five years, concentrating on production. Following freelance work at Shamask, he opened his own business in 1989.

Designing with a light touch, Zang Toi combines an Oriental sense of color and a taste for exotic details with the forthright flair of American sportswear. The result is a fresh twist for classic looks. The clothes are young and spirited, with a sophisticated attitude, while his preference for fabrics such as cashmere and silk and his innate sense of fantasy also means they are fashion of unabashed luxury.

Zang Toi at the 2002 CFDA Awards (above), and evening gown, Spring/ Summer 2003 (right).

Zoran

Born Belgrade, Yugoslavia, 1947

zoran beLongs to the fashion minimalists, confining himself to a few pure shapes, always in the most expensive, most luxurious fabrics. He studied architecture in Belgrade, moved to New York in 1971. His first fashion recognition came in 1977, when his designs were bought by Henri Bendel.

The early collections were based on squares and rectangles in silk crêpe de Chine, cashmere, and other luxurious fabrics. The designs have evolved from there, retaining their purity and luxury. Zoran works in a limited color range, usually black, gray, white, ivory, and red. It is a relaxed look, sophisticated and utterly simple, a perfection of understatement by a master of proportion and balance. He prefers not to use buttons and zippers and as far as possible avoids any extraneous detail. Because his customers lead a highly mobile life, he has produced a jet-pack collection of ten pieces that fit into a small bag so that a woman can look casual and glamorous wherever her travels take her. At a less costly level, Zoran has made daytime clothes in cotton knit, although evenings are still devoted to satin, velvet, and cashmere. Inevitably, his creations are for women of sophisticated tastes and well-filled bank accounts. With a devoted clientele and an independent attitude, Zoran does not hew to a rigid schedule of twice-yearly showings but shows his collections at such times as the spirit moves him.

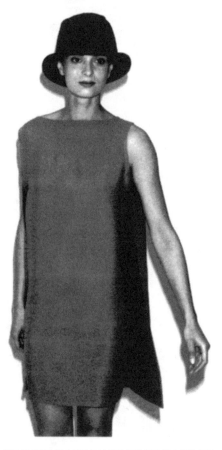

Zoran and a typically spare design from 1991.

The Stylemakers

Antonio

Richard Avedon

Cecil Beaton

Christian Bérard

Edna Woolman Chase

Bill Cunningham

Louise Dahl-Wolfe

Jessica Daves

Baron Adolf de Meyer

Carrie Donovan

Eric

Erté

Toni Frissel

Horst P. Horst

George Hoyningen-Huene

Man Ray

Martin Munkacsi

Irving Penn

Virginia Pope

Carmel Snow

Edward Steichen

Diana Vreeland

Antonio

Born Antonio Lopez; Puerto Rico, 1943
Died Los Angeles, California, March 17, 1987

Antonio was an illustrator of protean talent, sensitive to every social shift and art movement, changing styles innumerable times over his 24-year career. At the start, his work was elegant and relatively conventional fashion illustration, but by 1965 Pop Art had become the essence of his drawings, followed by Surrealism and by monumental figures clearly inspired by French artist, Fernand Léger. He later moved to a more fluid style, but each period was never less than flamboyant, dramatic in its use of black and white or color. In addition to women's and men's fashion, he also brought his unique point of view to bear on children's clothes.

When his family moved to New York, Antonio was nine years old but already committed to art—even as a very small child he would sketch little dresses to please his mother, a dressmaker. He attended the High School of Industrial Art (now the High School of Art and Design) and the Fashion Institute of Technology, from which he dropped out at nineteen to join *Women's Wear Daily.* He left *WWD* after only four months when he was refused permission to freelance and began working for *The New York Times.* During the 1960s he traveled back and forth to Europe working for *Elle* and *British Vogue* among others, eventually spending so much time in Europe that at the end of the decade he decided to move to Paris. Seven years later he moved back to New York. Other publications he worked for were *Harper's Bazaar, Vogue,* and *Interview.*

In 1964, Antonio undertook what became a five-year project, recording the life work of CHARLES JAMES under the direct supervision of the designer. He also was a molder and maker of fashion models, advising them on makeup and hairstyles to fit his ideas of their best look. He became interested in education and gave lectures and workshops to students of fashion illustration in the United States and the Dominican Republic. A retrospective of his work, 1963 to 1987, was mounted at F.I.T. in 1988.

Richard Avedon

Born New York City, May 15, 1923
Awards (partial list) Art Directors Show highest achievement medal, 1950 · Pratt Institute citation of dedication to fashion photography, 1976 · Art Directors Club Hall of Fame, 1982 · Council of Fashion Designers of America (CFDA) *Lifetime Achievement Award,* 1989

The son of a retail store owner, Avedon received his first photographic training in the merchant marine. He took a class in experimental photography at the New School for Social Research, taught by Alexey Brodovitch, art director of *Harper's Bazaar,* and in 1945 joined the staff of the magazine. Thus began his long and distinguished career in fashion and commercial photography and an association with *Harper's Bazaar* that endured for twenty years. During that time he had non-fashion assignments from other publications, including *Theatre Arts.* In 1966 he moved to *Vogue,* remaining there until 1990.

His fashion photography, notable for its sense of style, freedom, and drama, captured the tone of the 1960s and recorded the sexual revolution. He took the action photography of MARTIN MUNKACSI to a more sophisticated level, working in the studio, and, for his simulated photojournalism, on location. He also did photo-collages using the illustrations of Katerina Danzinger, was a visual consultant on the Fred Astaire film, *Funny Face,* and has been a TV consultant. Since leaving *Vogue,* he has been staff photographer at *The New Yorker,* their first, providing them with aggressively anti-glamour portraits. One-man shows of his work have been held at, among other venues, the Museum of Modern Art in 1975, the Metropolitan Museum of Art in 1978 and 2002, and in 1994 at the Whitney Museum. This last was a retrospective placing emphasis on his non-fashion work, which presumably, he considered more serious than the fashion.

Cecil Beaton

Born London, England, January 14, 1904
Died Broad Chalke, Wiltshire, England, January 18, 1980
Awards Antionette Perry (Tony) Award: *Quadrille,* 1955; *My Fair Lady,* 1957; *Coco,* 1970. Neiman Marcus Award, 1956 · Commander of the British Empire (C.B.E.), 1957 · Motion Picture Academy Award: *Gigi,* 1958; *My Fair Lady* (sets and costumes), 1965. *Légion d'Honneur,* 1960

Photographer, artist, costume and set designer, writer, Beaton was educated at Harrow and at Cambridge University. In 1928 he began a long affiliation with *Vogue* magazine, where his first contributions were spidery sketches, caricatures of well-known London actresses, and drawings of clothes worn at society parties; photographs appeared later. In her memoirs, Edna Woolman Chase of *Vogue* describes him at their first meeting as "...tall, slender, swaying like a reed, blond, and very young..." He gave an impression that was "an odd combination of airiness and assurance." And later, "What I like best is his debunking attitude toward life and his ability for hard work." In photography he did both fashion and portraiture, and became the favored photographer of the British royal family. During World War II, he photographed for the Ministry of Information, traveling to North Africa, Burma, and China.

Beginning in 1935, Beaton designed scenery and costumes for ballet, opera, and theatrical productions in both London and New York. Among his credits: *Lady Windermere's Fan, Quadrille, The Grass Harp,* and *The School for Scandal* (Comédie Française). He did the costumes for the New York, London, and film productions of *My Fair Lady,* costumes for the films *Gigi* and *The Doctor's Dilemma.* He also designed hotel lobbies and club interiors.

A prolific writer and diarist, Beaton published many books, illustrating them and those of others with drawings and photographs. He was knighted by Queen Elizabeth II in 1972. In 1975 he suffered a stroke, which left him partially paralyzed, but he learned to paint and take photographs with his left hand. From 1977 until his death, he lived in semi-retirement at his house in Wiltshire.

Christian Bérard

Born Paris, France, 1902
Died Paris, France, 1949

Bérard's fashion reputation is based largely on his work for *Vogue* in the 1930s but as artist, decorator, costume designer, his life was intertwined with the creative lives of the Paris of his time and his influence extended far beyond his illustrations. In great demand for comments and suggestions as well as technical advice, he was a familiar figure in creative circles, rumpled, disheveled, and not always entirely clean, a marked contrast to the refinement and beauty of his work.

Jean Cocteau was a close friend and Bérard, recognized as one of the great stage designers of his time in the French theater, designed many of Cocteau's productions, both scenery and costumes, from the first *La Voix Humaine* (1930) to *La Folle de Chaillot* (1949). In addition, he designed for the Comédie Française and also collaborated with actor-producer Louis Jouvet, with whom he was working at the time of his death.

Edna Woolman Chase

Born Asbury Park, New Jersey, March 14, 1877
Died Locust Valley, New York, March 20, 1957
Awards *Légion d'Honneur*, 1935 · Neiman Marcus
Award, 1940

The child of divorced parents, Edna was raised by her Quaker grandparents, whose principles and plain style of dress were to prove a lasting influence. In 1895, when she was eighteen, she went to work in the Circulation Department of *Vogue,* then just two years old, with a salary of $10 a week. She was to spend 56 years at *Vogue,* 37 of them as editor.

She fell in love with the magazine immediately. As she was enthusiastic, hard-working, and willing to take on any and all chores, she acquired more and more responsibility. By 1911 she was the equivalent of managing editor. Her name first appeared on the masthead as editor in February 1914. British and French *Vogue* were born in 1916 and 1920 respectively; Mrs. Chase was editor-in-chief of all three editions. During World War I she began to feature American designers in *Vogue's* pages, and is credited with originating the modern fashion show in 1914 when *Vogue* produced a benefit "Fashion Fête" sponsored by prominent society women.

During her tenure, *Vogue* survived two world wars, a depression, and tremendous social changes. With Condé Nast, who bought it in 1909, she helped shape the magazine according to her own strong sense of propriety and high standards of professionalism. She suffered the second-rate badly, respected talent and industriousness; she herself wrote directly to the point. Taste, business ability, and a capacity for hard work brought her to the top of her profession and kept her there for an amazing time span. She retired as editor-in-chief in 1952 and became chairman of the editorial board. Her requirements for success are still worth considering by those thinking of a career in fashion. They were: taste, sound judgment, and experience—the training and knowledge gained from actually working in a business, which she valued above formal course-taking.

She was married to and divorced from Francis Dane Chase and had one child, the writer and actress Ilka Chase. A second marriage in 1921 to Richard Newton ended with his death in 1950.

Bill Cunningham

Born Boston, Massachusetts, ca. 1929
Awards Council of Fashion Designers of America (CFDA)
Eugenia Sheppard Award for Fashion Journalism, 1993

A familiar New York figure in his beret, corduroys, and parka, camera unobtrusively at the ready, Bill Cunningham observes and records fashion, not as worn on the runway, but as it appears in the real world on real people. In fair weather or foul, from one of his favorite posts at 57th Street and Fifth Avenue, in SoHo, or at the Green Market or flea market, he catches the passing scene for his "On the Street" column in the Sunday *New York Times;* his second feature, "Evening Hours," chronicles benefits, art show openings, and other social events.

Bill Cunningham's early attraction to fashion was totally alien to his conservative New England background. In Boston he worked after school at Bonwit Teller, and when he moved to New York after graduation, went to work for Nona Park and Sophie Shonnard in their Chez Ninon boutique at the New York Bonwit's. It was there he first saw the fashionable women who later became his photographic subjects. On his own time he made masks and headdresses for ladies attending the then-popular masked balls, and later opened his own hat shop called William J., backed by Rebecca Harkness, the noted ballet patron. Drafted into the Army, he was stationed in the South of France and was able to join his former employers, Nona and Sophie, in Paris when they were there shopping for their clients.

Once out of the Army he was hired by *Women's Wear Daily's* John Fairchild to write a twice-weekly column, leaving after nine months to write about fashion for the *Chicago Tribune.* A friend, the illustrator ANTONIO, suggested that he use a camera to make notes, a move that opened his world and was the beginning of a new career. In the mid-70s, he began freelancing at *The New York Times* and in 1993 went on staff. To attract his photographic attention, a subject must have more than mere perfection, which he finds uninteresting. For him, a person with style must have "something extra. Something so personal—flawless but with a dash."

Louise Dahl-Wolfe

Born San Francisco, California, 1895
Died Allendale, New Jersey, December 13, 1989

ACCOMPLISHED in both fashion and portrait photography, Louise Dahl-Wolfe attended the California School of Design (now San Francisco Institute of Design). Before buying her first camera in 1923, she worked at everything from designing electric signs to decorating. After travels to Europe and Africa, during which she met future husband, Mike Wolfe, she moved to San Francisco, then to the Great Smoky Mountains of Tennessee. Her first published photographs were documentary shots of her Tennessee neighbors, which were bought by Frank Crowninshield and appeared in *Vanity Fair* in 1933.

Dahl-Wolfe's first black-and-white fashion photography appeared in *Harper's Bazaar* in 1936, her first color in 1937; her elegant photographs graced the magazine until 1958. With dramatic lighting and backgrounds ranging from intricate Chinese screens to seamless paper, she caught the essence of individual fashions as simple as a CLAIRE MCCARDELL linen sundress, as structured as a pair of satin ball gowns by CHARLES JAMES. She was the first to use color effectively in fashion photography, driving both the color separators and Art Director Alexey Brodovitch to distraction with her insistence on perfection. Unlike many of her peers, she never considered photography as art but rather as a commercial medium. She left *Harper's Bazaar* after Carmel Snow and Brodovitch resigned, worked for a few months at *Vogue*, then retired to Frenchtown, New Jersey, with her artist husband, who died in 1985.

Jessica Daves

Born Cartersville, Georgia, February 20, 1898
Died New York City, 1974

JESSICA DAVES arrived in NEW YORK in 1921. She worked in the advertising departments of various New York stores, including Saks Fifth Avenue, writing fashion copy and learning about fashion merchandising. In 1933 she went to *Vogue* magazine as fashion merchandising editor, where her ability was spotted by EDNA WOOLMAN CHASE, then editor-in-chief. In 1936 she was made managing editor, and she became editor in 1946. Upon Mrs. Chase's retirement in 1952, Daves became editor-in-chief of American *Vogue*. She was a director of Condé Nast Publications from 1946 until she retired in 1963, served as editorial consultant for a year then worked on specialized books until November 1966.

An accomplished writer and editor, Miss Daves could fix a piece of ailing copy in minutes. She was known for clearheadedness and sound judgment—of all the great fashion editors she was probably the most astute at business. The years of her editorship coincided with a phenomenal growth of the American ready-to-wear industry. She recognized its increasing importance and broadened the magazine's coverage of domestic ready-to-wear, including more moderately priced clothes. Under her direction *Vogue* assumed a more serious tone and ran more articles of intellectual interest than before.

Short and plump, Miss Daves dressed well, but her figure precluded real style. Her manner was warm, and her voice retained charming overtones of her southern origin. In her later years she became rather regal with something of a queen mother effect. She was married to Robert A. Parker, a writer, who died in 1970. They had no children.

Baron Adolf de Meyer

Born 1868
Died Los Angeles, California, 1949

Baron de Meyer is considered the first true fashion photographer, the one who transformed fashion photography from a photographic sideline to a major artistic expression. Born Adolf Meyer-Watson, he was of German extraction, the possessor of a modest fortune sufficient to allow him to circulate in fashionable English circles. He dropped the Watson from his name, gained a Saxon title, and in 1899, married Olga Alberta Caracciolo, the godchild of Edward VII of England and, it was rumored, his illegitimate daughter. The marriage opened society to de Meyer and the couple devoted themselves to the pleasures and pursuits of the English upper crust until the King's death in 1910 made it necessary to earn some money. De Meyer soon established a reputation as a photographer in Paris and London; his early pictures of Diaghilev's Ballets Russes captured the dazzling splendor and drama that so captivated the European avant-garde. In 1913, the imminent onset of World War I persuaded de Meyer and his wife to leave for New York where he went to work for the Condé Nast publications, *Vogue* and *Vanity Fair.* In 1923 he was hired away by Hearst, lured by more money and the opportunity to live and work in Paris, a privilege denied him by Condé Nast; it was a move he later regretted.

De Meyer's primary interest was in creating an ideal of feminine beauty and softness, of luxury and romance. His photographs relied on glamorous backgrounds and elaborate settings, reflecting a life of opulent ease and aristocratic idleness. They embodied the painterly traditions of 19th-century art with their emphasis on glowing light and romantic atmosphere. He employed soft focus, using a lens that was sharp in the center, soft at the edges, and sometimes stretched silk gauze over the lens. He made much use of backlighting, his most famous and influential technique. Many other photographers imitated his approach but failed to achieve the same extravagantly flattering and glamorously snobbish results. His influence declined with the disappearance of the way of life he glorified so brilliantly and with the liberation of women. A new age had begun and he could not move with the times.

Carrie Donovan

Born Carolyn Gertrude Amelia Donovan, Lake Placid, New York, March 22, 1928
Died November 12, 2001

The Last of a Line of fashion editors with larger-than-life fashion personalities that includes DIANA VREELAND and CARMEL SNOW, Donovan had a more than usually varied career that lasted nearly 50 years. Her first ambition was to be a designer and she studied dressmaking at Parsons School of Design in New York, from which she graduated in 1950. Deciding in 1955 that she lacked the necessary talent, she then turned to fashion journalism, working first at *The New York Times* before going to *Vogue* under Mrs. Vreeland. In 1972, when Mrs. Vreeland was fired from the magazine, Donovan moved to *Harper's Bazaar* as fashion editor, leaving in 1976 to become vice president for communications at Bloomingdale's.

Retailing proved not to be her forte and she returned to the *Times* in 1977 as style editor for the *New York Times Magazine.* There she stayed until her retirement in 1995, but she had not lost her love of fashion and wrote a column for *Allure* magazine before undertaking a new career in 1997 as spokesperson for Old Navy. For the store she appeared in newspaper ads and television spots wearing her trademark pearls and oversize black-framed glasses, and thus became a celebrity in the world beyond the small one of fashion, recognized on the street by people of all ages who sometimes saluted her by singing an Old Navy jingle.

Donovan was not content to simply report on the fashion world, she was actively engaged in promoting new talent, introducing designers such as DONNA KARAN and PALOMA PICASSO to her readers and acting as matchmaker between designer and prospective employer. She was instrumental in bringing ELSA PERETTI with her modern jewelry approach to Tiffany, a bastion of tradition. She never learned to use a typewriter (or a computer) and always wrote her copy by hand. With her enthusiasm and outgoing personality, she had a wide circle of friends in the fashion community and even those who knew her only slightly would find their world a little less colorful with her passing.

Eric

Born Carl Erickson, Joliet, Illinois, 1891
Died 1958

The son of Swedish immigrants, Eric studied at the Art Institute of Chicago before heading for Paris to become a painter. After he married a fashion artist on the staff of French *Vogue,* his seemingly off-hand fashion sketches began appearing in *Vogue's* pages. There, during the 1930s and 1940s he influenced fashionable life with his elegant watercolors of chic, super-slim women, often shown from the back, and set against a background of elegant restaurants, exclusive resorts, and other haunts of the rich and famous. In her book, *In My Fashion,* the fashion editor Bettina Ballard wrote, "His drawings over the years evoked a promise of beauty that photographs could never equal." The sketches are still coveted by collectors.

Erté

Born Romain de Tirtoff, St. Petersburg, Russia,
   November 10, 1892
Died Paris, France, April 21, 1990

The son of an admiral in the Russian Imperial Navy, Erté studied painting in Russia, went to Paris in 1912 to study at Académie Julian. He took a new name for himself from the French pronunciation of his initials R.T. (air-tay), got a job sketching for PAUL POIRET, went on to design for opera and theater, creating costumes for such luminaries as the opera soprano Mary Garden.

From 1914 into the 1930s, he produced illustrations and covers for various magazines, including *Harper's Bazaar.* He designed for the Folies Bergère, came to the United States in the 1920s to work for Ziegfeld and other impresarios, and tried Hollywood briefly in 1925. There he created beautiful and esoteric costumes for several silent films, including *The Mystic, Ben Hur,* and King Vidor's *La Boheme,* but impatient with financial restrictions placed on him, returned to Paris after eight months.

In 1967, to celebrate his eightieth birthday, Erté selected over a hundred of his designs for clothes, jewelry, and accessories, to be shown in London and at the Grosvenor Gallery in New York. The exhibition contained some of the most elegant and individual designs of the Art Deco period. The New York exhibition was bought in its entirety by the Metropolitan Museum of Art.

Toni Frissell

Born New York City, March 10, 1907
Died Saint James, New York, May 17, 1988

Before taking up photography, Toni Frissell worked for a painter and trained as an actress; she also worked in the advertising department of Stern Brothers and in 1929 went to work for *Vogue* as a caption writer. She had dabbled in photography but did not take it seriously until after the death of her brother, a documentary filmmaker, in an accident on location. It was at *Vogue* that she took her first fashion photographs in the informal style described by the magazine as "sunlit, windblown records of action outdoors." Outdoor work was her specialty: she would tilt her camera to achieve dramatic diagonals, and would often shoot from below with a short-focus lens to elongate the model's body. After World War II, Frissell did some location work but soon abandoned fashion. She worked for *Sports Illustrated* during its first four years and undertook assignments for *Life* and *Look,* as well as some documentary projects.

Horst P. Horst

Born Horst Paul Albert Bohrman, Weissenfels-an-der-Saale, Germany, August 14, 1906
Died Palm Beach Gardens, Florida, November 18, 1999

Horst studied furniture design with Walter Gropius at the School for Applied Arts in Hamburg, went to Paris in 1930 to study architecture with Le Corbusier. In Paris he met and modeled for HOYNINGEN-HUENE, who became a life-long friend, and took up photography himself. He photographed for French *Vogue,* then was brought to New York to work for American *Vogue.* He joined the Army during World War II, working as a photographer. Because his name, Bohrmann, was too close that of Hitler's close associate, he had it changed legally.

At the time Horst went to work for the magazine, *Vogue* publisher Condé Nast exerted rigid control over photography, demanding that all work be done on large-format studio cameras. Sets were elaborate and each detail was expected to be perfect, resulting in refined, but static images. Despite these limitations, Horst introduced energy into his photographs through dramatic lighting and camera angles, and managed to take risks, giving an edge to the required elegance. With the acceptance of smaller cameras he moved outdoors and brought action into his shots. His influences include both HOYNINGEN-HUENE and EDWARD STEICHEN, although he considered Steichen better at portraits than at fashion. In addition to fashion, he also photographed interiors for *Vogue.* His last fashion commission for the magazine was in 1992.

George Hoyningen-Huene

Born St. Petersburg, Russia, 1900
Died Los Angeles, California, 1968

Baron George Hoyningen-Huene was the son of the chief equerry to the Tsar; his mother was the daughter of a former American ambassador to Russia. His family fled the Russian Revolution, ending up in London. During World War I he served with the British, after the war moved to Paris where he supported himself with odd jobs, including work as an extra in the infant movie industry. It was there that he was able to observe and learn lighting techniques that were the basis for his later photographic work. He worked as a sketch artist in his sister's dressmaking firm, in 1925 was designing and preparing backgrounds in the photo studios of French *Vogue,* and by 1926 was taking photographs. He was discovered by Mainbocher, then the magazine's editor, became chief photographer, was brought to New York briefly, then returned to Paris. In 1935 he moved to New York and went to work for *Harper's Bazaar.* He lost interest in fashion during the 1940s, moved to Los Angeles in 1946 and taught photography at Art Center School. He was also color consultant to George Cukor. He traveled widely, taking what he called "archeological photographs" in Greece, Egypt, and Mexico, and subsequently published them in books.

At the start of his career, Hoyningen-Huene was influenced by Steichen but rapidly developed his own style. His photographs have an aristocratic assurance and innate, unforced elegance, which seem to come from within rather than be imposed from without. He was quite at home with his sitters, usually society women or other celebrities as there was at that time no corps of professional models, and this rapport may have contributed to the atmosphere. The later, non-fashion photographs have this same quality of confident communication.

Man Ray

Born Philadelphia, Pennsylvania, August 27, 1890
Died Paris, France, November 18, 1976

More interested in art than in commercial photography, Man Ray was nevertheless one of the fashion world's most innovative photographers, introducing elements of surrealism into his fashion work. He first worked for Paul Poiret around 1921 or 1922, using glass plates and operating out of Poiret's darkroom. He photographed the couture section of the 1925 Decorative Arts Exposition in Paris. After working in New York, he returned to Paris with American models, who brought an American accent to his work. He photographed the Paris collections from 1938 to 1940, sometimes during air raid warnings, before returning to the United States. After World War II he abandoned fashion to devote himself to art, including experimental photography.

Martin Munkacsi

Born Cluj, Romania, May 18, 1896
Died Randalls Island, New York, July 14, 1963

Munkacsi became a news photographer in 1923 after an abbreviated apprenticeship as a housepainter and work on a sporting paper in Budapest. Within a few years he had risen to the top of his profession and was Hungary's highest-paid photojournalist. He left Europe in 1934 because of the rise of Nazism, and came to the United States with a contract with Hearst Press. His first fashion work appeared in *Harper's Bazaar* in April 1934, revolutionary action shots that are the ancestors of all the spontaneous, outdoor-action, fashion photography since. His career peaked in the early 1940s, when he claimed to be the world's highest-paid photographer. Witty and charming, Munkacsi could also be arrogant, and his hot temper alienated many. He considered his work as business, not art, and is quoted as saying "A photograph is not worth a thousand words, it's worth a thousand dollars."

Irving Penn

Born Plainfield, New Jersey, June 16, 1917

A major figure in the field of fashion photography, Irving Penn attended the Philadelphia Museum School of Industrial Art, studied design from 1934 to 1938 with *Harper's Bazaar's* renowned artistic director and developer of talent, Alexey Brodovitch. Penn worked as art director in a New York store and, from 1937 to 1939, freelanced as an artist for *Harper's Bazaar.* In 1942 he spent a year painting in Mexico. His first *Vogue* photographs appeared in 1943, the beginning of a long and fruitful relationship. After war service in the American Field Service in Italy and India, his career blossomed, resulting in a wide variety of photographs of fashion, personalities, and travel. In addition to Condé Nast publications, his client roster included international advertising agencies. In 1947, he married model Lisa Fonssagrives, with whom he first collaborated in 1950 for photographs of the Paris collections; these were unadorned but rich in feeling. Their later location trip to Morocco foreshadowed his future interests and so-called anthropological pictures.

At a time when fashion photography was marked by elaborately artificial lighting, Penn used his lights to simulate daylight, an important and influential move. Posing his models against the plainest backgrounds, he achieved a monumental simplicity and clarity, an elegant femininity. On his location trips, he employed the same economy of means for portraits of native people. In the manner of 19th-century photographers he used a portable studio he built to ensure the desired working conditions in the Cameroons, Peru, and other areas where no studios existed. His work has been exhibited in one-man shows at the Museum of Modern Art in New York and the Metropolitan Museum of Art, and is in the permanent collections of both. He is also the author of numerous photographic books, from 1960 with *Moments Preserved,* through 1991 with *Passage.*

Virginia Pope

Born Chicago, Illinois, June 29, 1885
Died New York City, January 16, 1978

AS fashion editor at *The New York Times* from 1933 to 1955, Virginia Pope is credited with practically inventing fashion reportage. One of the first to look for news in the wholesale market, she reported on the people who made clothes at a time when only Paris fashion was considered newsworthy. She encouraged the American fashion industry in its early years, originating the "Fashions of The Times" fashion show in 1942 as a showcase for American designers and staging the show each fall for the next nine years. In 1952 the show became a twice-yearly fashion supplement of the same name still published by *The Times.*

Following her father's death, the five-year-old Virginia was taken to Europe by her mother; together they toured the continent for the next 15 years. She became fluent in French, German, and Italian, and familiar with the best of European art and music. They returned to Chicago in 1905. Virginia served in the Red Cross during World War I, and then tried various careers in Chicago and New York, including social work, the theater, book translations, and writing.

A late starter in journalism, Miss Pope had a long run. Her first published pieces, which ran in *The New York Times,* were interviews with a visiting German theater group and articles about an Italian neighborhood, results of her facility in languages. She joined *The Times* as a member of the Sunday staff in 1925 and eight years later became fashion editor, a position she held and developed for 22 years. Following her retirement, Miss Pope joined the staff of *Parade* magazine as fashion editor; her name remained on the masthead until her death.

In addition, she held the Edwin Goodman chair established by Bergdorf Goodman at the Fashion Institute of Technology, giving a course on "Fashion in Contemporary Living." She could often be seen on Seventh Avenue with her students, escorting them to fashion shows and behind the scenes to see how a business worked. And because she believed that exposure to culture was essential to a designer's development, she regularly took students to performances of the Metropolitan Opera. While her personal style was of the establishment, she understood innovation and could look at clothes objectively. Referring to her conservative appearance and "grande dame" reputation, a fellow editor once said, "she could play the Queen of England without rehearsal."

Carmel Snow

Born Dublin, Ireland, 1888
Died New York City, May 9, 1961

CARMEL SNOW WAS RAISED IN the fashion business—her mother came to the United States to promote Irish industries at the 1893 Chicago World's Fair and stayed on to found a dressmaking business, Fox & Co. One of the exhibitors at *Vogue's* first "Fashion Fête" in 1914, the firm made the dress worn on that occasion by *Vogue's* editor, EDNA WOOLMAN CHASE. A friendship developed and in 1921 Mrs. Chase offered Carmel a job in the magazine's fashion department. In 1929 she became editor of American *Vogue.*

In 1932, in a move that sent shock waves through the fashion world, Mrs. Snow went as fashion editor to *Harper's Bazaar, Vogue's* great rival. *Vogue's* publisher, Condé Nast, never spoke to her again. She remained with *Bazaar,* first as fashion editor then as editor, until 1957, when she became chairman of the editorial board. Her successor was Nancy White, her niece and godchild.

Tiny in stature but a major fashion presence and forceful personality, Mrs. Snow was a woman of wit and intelligence, of strong views expressed frankly and with passion. She dressed in great style in clothes from the Paris couture and like a high priestess of fashion, championed each change as it appeared. She recognized BALENCIAGA'S genius and well before the majority of the fashion press promoted him indefatigably; CHRISTIAN DIOR spoke of her "marvelous feeling for what is fashion today and what will be fashion tomorrow." A loyal and powerful champion of the talented, she demanded their best and received their finest efforts. After World War II, she took a leading role in helping the French and Italian textile and fashion industries get back on their feet. She was the stuff of legends: it was said that even when she dozed off at showings, her eyes would snap open when a winner appeared and that she had total ocular recall. It is a fact that Christian Dior delayed openings until she arrived. Even after she no longer had official connections and despite precarious health, she continued to go to Paris twice yearly for the collections.

She married George Palen Snow in 1926 and had three children. Her Irish accent never completely disappeared nor her attachment to the country of her birth. She worked there and in New York on her memoirs published in 1962, written in collaboration with Mary Louise Aswell, a fiction editor at *Bazaar* for 11 years.

The Stylemakers

Edward Steichen

Born Luxembourg, March 27, 1879
Died West Redding, Connecticut, May 25, 1973

BROUGHT TO THE UNITED STATES as an infant, Steichen grew up in the Midwest and studied art at the Milwaukee Art Students League (1894-1898), during which time he was a lithography apprentice and began to teach himself photography. He became a U.S. citizen in 1900, lived in Paris, painting and doing photography from 1900 till 1902, and again from 1906 to 1914. During World War I he served in the U.S. Army Expeditionary Forces (1917-1919) as commander of a photo division. Around 1922, he abandoned painting and committed himself entirely to photography.

His first fashion photographs were made in 1911 for PAUL POIRET; it was not until after he was hired by Condé Nast in 1923 as photographic editor-in-chief that he developed his mature style, deeply influenced by his involvement with modern art. He replaced the pictorialism of his predecessor, BARON DE MEYER, with a modernism based on strong, clean lines, plain backgrounds, and an all-new model, the "flapper." He also worked for the advertising agency, J. Walter Thompson.

Steichen essentially abandoned his own photography in 1947 when he became director of the Department of Photography at New York's Museum of Modern Art, a post he held until his retirement in 1962. His best-known show from that era was "The Family of Man," which traveled to a number of other museums around the country. During his long and distinguished career he accumulated a staggering list of honors and affiliations.

Diana Vreeland

Born Paris, France, ca. 1906
Died New York City, August 22, 1989
Awards Chevalier of the National Order of Merit of France, 1970 · *Légion d'Honneur,* 1976 · Lord & Taylor Dorothy Shaver "Rose" Award, 1976 · Parsons School of Design Honorary Doctor of Fine Arts Degree, 1977

FOR NEARLY FIVE DECADES, DIANA VREELAND was a powerful influence on the American fashion consciousness, first as fashion editor and last as museum consultant. Born in Paris to an American mother and English father, raised in a milieu saturated with fashion and the arts, she was by both nature and nurture ideally fitted for her eventual vocation. As a child, she was exposed to extraordinary people and events—Diaghilev, Nijinsky, Ida Rubinstein, Vernon and Irene Castle were all guests in her parents' apartment—and she remembered being sent to London in 1911 for the coronation of George V. Her family moved to America at the outbreak of World War I. Married in 1924 to Thomas Reed Vreeland, she accompanied her husband as his job took him to Albany, New York, on to London, then back to New York City in 1937. The same year, at the invitation of Carmel Snow, she went to work for *Harper's Bazaar.*

At *Bazaar,* she first wrote "Why Don't You," a column that quickly became a byword for such suggestions as "Why Don't You ... rinse your blonde child's hair in dead champagne to keep it gold as they do in France...?" After six months she became fashion editor, working closely with Mrs. Snow and art director Alexey Brodovitch to make *Bazaar* the exciting, influential publication it was. In 1962 she left the magazine to go to *Vogue* as associate editor, then editor-in-chief, a post she held until 1971. After 1971 she was a consulting editor at *Vogue* and began a new career as consultant to the Costume Institute of the Metropolitan Museum of Art. There she mounted a series of outstanding exhibitions on such subjects as "BALENCIAGA," "American Women of Style," The Glory of Russian Costume," "Vanity Fair," "Man and the Horse."

Mrs. Vreeland, who as a child felt like an ugly duckling, recreated herself as an elegant, completely individual woman with a strong personal style: jet black hair, heavily rouged cheeks, and bright red lips. For day and small dinners she dressed in simple uniforms—sweaters and skirts or sweaters and pants—appearing for big evenings in dramatic gowns from favorite designers: SAINT LAURENT, GRÈS, GIVENCHY. Her writing styles and conversation were as original as her appearance—dramatic, exaggerated, and quite inimitable. In her time at *Vogue,* the Vreeland memos were cherished, copied, and passed around among the staff.

As an editor she not only reported fashion but promoted it vigorously, showing something she believed in repeatedly until it took hold. Perhaps her greatest achievement was her ability to understand the era of the 1960s with all its upheavals. To whatever she did she brought her sense of drama, her immense energy, and above all, her unquenchable enthusiasm for the unique and the beautiful. She credited her success to conscientiousness, thoroughness, and an inability to take short cuts. A fund in her name has been established to benefit the Metropolitan Museum of Art's Costume Institute.

The Luxury Conglomerates

Apparel is only one element of the new luxury conglomerate—its holdings can include everything from makers of the finest watches, shoes, and fine jewelry to wine, spirits, and art magazines—every conceivable aspect of the well-appointed life, including clothes. During the 1990s the financial affairs of the luxury conglomerates and their struggles for power were reported in the business sections of newspapers as avidly as in the fashion pages, and the corporations' names and those of their principals became as familiar as the famous brands they collected so tirelessly. Here, we'll consider a handful of the best known, whose high-profile acquisitions have made them household names.

LVMH Moët Hennessy Louis Vuitton—the largest of the luxury conglomerates and probably the best known, owes its fame not only to the stellar names in its portfolio, but also to the charisma of the man at the top, **Bernard Arnault**, reputedly the richest man in fashion. An engineer by training, he became chairman of LVMH in the late 1980s, embarking on a campaign of acquisitions and adding steadily to his domain during the next decade. At last count, there were over 50 brands under the LVMH banner.

The first initials in the logo belong to Louis Vuitton with its long history as a maker of top-drawer luggage; Moët Champagne and Hennessy cognac account for the other two initials. The LVMH fashion properties include couture and ready-to-wear clothes and accessories for both women and men—Christian Dior, Givenchy, Christian Lacroix, Celine, Kenzo—even Louis Vuitton has branched out into ready-to-wear. There is Thomas Pink for shirts, Chaumet and Fred Joaillier in jewelry, TAG Heuer watches, Madrid-based Loewe leather goods and women's fashion, Veuve Cliquot Champagne, and Sephora beauty products.

In Italy LVMH owns PUCCI and FENDI, and in the United States controls DONNA KARAN and MARC JACOBS. For most of these brands there are splendid retail shops in the world's great cities. At one time or another the list has also included auction houses, a cruise line, and duty free shops.

Richemont. Second to LVMH in size, Richemont has not had nearly the press coverage, perhaps due to the lack of a major personality at the top, or perhaps because of a quieter Swiss way of doing business. The firm bills itself as the world's largest proprietor of luxury watch brands and has much deeper holdings there than in fashion. Chloé is its most prominent name in women's clothes.

Among Richemont's prestigious possessions, Cartier, Jaeger-LeCoultre, Montblanc, Baume Mercier, Piaget, Vacheron Constantin, and Van Cleef and Arpels are internationally famous. Hackett, for traditional men's clothing, and Purdey, maker of fine guns and rifles, are revered English institutions. They have Dunhill, Sulka, Italy's Montegrappa fine writing instruments, Old England (a French firm with fashion for men, women, children, and the home), and Shanghai Tang. Lancel luggage and leathers, and watchmakers A. Lange & Sohne and IWC of Germany and the Italian Officine Panerai complete the list.

Gucci. Founded in Italy by the Gucci family in 1923, the firm has gone from a stodgy luggage and leather company on the verge of bankruptcy to a major and highly successful global fashion presence. Recognizing its potential in the 1990s, LVMH under Bernard Arnault began a takeover campaign, successfully resisted by Gucci under the direction of chairman and chief executive **Domenico De Sole**, an Italian who studied law at Harvard. Together with designer TOM FORD, and with the aid of a large cash infusion by **François Pinault**, one of the richest men in France, De Sole fought off the LVMH advances to remain independent and then went on an acquisition campaign of his own. The battle left a lasting residue of bad feeling between the two.

Starting in 1999 Gucci began acquiring a series of great names in the luxury category—first and most prominently YVES SAINT LAURENT. Others in the clothing category include a majority interest in BALENCIAGA and financial backing in their own businesses for STELLA MCCARTNEY and ALEXANDER MCQUEEN. Gucci also owns Boucheron jewelry, Sergio Rossi shoes, and Italy's Bottega Veneta fine leather goods. In keeping with the trend toward globalization, elegant retail stores for the individual brands have appeared in the world's great shopping cities, from Tokyo to New York to Paris to Milan to Los Angeles.

Prada. Founded in 1913 as a maker of luxury leather goods by Mario Prada, the grandfather of MIUCCIA PRADA, the company moved into the modern era and added apparel under her creative direction. In the 1990s an ambitious expansion program was initiated by her husband, **Patrizio Bertelli,** chief executive of the Prada Group.

Beyond their signature Prada and the younger Miu Miu, both with ready-to-wear for women and men, their roster includes a controlling interest in the designers HELMUT LANG and AZZEDINE ALAÏA, in Italy's Carshoe athletic shoes, English Church's shoes, and the Genny group. After a very public parting-of-the-ways with designer JIL SANDER, a part interest in that firm became full ownership. The rift has since been healed and Sander has returned as designer.

In December 2001 Prada opened a huge store in New York's SoHo, a veritable temple of retailing designed by world-class architect Rem Koolhaus. It became an instant tourist attraction and Saturday-night destination for young New Yorkers. Other flagship stores were scheduled for San Francisco, Los Angeles, Paris, and Tokyo.

Appendix

Council of Fashion Designers of America (CFDA) Awards

DESIGNER/AWARDEE	AWARD	YEAR
Joseph Abboud	Menswear Designer of the Year	1989
Joseph Abboud	Menswear Designer of the Year	1990
Victor Alfaro	Perry Ellis Award for Womenswear (tie with Cynthia Rowley)	1994
Giorgio Armani	CFDA International Award	1983
Giorgio Armani	Lifetime Achievement Award	1987
Richard Avedon	Lifetime Achievement Award	1988
Jhane Barnes	Outstanding Menswear Designer	1981
John Bartlett	Perry Ellis Award for Menswear	1993
John Bartlett	Menswear Designer of the Year	1997
Geoffrey Beene	Special Award Individual Approach to High Quality Clothing	1985
Geoffrey Beene	Special Award Outstanding Designer of the Year	1986
Geoffrey Beene	Special Award Fashion as Art	1988
Geoffrey Beene	Lifetime Achievement Award	1997
Manolo Blahnik	Special Award Outstanding Excellence in Accessory Design	1987
Manolo Blahnik	Accessory Award	1990
Manolo Blahnik	The Stiletto Award	1997
Bill Blass	Lifetime Achievement Award	1986
Bill Blass	Dom Perignon Award	1995
Bill Blass	Special Award, The Dean of American Fashion	2000
(Daphne Gutierrez & Nicole Noselli) Bruce	Perry Ellis Award for Womenswear	2001
Edmundo Castillo	Perry Ellis Award for Accessories	2001
Liz Claiborne	Special Award Good Fashion at Reasonable Prices	1985
Liz Claiborne, for the Liz Claiborne and Art Ortenberg Foundation	Humanitarian Award	2000
Kenneth Cole	Dom Perignon Award	1996
Bill Cunningham		1982
Bill Cunningham	Eugenia Sheppard Award for Journalism	1993
Sandy Dalal	Perry Ellis Award for Menswear	1997
Oscar de la Renta	Lifetime Achievement Award	1989
Oscar de la Renta	Womenswear Designer of the Year	2000
Carrie Donovan	Eugenia Sheppard Award for Journalism	1989
Carrie Donovan	Lifetime Achievement Award	1994
Perry Ellis	Outstanding Designer in Women's Fashion	1981
Perry Ellis	Outstanding Designer in Men's Fashion	1982
Perry Ellis	Outstanding Designer in Men's Fashion	1983
Tom Ford	International Award	1995
Tom Ford	Womenswear Designer of the Year	2001
James Galanos	Lifetime Achievement Award	1984
John Galliano	International Award	1997
Jean-Paul Gaultier	International Designer of the Year	2000

DESIGNER/AWARDEE	AWARD	YEAR
Rudi Gernreich	Special Tribute	1985
Nicolas Ghesquière for Balenciaga	International Designer of the Year	2001
Hubert de Givenchy	Lifetime Achievement Award	1995
Halston	Special Tribute	1990
Tommy Hilfiger	Menswear Designer of the Year	1995
Horst	Lifetime Achievement Award	1987
Marc Jacobs	Perry Ellis Award for New Fashion Talent	1987
Marc Jacobs	Womenswear Designer of the Year	1997
Marc Jacobs	Accessory Designer of the Year	1998/1999
Betsey Johnson	Special Award for Her Timeless Talent	1998/1999
Norma Kamali	Outstanding Women's Fashion	1982
Norma Kamali	Special Award Innovative Uses of Video in Presentation and Promotion of Fashion	1985
Donna Karan	Special Award Sophisticated Approach to Contemporary Dressing	1985|
Donna Karan	Special Award Impact on the Total Head-to-Toe Look of Fashion	1986
Donna Karan	Womenswear Designer of the Year	1990
Donna Karan	Menswear Designer of the Year	1992
Donna Karan	Womenswear Designer of the Year	1996
Barry Keiselstein-Cord	Excellence in Design	1981
Calvin Klein	Best American Collection	1981
Calvin Klein	Outstanding American Talent of the Year for Women's Apparel	1983
Calvin Klein	Best American Collection	1987
Calvin Klein	Womenswear Designer of the Year	1993
	Menswear Designer of the Year	1993
Calvin Klein	Menswear Designer of the Year	1998/1999
Calvin Klein	Lifetime Achievement Award	2001
Michael Kors	Womenswear Designer of the Year	1998/1999
Karl Lagerfeld	Special Award	1982
Karl Lagerfeld	Special Award for House of Chanel	1988
Helmut Lang	International Award	1996
Helmut Lang	Menswear Designer of the Year	2000
Ralph Lauren	Special Award	1981
Ralph Lauren	Special Award Outstanding Concept Design of a Retail Store	1986
Ralph Lauren	Lifetime Achievement Award	1991
Ralph Lauren	Womenswear Designer of the Year	1995
Ralph Lauren	Menswear Designer of the Year	1996
Ralph Lauren	Dom Perignon Award	1997

Appendix

DESIGNER/AWARDEE	AWARD	YEAR
Judith Leiber	Lifetime Achievement Award	1993
Antonio Lopez		1982
Antonio Lopez		1983
Bob Mackie	Special Award for His Fashion Exuberance	2001
Gene Meyer	Accessory Award for Men	1994
Gene Meyer	Perry Ellis Award for Menswear	1996
Issey Miyake	International Award	1983
Isaac Mizrahi	Perry Ellis Award for New Fashion Talent	1988
Isaac Mizrahi	Womenswear Designer of the Year	1989
Isaac Mizrahi	Womenswear Designer of the Year	1991
Isaac Mizrahi	Special Award With Douglas Keeve for *Unzipped*	1995
Robert Lee Morris	Special Award for Founding Artwear and for Jewelry Design	1985
Robert Lee Morris	Accessory Award for Women	1994
Todd Oldham	Perry Ellis Award for New Fashion Talent	1991
Elsa Peretti	Accessory Designer of the Year (for Tiffany & Co.)	1996
Miuccia Prada	International Award for Accessories	1993
Emilio Pucci	Special Award	1990
Richard Edwards (Richard Benson & Edward Pavlick)	Perry Ellis Award for Menswear (tie with Richard Tyler)	1995
Narciso Rodriguez	Perry Ellis Award for Womenswear	1997
Christian Francis Roth	Perry Ellis Award for New Fashion Talent	1990
Cynthia Rowley	Perry Ellis Award for Womenswear (tie with Victor Alfaro)	1994
Yves Saint Laurent	International Fashion Award	1981
Yves Saint Laurent	Lifetime Achievement Award	1998/1999
Fernando Sanchez	Special Award Lingerie and At-Home Wear	1981
Giorgio di Sant'Angelo	Special Award Contribution to Evolution of Stretch Clothing	1987
Arnold Scaasi	Special Award Extravagant Evening Dress	1987
Arnold Scaasi	Lifetime Achievement Award	1996
Ronaldus Shamask	Menswear Designer of the Year	1987
Kate Spade	Perry Ellis Award for Accessories	1995
Kate Spade	Accessory Designer of the year	1997
Stephen Sprouse	Special Award	1984
Anna Sui	Perry Ellis Award for New Fashion Talent	1992
Pauline Trigère	Lifetime Achievement Award	1992
Richard Tyler	Perry Ellis Award for Womenswear	1993
Richard Tyler	Womenswear Designer of the Year	1994
Richard Tyler	Perry Ellis Award for Menswear (tie with Richard Edwards)	1995
Patricia Underwood		1983
Valentino	Lifetime Achievement Award	2000
John Varvatos	Perry Ellis Award for Menswear	2000
John Varvatos	Menswear Designer of the Year	2001

Council of Fashion Designers of America (CFDA) Awards cont.

DESIGNER/AWARDEE	AWARD	YEAR
Gianni Versace	International Award	1992
Gianni Versace	Special Tribute	1997
Diana Vreeland	Special Award	1984
Yohji Yamamoto	International Award	1998/1999

Coty American Fashion Critic's Awards

DESIGNER	AWARD	YEAR
Adolfo	Special Award (millinery)	1955, 1969
Adri	"Winnie"	1982
John Anthony	"Winnie"	1972
John Anthony	Return Award	1976
Jhane Barnes	Men's Wear	1980
Jhane Barnes	Men's Wear Return Award	1984
Geoffrey Beene	"Winnie"	1964
Geoffrey Beene	Return Award	1966
Geoffrey Beene	Hall of Fame	1974
Geoffrey Beene	Hall of Fame Citation	1975
Geoffrey Beene	Hall of Fame Citation	1977
Geoffrey Beene	Hall of Fame Citation	1979
Geoffrey Beene	Hall of Fame Citation	1981
Geoffrey Beene	Hall of Fame Citation	1982
Bill Blass	"Winnie"	1961
Bill Blass	Return Award	1963
Bill Blass	First Coty Award for men's wear	1968
Bill Blass	Hall of Fame	1970
Bill Blass	Hall of Fame Citation	1971
Bill Blass	Special Award (furs for Revillon America)	1975
Bill Blass	Hall of Fame Citation	1982
Bill Blass	Hall of Fame Citation	1983
Stephen Burrows	Special Award (lingerie)	1974
Stephen Burrows	"Winnie"	1977
Bonnie Cashin	"Winnie"	1950
Bonnie Cashin	Special Award (leather and fabric design)	1961
Bonnie Cashin	Return Award	1968
Bonnie Cashin	Hall of Fame	1972
Sal Cesarani	Special Award (men's wear)	1974
Sal Cesarani	Men's Wear Award	1976
Sal Cesarani	Men's Wear Return Award	1982
Aldo Cipullo	Men's Wear (jewelry)	1974
Lilly Daché	Special Award (millinery)	1943
Oscar De la Renta	"Winnie"	1967
Oscar De la Renta	Return Award	1968
Oscar De la Renta	Hall of Fame	1973
Louis Dell'Olio	First Citation (women's wear with Donna Karan)	1984
Louis Dell'Olio	"Winnie" (with Donna Karan)	1977
Louis Dell'Olio	Hall of Fame (with Donna Karan)	1982

DESIGNER	AWARD	YEAR
Perry Ellis	"Winnie"	1979
Perry Ellis	Return Award	1980
Perry Ellis	Hall of Fame	1981
Perry Ellis	Men's Wear Award	1981
Perry Ellis	Hall of Fame Citation (women's wear)	1983
Perry Ellis	Men's Wear Return Award	1983
Perry Ellis	Hall of Fame (men's wear)	1984
Perry Ellis	Hall of Fame (women's wear)	1984
Anne Fogarty	Special Award (dresses)	1951
James Galanos	"Winnie"	1954
James Galanos	Return Award	1956
James Galanos	Hall of Fame	1959
Rudi Gernreich	Special Award (innovative body clothes)	1960
Rudi Gernreich	"Winnie"	1963
Rudi Gernreich	Return Award	1966
Rudi Gernreich	Hall of Fame	1967
Halston	Special Award (millinery)	1962, 1969
Halston	"Winnie"	1971
Halston	Return Award	1972
Halston	Hall of Fame	1974
Joan Helpern	Special Award (footwear)	1978
Carol Horn	"Winnie"	1975
Charles James	"Winnie"	1950
Charles James	Special Award (innovative cut)	1954
Mr. John	Special Award	1943
Betsy Johnson	"Winnie"	1971
Alexander Julian	Men's Wear Trophy	1977
Alexander Julian	Men's Wear Return Award	1979
Alexander Julian	Hall of Fame Award	1980
Alexander Julian	First Citation	1983
Alexander Julian	Second Citation	1984
Robin Kahn	Special Award (belt and buckle designs for men's wear)	1984
Norma Kamali	"Winnie"	1981
Norma Kamali	Return Award	1982
Norma Kamali	Hall of Fame	1983
Donna Karan	"Winnie" (with Louis, Dell'Olio)	1977
Donna Karan	Hall of Fame (with Louis, Dell'Olio)	1982
Donna Karan	First Citation (women's wear with Louis Dell'Olio)	1984
Herbert Kasper	"Winnie"	1955
Herbert Kasper	Return Award	1970
Herbert Kasper	Hall of Fame	1976

Appendix

DESIGNER	AWARD	YEAR
Barry Kieselstein-Cord	Outstanding, Jewelry Design	1979
Barry Kieselstein-Cord	Special Award (belts and jewelry)	1984
Anne Klein	"Winnie"	1955
Anne Klein	Return Award	1969
Anne Klein	Hall of Fame	1971
Calvin Klein	"Winnie"	1973
Calvin Klein	Return Award	1974
Calvin Klein	Hall of Fame	1975
Calvin Klein	Special Award (fur design for Alexandre)	1975
Calvin Klein	Special Award (contribution to international status of American fashion)	1979
Kenneth Jay Lane	Special Award (jewelry)	1966
Ralph Lauren	Men's Wear	1970
Ralph Lauren	Return Award	1973
Ralph Lauren	"Winnie"	1974
Ralph Lauren	Second Citation	1984
Ralph Lauren	Return Award	1976
Ralph Lauren	Hall of Fame (men's wear)	1976
Ralph Lauren	Hall of Fame (women's wear)	1977
Ralph Lauren	First Citation (men's wear)	1981
Judith Leiber	Special Award (handbags)	1973
Tina Leser	"Winnie"	1945
Vera Maxwell	Special Award (coats and suits)	1951
Claire McCardell	"Winnie"	1944
Claire McCardell	Hall of Fame (posthumous)	1958
Mary McFadden	"Winnie"	1976
Mary McFadden	Return Award	1978
Mary McFadden	Hall of Fame	1979
Robert Lee Morris	Special Award (jewelry for Calvin Klein)	1981
Norman Norell	First "Winnie"	1943
Norman Norell	First Return Award	1951
Norman Norell	First designer elected to Hall of Fame	1956
Emeric Partos	Special Award (furs)	1957
Sylvia Pedlar	Special Award (lingerie)	1951
Sylvia Pedlar	Return Special Award (lingerie)	1964
Elsa Peretti	Special Award (jewelry)	1971
Fernando Sanchez	Special Award (lingerie)	1974, 1977
Fernando Sanchez	Special Award (fur for Revillon)	1975
Giorgio Sant Angelo	Special Award (fantasy accessories and ethnic fashions)	1968
Giorgio Sant Angelo	"Winnie"	1970
Arnold Scaasi	"Winnie"	1958
Jean Schlumberger	Special Award (the first given for jewelry)	1958
Ronaldus Shamask	"Winnie"	1981

DESIGNER	AWARD	YEAR
Adele Simpson	"Winnie"	1947
Willi Smith	"Winnie"	1983
Viola Sylbert	Special Award (fur design)	1975
Gustave Tassell	"Winnie"	1961
Bill Tice	Special Award (loungewear)	1974
Monika Tilley	Special Award (swimsuits)	1975
Pauline Trigère	"Winnie"	1949
Pauline Trigère	Return Award	1951
Pauline Trigère	Hall of Fame	1959
Joan Vass	Special Award (crafted knit fashions)	1979
Adrienne Vittadini	"Winnie"	1984
Chester Weinberg	"Winnie"	1970
John Weitz	Special Men's Wear Award	1974

Appendix

Neiman Marcus Awards

DESIGNER	YEAR	DESIGNER	YEAR
Adrian	1943	Karl Lagerfeld	1980
Giorgio Armani	1979	Kenneth Jay Lane	1968
Pierre Balmain	1955	Ralph Lauren	1973
Cecil Beaton	1956	Judith Leiber	1980
Geoffrey Beene	1964, 1965	Tina Leser	1945
Bill Blass	1969	Vera Maxwell	1955
Giuliana Camerino	1956	Claire McCardell	1948
Hattie Carnegie	1939	Mary McFadden	1979
Bonnie Cashin	1950	Rosita & Ottavio Missoni	1973
Gabrielle Chanel	1957	Issey Miyake	1984
Edna Woolman Chase	1940	Hanae Mori	1973
Jules-Francois Crahay	1962	Jean Muir	1973
Lilly Daché	1940	Norman Norell	1942
Oscar De la Renta	1968	Sylvia Pedlar	1960
Christian Dior	1947	Clare Potter	1939
Florence Eiseman	1955	Miuccia Prada	1995
Perry Ellis	1979	Emilio Pucci	1990
Salvatore Ferragamo	1947	Yves Saint Laurent	1958
Anne Fogarty	1952	Arnold Scaasi	1987
James Galanos	1954	Elsa Schiaparelli	1940
Norman Hartnell	1947	Adele Simpson	1946
Irene	1947	Carmel Snow	1941
Charles James	1953	Pauline Trigère	1950
Mr. John	1938	Emanuel Ungaro	1969
Omar Kiam	1941	Valentino	1967
Anne Klein	1959, 1969	Roger Vivier	1961

Fashion Walk of Fame

The Fashion Walk of Fame, established in 1999 by leaders of the fashion industry, is the only permanent landmark paying tribute to the creative talents of American fashion. White bronze plaques, 2½ feet in diameter have been embedded in granite in the sidewak from 35th Street to 41st Street, on the east side of Seventh "Fashion" Avenue. Each plaque bears an original fashion sketch and the signature of the designer, with text describing his or her contribution to fashion. Eight designers were honored each year from 2001 to 2002—the three-year span of the project—for a total of 24 names.

DESIGNER	YEAR	DESIGNER	YEAR
Geoffrey Beene	2000	Charles James	2001
Bill Blass	2000	Betsey Johnson	2002
Stephen Burrows	2002	Norma Kamali	2002
Bonnie Cashin	2001	Donna Karan	2001
Lilly Daché	2002	Anne Klein	2001
Oscar De La Renta	2001	Calvin Klein	2000
Giorgio Sant' Angelo	2001	Ralph Lauren	2000
Perry Ellis	2002	Mainbocher	2002
James Galanos	2001	Claire McCardell	2000
Rudi Gernreich	2000	Norman Norell	2000
Halston	2000	Willi Smith	2002
Marc Jacobs	2002	Pauline Trigère	2001

Photo Credits

unless otherwise noted, photographs and permission to reprint them in this text have been obtained from the archives of *W, Women's Wear Daily,* and *Daily News Record,* Fairchild Publications, Inc. The author wishes to especially thank Delcina Charles, in the Library Information Department at Fairchild, for her patience and persistence in gathering the contact files from our extensive list of designers.

Color Plates

3 Genreich, The Metropolitan Museum of Art, Gift of Rudi Genreich Revocable Trust, 1985.

5 Chanel, The Metropolitan Museum of Art, Purchase, Irene Lewisohn Bequest, Catherine Breyer Von Bomel Foundation Fund; Hoeschst Fiber Industries Fund; Chauncey Stillman Fund, 1984.

7 Callot Soeurs, The Metropolitan Museum of Art, Gift of Isabelle Shults, 1944.

9 Mainbocher, Photograph by Louise Dahl-Wolfe. Fashion Institute of Technology, New York.

10 Fortuny, The Metropolitan Museum of Art, Gift of C. J. Vincent Minette, 1972.

13 James, Photograph by Louise Dahl-Wolfe. Fashion Institute of Technology, New York.

14 Beaton, The Kobal Collection.

15 Poiret, The Metropolitan Museum of Art, Gift of Mrs. Muriel Draper, 1943.

16 McCardell, The Metropolitan Museum of Art, Gift of Irving Drought Harris, in memory of Claire McCardell Harris, 1958.

20 Adrian, Norell, McCardell, The Metropolitan Museum of Art. Photograph by Sheldon Collins.

21 Balenciaga, The Metropolitan Museum of Art, Gift of Louis Rorimer Dushkin, 1980.

A Amies, p. 10: AP/Wide World Photos.

B Balenciaga, p. 18: © Hearst Corporation, *Harper's Bazaar*, 1965. Banton, p. 20: The Kobal Collection. Brooks, p. 32: AP/Wide World Photos. Burrows, p. 34: Henri Bendel, New York.

C Cashin, pp. 44-45: Bonnie Cashin. Cesarani, p. 48: Photograph by Richard Reed. Cipullo, p. 52: Tiffany & Co. Cole, p. 55: Anne Cole. Kenneth Cole, p. 56; Photographer: Timothy Greenfield-Sanders.

D Dior, p. 68: © 1995 Artists Rights Society (ARS), New York/ADAGP, Paris. Photograph of Dior's New Look by Willy Maywald.

E Emanuel, p. 78: UPI/Bettmann.

F Fath, p. 81: © Robert Capa, Magnum Photos, Inc. Ferragamo, p. 83: LOCCHI. Fogarty, p. 85: AP/Wide World Photo.

G Galanos, p. 90: James Galanos, California. Grés, p. 99: Photograph by Eve Arnold, Magnum Photos Inc.

H Hartnell, p. 105: AP/Wide World Photos. Head, p. 106: The Kobal Collection. Helpern, p. 107: Joan and David. Tommy Hilfiger, p. 109: Tommy Hilfiger.

K Gemma Kahng, p. 120: Gemma Kahng. Kieselstein-Cord, p. 127: Barry Kieselstein-Cord. Kökin, p. 131: Kokin.

L Leroux, p. 143: Hervé Leroux, SA.

M Mackie, p. 151-152: UPI/Bettmann. Mainbocher, p. 153: © 1931 The Hearst Corporation, *Harper's Bazaar*. Maxwell, p. 155: NYT Pictures. McCardell, p. 157 (right): The Brooklyn Museum. Gift of Miss Sally Kirkland. Molyneux, p. 168: © 1931 The Hearst Corporation, *Harper's Bazaar*. Morris, p. 171: Robert Lee Morris.

N Norell, p. 177: AP/Wide World Photos. p. 178: The Brooklyn Museum. Gifts of Gustave Tassell and Norman Norell, Inc.

P Pipart, p. 190: Nina Ricci & Co.

Q Quant, p. 198: AP/Wide World Photos.

R Rabanne, p. 200: AP/Wide World Photos. Rhodes, p. 202: Photographs of designer and 1994 costume by Polly Estes, Zandra Rhodes LTD. Alice Roi, p. 206: Alice Roi/Denise Williamson Showroom.

S Schiaparelli, p. 220: © Robert Capa, Magnum Photos, Inc. Schlumberger, p. 221: Tiffany & Co. Sharaff, p. 224: The Kobal Collection.

W Weitz, p. 262: J. Schoeneman Inc. Worth, p. 266: Doyle New York, Auctioneers & Appraisers.

Bibliography

This bibliography is compiled to help the reader in the study of fashion. Not all the listed books contributed to this edition of Who's Who in Fashion.

The Age of Worth. New York; Brooklyn Museum of Arts, 1982.

Amies, Hardy. *Just So Far.* St. James Place, London: Collins, 1984.

———. *ABC of Men's fashion.* London: Newnes, 1964.

———. *Still Here.* London: Weidenfeld and Nicolson, 1984.

Anscombe, Isabelle. *A Woman's Touch: Women in Design from 1860 to the Present Day.* London: Virago, 1984.

Ash, Juliet and Elizabeth Wilson, eds. *Chic Thrills.* Berkeley, CA: University of California Press, 1993.

Bailey, M.J. *Those Glorious, Glamour Years: The Great Hollywood Costume Designs of the Thirties.* Secaucus, NJ: Citadel Press, Reissue, 1988.

Baillen, C. *Chanel: Solitaire.* Translated by Barbara Bray. New York: Quadrangle/The New York Times Book Co., 1974.

Ballard, Bettina. In My Fashion. New York: David McKay Co., Inc., 1960.

Balmain, Pierre. My Years and Seasons (autobiography). Translated by E. Lanchbery and G.Young. London: Cassell & Co. Ltd., 1964. New York: Doubleday & Company, Inc., 1965.

Beaton, Cecil. *The Glass of Fashion.* London: Casssell, 1989.

———. *Fair Lady.* New York: Holt, Rinehart & Winston, 1964.

———. *Cecil Beaton: Memoirs of the 40s.* New York: McGraw-Hill Book Co., 1977.

———. *The Book of Beauty.* London: Duckworth, 1930.

——— *Cecil's Beaton's New York.* London: Batsford, 1938.

———. *Persona Grata* (with Kenneth Tynan). London: G. P. Putnam's Sons, 1954.

Beaton, Cecil. *The Glass of Fashion.* London: Weidenfeld & Nicolson, 1954.

——— *Cecil Beaton's Diaries—1922-1929, The Wandering Years* (1961); *1939-1944, The Years Between* (1965); *1948-1955, The Strenuous Years* (1973). London; Weinfeld & Nicolson.

———. *The Gainsborough Girls,* a play. 1951.

Bender, Marylin. *Beautiful People.* New York: Coward, McCann & Geoghegan, Inc., 1967.

Bernhard, Barbara. *Fashion in the 60s.* New York: St. Martin's Press, 1978.

Bertin, Celia. *Paris à la Mode.* London: Gollancz, 1956.

Bianchino, Gloria, Grazietta Butazzi. Alessandra Mottola Molfino, and Arturo Carlo Quintavalle. *Italian Fashion.* New York: Rizzoli International Publications, 1988.

Black, J. Anderson and Madge Garland. *A History of Fashion.* New York: Morrow, 1980.

Blum, Stella. *Designs by Erté. Fashion Drawings & Illustrations from Harper's Bazaar.* New York: Harry N. Abrams, 1987.

Bond, David. *The Guinness Guide to Twentieth Century Fashion.* Middlesex, England: Guinness Superlatives Ltd., 1989.

Borrelli, Laird. *Stylishly Drawn: Contemporary Fashion Illustration.* New York: Harry N. Abrams, Inc., 2001.

Boucher, François with Yvonne Deslandres. *20,000 Years of Fashion: The History of Costume and Personal Adornment,* Expanded Edition. New York: Harry N. Abrams, 1987.

Brady, James. *Super Chic.* Boston: Little, Brown & Co., 1974.

Brogden, J. *Fashion Design.* London: Studio Vista, 1971.

Burris-Meyer, Elizabeth. *This is Fashion.* New York: Harper, 1943.

Byers, Margaretta. *Designing Women.* New York: Simon & Schuster, 1938

Calasibetta, Charlotte Mankey and Phyllis G. Tortora. *Fairchild's Dictionary of Fashion, 3rd ed.* New York: Fairchild Publications, 2003.

Carter, Ernestine. *Magic Names of Fashion.* New Jersey: Prentice-Hall, Inc., 1980.

———. *Twentieth Century Fashion, a Scrapbook: 1900 to Today.* London: Eyre Methuen, 1975.

———. *The Changing World of Fashion.* New York: G.P. Putnam's Sons, 1977.

Chapkis, Wendy and Cynthia Enloe. *Of Common Cloth: Women in the Global Textile Industry.* Amsterdam: Transnational Institute, 1983.

Charles-Roux, Edmonde. *Chanel: Her Life, Her World, and the Woman Behind the Legend She Herself Created.* New York: Random House, 1976..

———. *Chanel and Her World.* London: Weidenfeld & Nicolson, 1979.

Chase, Edna Woolman and Ilka Chase. *Always in Vogue.* New York: Doubleday & Company, Inc., 1954.

Coleman, Elizabeth Ann. *The Genius of Charles James.* Published for the exhibition at the Brooklyn Museum. New York: Holt, Rinehart and Winston, 1982.

———. *Changing Fashions, 1800-1970.* New York: Brooklyn Museum, 1972.

———. *The Opulent Era: Fashions of Worth, Doucet and Pingat.* London: Thames and Hudson, 1992.

Creed, Charles. *Made to Measure.* London: Jarrolds, 1961.

Daché, Lilly. *Talking through My Hats.* Edited by Dorothy Roe Lewis. New York: Coward-McCann, Inc., 1946.

———. *Lilly Dache's Glamour Book.* 1957.

Dars, Celestine. *A Fashion Parade: The Seeberger Collection.* London: Blond & Briggs, 1979.

Davenport, Millia. *The Book of Costume.* New York: Crown Publishers, Inc., 1976.

Daves, Jessica. *Ready-Made Miracle.* New York: G.P. Putman's Sons, 1967.

The World in Vogue. Compiled by the Viking Press and Vogue Magazine, 1963.

DeGraw, Imelda G. *25 Years, 25 Couturiers.* Denver: Denver Museum, 1975.

De Marly, Diana. *Costume on the Stage.* Summit, PA: Rowman & Littlefield, 1982.

———. *The History of Haute Couture, 1850-1950.* New York: Holmes and Meir, 1994.

———. *Worth, Father of Haute Couture.* New York: Holmes and Meir, 1994.

Demornex, Jacqueline. *Madeleine Vionnet.* Translated by Augusta Audubert. New York: Rizzoli International Publications, 1991.

De Osma, Guillermo. *Mariano Fortuny: His Life and Work.* New York: Rizzoli International Publications, 1994.

Derrick, Robin and Robin Muir, eds. *Unseen Vogue: The Secret History of Fashion Photography.* London: Little, Brown and Company, 2002.

Deschodt, Anne-Marie. *Mariano Fortuny, un Magicien de Venise.* Tours, France: Editions du Regard, 2000.

Deschodt, Anne-Marie and Daretta Davanzo Poli. *Fortuny.* New York: Harry N. Abrams, 2002.

Deslandres, Yves. *Poiret.* New York: Rizzoli International Publications, Inc., 1987.

Devlin, P. *Fashion Photography in Vogue.* London: Thames and Hudson, 1978.

Diamonstein, Barbaralee. *Fashion: The Inside Story.* New York: Rizzoli International Publications, Inc., 1985.

Dior, Christian. *Talking about Fashion.* Translated by Eugenia Sheppard. New York: G.P. Putnam's Sons, 1954.

———. *Christian Dior and I.* Translated by Antonia Fraser. New York: E.P. Dutton & Company, Inc., 1957.

_____. *Dior by Dior.* Translated by Antonia Fraser. London: Weidenfeld & Nicolson, 1957. Harmondsworth, England: Penguin Books, 1968.

Dixon, H. Vernon. *The Rag Pickers.* New York: Avon, 1971.

Dorner, Jane. *Fashion: The Changing Shape of Fashion through the Years.* London: Octopus Books, 1974.

_____. *Fashion in the 40s and 50s.* London: Ian Allen, 1975.

Duncan, N.H. *History of Fashion Photography.* New York: Alpine Press, 1979.

Élegance et Création: Paris 1945-1975. Paris: Musée de la Mode et du Costume, 1977.

Emanuel, David and Elizabeth. *Style for All Seasons.* London: Pavilion: Michael Jospeh, 1983.

Erté. *Erté Fashions.* New York: St. Martin's Press, 1972.

_____. *Erté - Things I Remember* (autobiography). London: Peter Owen Limited, Reissue, 1983.

Etherington-Smith, Meredith. *Patou.* New York: St. Martin's Press, 1984.

Ewing, Elizabeth and Alice Mackrell. *History of 20th Century Fashion.* Rev. 4th ed. New York: Quite Specific Media Group Ltd., 2002.

Fairchild, John. *The Fashionable Savages.* New York: Doubleday & Company, Inc., 1965.

Farber, R. *The Fashion Photographer.* New York: Watson Guptill, 1981.

Fashion, 1900-1939. London: Scottish Arts Council; Victoria and Albert Museum, 1975.

Fashion Illustration. New York: Rizzoli International Publications, 1979.

Ferragamo, Salvatore. *Shoemaker of Dreams: The Autobiography of Salvatore Ferragamo.* 3rd ed. Florence: Centro Di, 1985.

Fine Fashion. Philadelphia: Museum of Art, 1979.

Fogarty, Anne. *Wife-Dressing.* New York: Julian Messner Inc., 1959.

Fortuny. New York: Fashion Institute of Technology, 1981.

Fortuny nella Belle Epoque. Milan: Electa, 1984.

Forty Years of Italian Fashion, 1945-1980. (organized by Bonizza Giordani Aragno). Rome: Fidevrart, 1983.

Fraser, Kennedy. *The Fashionable Mind.* Boston: David R. Godine, 1985.

Gaines, S. *Simply Halston.* New York: Jove Publications, 1993.

Galante, Pierre. *Mademoiselle Chanel.* Chicago: Regency, 1973.

Garland, Madge. *Fashion.* London: Penguin Books, 1962.

_____. *The Changing Form of Fashion.* London: J.M. Dent & Sons, 1970.

Giroud, François. *Dior.* New York: Rizzoli International Publications, 1987.

Glynn, Prudence. *In Fashion: Dress in the Twentieth Century.* New York: Oxford University Press, 1978.

_____. *Skin to Skin.* New York: Oxford University Press, 1983.

Gold, Annalee. *75 Years of Fashion.* New York: Fairchild Publications, 1975.

_____. *What People Wore: 1,800 Illustrations from Ancient Times to the Early Twentieth Century.* New York: Dover Publications, 1994.

_____. *One World of Fashion.* 4th edition. New York: Fairchild Publications, 1986.

Gorsline, Douglas Warner. *What People Wore: A Visual History of Dress from Ancient Times to 20th Century America.* New York: Random House Value Publishing, 1987.

_____. *90 Years of Fashion.* New York: Fairchild Publications, Inc., 1990.

Haedrich, Marcel. *Coco Chanel: Her Life, Her Secrets.* Boston: Little, Brown & Co., 1972.

Hartnell, Norman. *Silver and Gold* (autobiography). London: Evans Brothers, 1955.

_____. *Royal Courts of Fashion.* London: Cassell & Co. Ltd., 1971.

Haute Couture: Notes on Designers and Their Clothes in the Collection of the Royal Ontario Museum. Toronto: Royal Ontario Museum, 1969.

Hawes, Elizabeth. *Fashion is Spinach.* New York: Random House, 1938.

_____. *It's Still Spinach.* Boston: Little, Brown and Co., 1954.

Head, Edith. *The Dress Doctor.* Boston: Little, Brown and Co., 1959.

A History of Fashion. London: House of Worth.

Hommage à Schiaparelli. Paris: Musée de la Mode et du Costume, 1984.

Horst. *Salute to the Thirties.* New York: Viking Press, 1971.

Houck, Catherine. *The Fashion Encyclopedia.* New York: St. Martin's Press, 1982.

The House of Worth: The Gilded Age, 1860-1918. New York: Museum of the City of New York, 1982.

Howell, Georgina. *In Vogue: Six Decades of Fashion.* New York: Viking Press, 1979.

Hulanicki, Barbara. *From A to Biba.* London: Hutchinson, 1983.

Immagini e Materiali del Laboratorio Fortuny. Venice: Comune di Venezia Marsilio Edition, 1978.

Jachimowicz, Elizabeth. *Eight Chicago Women and Their Fashion, 1860–1926.* Chicago: Chicago Historical Society, 1978.

Jouve, M. *Balenciaga (Universe of Fashion).* New York: Universe Books, 1998.

Karan, Donna. *An American Woman Observed.* 1987.

Keenan, Brigid. *Dior in Vogue.* New York: Random House Value Publishing, 1983.

Kellogg, A., Amy T. Peterson, Stefani Bay, and Natalie Swindell. *In an Influential Fashion: An Encyclopedia of Nineteenth- and Twentieth-Century Fashion Designers and Retailers Who Transformed Dress.* Westport, CT: Greenwood Publishing Group, Inc., 2002.

Kennedy, Shirley. *Pucci: A Renaissance in Fashion.* New York: Abbeville Press, 1991.

Kennett, Frances. *The Collector's Book of Fashion.* New York: Crown Publishers, Inc., 1983.

Khornak, Lucille. *Fashion 2001.* New York: Viking Press, 1982.

Kybalova, Ludmila, Olga Herbenova and Milena Lamorova. *The Pictorial Encyclopedia of Fashion,* 2nd Edition. Translated by Claudia Rosoux. England: Hamlyn Publishers, 1968. New York: Crown Publishers, Inc., 1969.

Lagerfeld, Karl. *Lagerfeld's Sketchbook: Karl Lagerfeld's Illustrated Fashion Journal of Anna Piaggi.* London: Weidenfeld & Nicolson, 1988.

Lambert, Eleanor. *World of Fashion: People, Places and Resources.* 2nd ed. New York: R.R. Bowker Company, 1979.

Langlade, Emile. *Rose Bertin: The Creator of Fashion at the Court of Marie-Antoinette.* Adapted from the French by Dr. Angelo S. Rappoport. New York: Charles Scribner's Sons, 1913.

Latour, Anny. *Kings of Fashion.* Translated by Mervyn Saville. London: Weidenfeld & Nicolson, 1958.

———. *Paris Fashion.* London: Michael Joseph, 1972.

Laver, James. *Taste and Fashion.* London: George G. Harrap & Co. Ltd., 1937.

———. *A Concise History of Costume.* New York: Oxford University Press, 1988.

———. *Fashion, Art and Beauty.* New York: Costume Institute, Metropolitan Museum of Art, 1967.

Laver, James, et. al. *Costume and Fashion: A Concise History.* 4th ed. London: Thames & Hudson, 2002.

Lavine, W. Robert. *In a Glamorous Fashion.* New York: Charles Scribner's Sons, 1980.

Lee, Sarah Tomerlin, editor. *American Fashion: The Life and Lines of Adrian, Mainbocher, McCardell, Norell & Trigère.* New York: Quadrangle/The NY Times Book Co., 1975.

Leese, Elizabeth. *Costume Design in the Movies.* New York: Frederick Ungar Publishing Co., 1977.

Levin, Phyllis Lee. *The Wheels of Fashion.* New York: Doubleday & Company, Inc., 1965.

Ley, S. *Fashion for Everyone: The Story of Ready-to-Wear.* New York: Charles Scribner's Sons, 1975.

Leymarie, Jean. *Chanel.* New York: Rizzoli International Publications, 1987.

Lynam, Ruth, editor. *Couture.* New York: Doubleday & Company, Inc., 1972.

Madsen, Axel. *Chanel: A Woman of Her Own.* New York: Henry Holt and Co., Reprint, 1991.

———. *Living for Design: Yves Saint Laurent Story.* New York, 1979.

———. *Chanel, A Woman of Her Own.* New York: Henry Holt Co., 1990.

Martin, R. and H. Koda. *Giorgio Armani: Images of Man.* New York: Rizzoli International Publications, 1990.

Maxwell, Elsa. *R.S.V.P. Elsa Maxwell's Own Story.* Boston: Little, Brown & Co., 1954.

McCardell, Claire. *What Shall I Wear?.* New York: Simon & Schuster, 1956.

McConathy, D. with D. Vreeland. *Hollywood Costume.* New York: Harry N. Abrams, 1976.

McDowell, Colin. *McDowell's Directory of Twentieth Century Fashion.* New Jersey: Prentice-Hall, Inc., 1985.

Mendes, Valerie D. *Twentieth Century Fashion: An Introduction to Women's Fashionable Dress, 1900-1980.* London: Victoria and Albert Museum, 1996.

Mendes, Valerie D. and Amy de la Haye. *20th Century Fashion.* London: Thames & Hudson, 1999.

Milbank, Caroline Rennolds. *Couture: The Great Designers.* New York: Stewart, Tabori & Chang, Inc., 1997.

———. *New York Fashion: The Evolution of American Style.* New York: Harry N. Abrams, 1989.

Milinaire, Caterine. *Cheap Chic: Update.* Rev. ed. New York: Outlet Book Company, 1978.

Mirabella, Grace. *In and Out of Vogue.* New York: Doubleday, 1995.

Miyake, Issey. *Issey Miyake Meets West.* Tokyo: Shogaku Kan Publishing Co. Ltd., 1978.

———. *Issey Miyake Bodyworks.* Tokyo: Shokagu Kan Publishing Co. Ltd., 1983.

Miyake, Issey, Kazuko Sato, Herve Chandes, Fondation Cartier, and Raymond Meier. *Issey Miyake: Making Things.* New York: Scalo Verlag, 1999.

Moffitt, P. et al. *The Rudi Gernreich Book.* New York: Taschen America, LLC. 1999.

Mohrt, Françoise. *30 Ans D'Elegance et de Créations Rochas Mode, 1925-1955.* Paris: Jacques Damase, 1983.

Morris, Bernadine. *The Fashion Makers: An Inside Look at America's Leading Designers.* New York: Random House, 1978.

Mugler, Thierry. *Thierry Mugler.* New York: Rizzoli International Publications, 1988.

Nicolson, Nigel. *Mary Curzon.* New York: Harper & Row, 1977.

O'Hara, Georgina. *The Encyclopedia of Fashion.* New York: Harry N. Abrams, Inc., 1986.

Osma, G. *Fortuny. His Life and Work.* New York: Rizzoli International Publications, 1980.

Payne, Blanche. *History of Costume: From the Ancient Egyptians to the Twentieth Century.* New York: Harper & Row, 1965.

Payne, Blanche, Geitel Winakor, and Jane Farrell-Beck. *History of Costume: From Ancient Mesopotamia through the Twentieth Century.* 2nd ed. Boston: Addison-Wesley, 1997.

Pelle, M. Valentino. *Thirty Years of Magic.* New York: Abbeville Press, 1991.

Perkins, Alice K. *Paris Couturiers & Milliners.* New York: Fairchild Publications, 1949.

Picken, Mary Brooks. *A Dictionary of Costume and Fashion: Historic and Modern.* New York: Dover Publications, Inc., 1999.

———— and Dora Loves Miller. *Dressmakers of France: The Who, How and Why of French Couture.* New York: Harper & Brothers Publishers, 1956.

Poiret, Paul. *En Habillant l'Epoque.* Paris: Grasset, 1930.

Polan, Brenda, editor. *The Fashion Year, 1938.* London: Zomba Books, 1983.

Prichard, S. *Film Costume: An Annotated Bibliography.* Metuchen, NJ: Scarecrow, 1981.

————. *King of Fashion* (autobiography). Translated by Stephen Haden Guest. Philadelphia: J.B. Lippincott Company, 1931.

————. *Revenez-Y.* Paris: Lutetia, 1934.

Quant, Mary. *Quant by Quant.* London: Cassell & Co. Ltd., 1966.

Quant, Mary and Felicity Green. *Color by Quant: Your Complete Personal Guide to Beauty and Fashion.* New York: McGraw-Hill, 1985.

Rhodes, Zandra and Anne Knight. *The Art of Zandra Rhodes.* London: Michael O'Mara Books, Ltd., 1995.

Riley, Robert. *Givenchy: 30 Years.* New York: Fashion Institute of Technology, 1982.

Robinson, Julian. *Fashion in the Forties.* New York: St. Martin's Press, 1977.

————. *Fashion in the Thirties.* New York: Oresko Books, 1978.

Rochas, Marcel. *Twenty-Five Years of Parisian Elegance, 1925-1950.* Paris: Pierre Tisne, 1951.

Roshco, Bernard. *The Rag Race.* New York: Funk & Wagnalls, 1963.

Ross, Josephine. *Beaton in Vogue.* New York: Outlet Book Company, 1988.

Rykiel, Sonia. *And I Would Like Her Naked.* Paris: Bernard Grasset, 1979.

Salomon, Rosalie Kolodny. *Fashion Design for Moderns.* New York: Fairchild Publications, 1976.

Saunders, Edith. *The Age of Worth: Couturier to the Empress Eugenie.* Bloomington, IN: Indiana University Press, 1955.

Schiaparelli, Elsa. *Shocking Life.* New York: E.P. Dutton & Co., Inc., 1954.

————. *Elsa Schiaparelli: Empress of Paris Fashion.* New York: Rizzoli International Publications, Inc., 1986.

Schreier, Barbara. *Mystique and Identity: Women's Fashions in the 1950s.* Norfolk, VA: Chrysler Museum, 1984.

Seebohm, Caroline. *The Man Who Was Vogue.* New York: Viking Press, 1982.

Snow, Carmel and Mary Louise Aswell. *The World of Carmel Snow.* New York: McGraw-Hill Book Co., 1962.

Spencer, Charles. *Erté.* New York: Clarkson N. Potter, Inc., 1970.

Steele, Valerie. *Women of Fashion.* New York: Rizzoli Books International, 1991.

Sudjic, Deyan. *Rei Kawakubo and Comme des Garçons.* New York: Rizzoli, 1990.

Teboul, David, Christine Baute, and Pierre Berge. *Yves Saint Laurent: 5 Avenue Marceau, 75116 Paris, France.* New York: Harry N. Abrams, Inc., 2002.

Thornton, N. *Poiret.* New York: Rizzoli International Publications, 1979.

Tice, Bill (with Sheila Weller). *Enticements: How to Look Fabulous in Lingerie.* New York: The MacMillan Company, 1985.

Toklas, Alice B. *A New French Style.* Paris: J.F. Verly, 1946.

Tolstoy, Mary Koutouzov. *Charlemagne to Dior: The Story of French Fashion.* New York: Michael Slains, 1967.

Trachtenberg, J. *Ralph Lauren - Image-maker. The Man Behind the Mystique.* New York: Little, Brown and Co., 1988.

Trahey, Jane, editor. *Harper's Bazaar: Years of the American Female.* New York: Random House, 1967.

Vanderbilt, Gloria. *Woman to Woman.* New York: Doubleday, 1979.

Vecchio, Walter and Robert Riley. *The Fashion Makers: A Photographic Record.* New York: Crown Publishers, Inc., 1968.

Vickers, Hugo. *Cecil Beaton.* New York: Sterling Publishing Co., 2002.

Von Furstenberg, Diane. *Book of Beauty.* New York: Simon & Schuster, Inc., 1977.

Vreeland, Diana and Christopher Hemphill. *Allure.* Boston: Bullfinch Press, 2002.

———. *D.V.* New York: DeCapo Press, 1997.

"W": The Designing Life. Staff of W, edited by Lois Perschetz. New York: Clarkson N. Potter, Inc., 1990.

Walkley, C. *The Way to Wear 'Em: One Hundred Fifty Years of Punch on Fashion.* Chester Springs, PA: Dufour (P. Owen Ltd.), 1985.

Weitz, John. *Man in Charge.* New York: The MacMillan Company, 1974.

Weitz, John. *Sports Clothes for Your Sports Car.* New York: Arco Publishing Co., Inc., 1958.

White, Emily, editor. *Fashion 85.* New York: St. Martin's Press, 1986.

White, Palmer. *Point.* New York: Clarkson N. Potter, Inc., 1973.

Whiteman, Von. *Looking Back at Fashion.1901-1939.* West Yorkshire, England: EP Publishing, 1978.

Williams, Beryl Epstein. *Fashion Is Our Business.* Philadelphia: J.B. Lippincott Co., 1945.

———. *Young Faces in Fashion.* Philadelphia: J.B. Lippincott Co., 1945.

Wilcox, R. Turner. *The Mode in Costume.* London: MacMillan Publishing Co., 1983.

The World of Balenciaga. New York: Costume Institute, Metropolitan Museum of Art, 1972.

Worsley-Gough, Barbara. *Fashions in London:* Allan Wingate, 1952.

Worth, Jean Philippe. *A Century of Fashion.* Translated by Ruth Scott Miller. Boston: Little, Brown & Co., 1928.

Yarwood, Doreen. *The Encyclopedia of World Costume.* London: MacMillan Publishing Co., 1979.

Yoxall, H.W. *A Fashion of Life.* New York, Taplinger, 1967.

Yves Saint Laurent. New York: Costume Institute, Metropolitan Museum of Art, 1983.

Index of Designers

Designers listed in **boldface type** *are new to this edition.*

Index